MW00443886

SOUTHAMPTON SUMMERS

SOUTHAMPTON SUMMERS:

Stories Of Three Italian Families, Their Beach Houses, And The Five Generations That Enjoyed Them

Albert Marra

Contributing authors:

Sal Anselmo, Frances Maffei, Gilbert Maffei, Alex Marra,
Andrew Marra, Eugene Marra, Frank Marra, Peter Nardi,
Jonathan Resh, Ellen Saracino, Gregory Saracino, Linda Saracino,
Mark Saracino, Sylvia Saracino, Judith Marra Scott

New Dominion Press ● Norfolk ● Virginia

Southampton Summers:
Stories of Three Italian Families, Their Beach Houses, and the Five Generations that
Enjoyed Them.

Published by:

New Dominion Press
New Dominion Media/New Dominion Press
1217 Godfrey Avenue, Norfolk, Virginia 23504-3218
www.NewDominionPress.com

First Printing: March 2019

Cover Design, Graphic Design, and Typography by New Dominion Press
Cover Photographs by Albert Marra
Illustrations by John Del Russo, Sr. and Albert Marra
Copy editing by Linda Saracino

Publisher's Cataloging-in-Publication Data
provided by Five Rainbows Cataloging Services

Names: Marra, Albert, author, illustrator. | Del Russo, John, Sr., illustrator.
Title: Southampton summers : stories of three Italian families, their beach houses, and
    the five generations that enjoyed them / Albert Marra [and 15 others], authors ; John
    Del Russo, Sr. [and] Albert Marra, illustrators.
Description: First edition. | Norfolk, VA : New Dominion Press, 2019.
Identifiers: LCCN 2019931113 | ISBN 978-1-793-93063-7 (paperback) | ISBN 978-0-
578-47525-7 (hardcover) | ISBN 978-0-578-44727-8 (ebook)
Subjects: LCSH: Italian American families--Biography. | Families--History. | Family
    vacations. | Southampton (N.Y. : Town)--History. | Coming of age. | Essays. | BISAC:
BIOGRAPHY & AUTOBIOGRAPHY / Personal Memoirs. | BIOGRAPHY & AUTO
    BIOGRAPHY / Cultural, Ethnic & Regional / General. | HISTORY / United States /
    State & Local / Middle Atlantic (DC, DE, MD, NJ, NY, PA) | TRAVEL / United
    States / Northeast / Middle Atlantic (NJ, NY, PA)
Classification: LCC F129.S7 M37 2019 (print) | LCC F129.S7 (ebook) | DDC 974.7/25--
    dc23.

Every good story is of course both a picture and an idea,

and the more they are interfused the better.

— **Henry James**

DEDICATION

For my mother, Cecile, whose breakfast muffins made Southampton summer mornings memorable; for my father, Frank, who made us rest after meals before going swimming; for our courageous grandparents and their siblings, who explored Southampton, bought the land and, with our parents, built three family bungalows over sixty years ago; and for all our family members who made lifelong memories with us at the beach.

Top Photos: Cecile and Frank Marra
Bottom Photo (L to R): Frank, Cecile, Albert

TABLE OF CONTENTS

xi

ACKNOWLEDGMENTS

Adrienne Marra, my wife and life partner, for sticking *with* me for 48 years and for sticking it *to* me on a regular basis until I finally finished this book.

Cecile Marra, my mother, for the famous biscuits and waffles she made for us at our bungalow, and for teaching me important beach skills like digging for clams with your feet.

Frank Marra, my father, for teaching me many other useful skills, like how to rest and then "police the area" after evening suppers at our beach house.

Andrew Marra, my older son, who while spending a memorable father-son BMW top-down weekend at the beach planted the tiny seed that germinated into the writing of these stories.

Alex Marra, my younger son, whose stories of the times he spent at the beach with his grandparents still make me roll with endless laughter.

Eugene Marra, my younger brother, who wrote a fascinating story of childhood adventures and supplied me with details about some of his more recent outings at the beach.

Linda Saracino, my cousin, for her skillful editing of the copy for the original stories and for organizing them into a more logical presentation. Early on Linda became the best "idea man" I could possibly have had as to the format, content, and style of this book. Linda certainly made sure that every word counts.

Ellen Saracino, another cousin and Linda's sister, who provided me with many facts, figures and updates about Southampton on an almost continual basis.

Lorraine (Cioffi) Gargiulo, another Saracino cousin, who, before I put pen to paper, reminisced with me, set me in the right direction, and provided and validated several of my stories. And for many good times in Southampton and New York in the 1950s and 1960s.

Peter Nardi, lifelong family friend and professional colleague, whose prologue sets the tone for the contents of this book by inviting the reader to savor the stories that follow. He has also been helpful with final editing.

Contributing authors: my sons, **Andrew and Alex**, my brother, **Eugene**; my cousins, **Judith Marra Scott, Sal Anselmo, Linda Saracino, Ellen Saracino**, and **Frances Maffei**; my cousins in the fourth generation of the Saracino family, **Jon Resh** and **Mark and Gregory Saracino**.

John Del Russo, Sr., my dear friend and past president of Roma Lodge of Virginia Beach (Order Sons of Italy in America), for his original art work and his guidance designing and placing the illustrations contained in this book.

Chuck Christie, founder and president, New Dominion Press, my publisher, for his invaluable guidance and technical assistance, without which this project might never have concluded!

Members of the **Marra, Saracino, Maffei**, and **Genovese** families, who provided many photos.

My father's first cousins: **Sylvia Saracino**, who provided key historical details and information; and **Gilbert Maffei**, who strongly praised the work of our family's first Americans.

At the Town of Southampton, **Ms. Sundy Schermeyer**, Town Clerk, and **Ms. Julie Greene**, Town Historian, for their invaluable assistance concerning historical sites around Southampton.

Kathryn Menu, Editor, Sag Harbor Express, for her guidance locating and using the archived historical records of her newspaper.

Our beach friends, who, although not fully identified, created and share many of these memories.

My grandparents and great aunts and uncles, our family's hardy explorers and settlers. They showed courage when they came to the US. Their hard work and frugal lifestyle left us a true legacy that made Southampton and all of this possible for the rest of the family.

Albert Marra

PICTURESQUE

Southar

FIRST PRESBYTERIAN CHURCH, BUILT 1707

pton

OLD SAYRE HOUSE ERECTED 1648 STILL STANDING

SOUTHAMPTON ART MUSEUM, FOUNDED 1897 BY SAMUEL L. PARRISH.

The OLD and N

PROLOGUE:
A Big White Duck

Peter M. Nardi, Ph.D.

For many people driving east from New York City, the sight of a big oceanfront mansion may signal that they have officially arrived in the Hamptons. For me and my sister, Donna, in the mid-1950s, it took a big white duck past Riverhead, Long Island, to let us know we had really left the Bronx and arrived at what would be our rental for several summers.

When I think of that duck—*The Big Duck*—big as a house, selling various dairy products, and listed on the National Register of Historic Places, it brings back vivid memories of another time and place, just as the wonderful stories in this collection evoke details I had long forgotten. As you read about the experiences across over 60 years and five generations, you too may likely make connections to your own childhood summers, no matter where they were spent. When you listen to what the stories tell us, you can make those connections because this book is as much about rituals and customs of friendship and family as it is about summers in the Hamptons.

My connections begin at age seven. Donna was five. My parents rented a modest two-bedroom, one-bath, thousand square foot house. We were sure back then that the driveway was the size of an airport runway. At least it felt that way while sweeping it in anticipation of our dad's return trip to the beach each weekend. It was on Spring Lane off Noyac Road in walking distance to Long Beach. We always said we went to Sag Harbor, a small whaling village mentioned by Melville in *Moby Dick*, but after reading the touching stories in this collection, I realize we too may technically have been in Southampton. Who knew? I can now brag that we "summered" in Southampton, although Sag Harbor has become nearly as trendy in recent years.

But the lives we led in those late 1950s summers were not the glamorous ones depicted in today's Hamptons, neither in terms of the architecture nor the concept. Rather, we lived in a house that had a telephone but no dial. I can still hear the operator saying "number pull-ease" when we picked up the receiver. We didn't even have a car our first summer, and certainly no television. How could I watch the Mouseketeers? What would we do with our time?

Well, we did what others in this memoir did: we learned to swim in the Atlantic at Bridgehampton; we picked blueberries in the woods; we tried not to get ticks on us or scratch our feet on rocks; we walked to the local store for bottles of milk with our dog, Bingo; we saw movies at the tiny Sag Harbor theater; we went fishing with another Bronx Italian family who stayed nearby; we tickled the bellies of blowfish to watch them puff up; *Fishing, Sag Harbor, circa 1955* we ate pizza at Ma Bergman's in East Hampton; we stood in awe under the giant jawbone at the Sag Harbor whaling museum; we figured out how to use a crab trap and dig for clams; and we eagerly awaited friends and relatives visiting each weekend.

Our summers, although similar, were not exactly like those of the families depicted in this collection of stories. We did not have the tradition of multiple generations of large Italian families living side by side. Ours was a small family. While my grandparents, Pietro and Celestina, were also Italian, my father, Peter (often called Pierino, for Petey), was an only child. There were just two of his first cousins (also from single-child families) living nearby. You call that an Italian family?

Despite the differences, these terrific summer stories brought back some nostalgic memories of an earlier time and the relevance of rituals and cultural heritage often associated with prior generations. We too grew up in the Bronx in an Italian family, but only on my father's side. Because my mother Jeanne's Irish family lived in Buffalo, we witnessed more the full force of Italian immigrant life, not unlike what Albert Marra and his family contributors depict in this book. My grandparents were from the mountains outside Parma, so we rarely ate fish. But our meals were still an organizing force in our lives. We ate *risotto*, *polenta*, lamb, veal *scallopine*, homemade ravioli, *cappelletti*, *funghi*, and *torta*. We called it sauce, not gravy. And when we did eat fish, it was mostly during the summers in Sag Harbor and often the ones we caught.

Could those be our only similarities to the people in this memoir? Curiously, my connections to the Marra family weave throughout our lives in several other ways. My father was a physician colleague of Dr. Alfred Marra (one of the first of their family to visit the Hamptons), and the mother of my best grammar school friend worked for him in his office. More significantly, our neighbor was Adrienne Rinaldi, Albert's wife, and the mother of Andrew and Alex, whose stories illustrate another generation's summers at the beach. Adrienne, my sister Donna, and I were the founding (and the *only*) members of the notorious Bronx street gang, the PAD Club of Tenbroeck Avenue. Our gang put on magic shows, made an annual trip to Playland at Rye Beach, and in later years would try to terrorize the retirees on Jessamine Court in Deltona, Florida. Donna was Adrienne's maid of honor and we continued to see each other through the years, especially during their California days and our Florida visits.

For all I know, our paths may have crossed many other times. In Albert's stories, he recalls going to the movies in Sag Harbor. I wonder. Was he in the same theater when I saw Gregory Peck in "Moby Dick?" Or in the nearby 5 and 10 cent store when I was getting my Davy Crockett hat and other essential equipment for my summer of sand, woods and water? We were the same age and went to many of the same places, possibly at the same time, and with some shared familial experiences and rituals. I suppose it doesn't really matter if our summers overlapped, for like anyone who spends time in any vacation area, the memories of childhood sounds, smells, and sensations are so similar. That makes it all seem like a much simpler time than our overly complex adult world of today.

These memories of my own four Hamptons summers are recalled vividly through these beautiful and fun-filled stories. What strikes you is the invocation of that certain time and place—especially compared to today's internetted, Twittered, Facebooked world—when social media meant actually speaking to each other in the streets or the small shops of the nearby villages. While my connections are more with Albert's generation, what's most impressive in this collection is the continuity across five generations. You hear different stories from writers representing each of the three bungalows and two generations of cousins and their sons. I've spent my career as a sociologist (here I don this hat for some jargon that will not be on the final exam); the role of ritual in social institutions is one of the primary concepts we emphasize. Food, of course, is a central organizing piece of culture around which numerous traditions, rituals, and meanings are constructed. This is so evident in these memoirs as we experience—yes maybe even smell and taste—the foods so significant to memory. It's no wonder that it took only a *madeleine* and a cup of tea for Proust to write seven volumes!

The family members telling their stories reminisce about the houses, the neighbors, the elders, the phrases in standard and dialect Italian, the fish, the pasta, the espresso, the *machinetta,* the rocky beach, the smell and look of the place. Yes, their summers are not at all like those of any Hampton socialites. This is a memoir of a modest family, in a simpler time, when operators talked to you when you picked up the phone and edible wild blueberries and blackberries could be safely picked in the woods. We bring our own interpretations and meanings when recalling past events, so what we remember often changes over time. We recreate our biographies through the lenses of what we are today. There is, therefore, no one version, no one correct account, just lots of stories filled with collective and individual remembrances.

What you take from these narratives depends on where you are in time and place when you read them and how you listen to and process what is said and what goes unsaid. I guarantee they will evoke some significant memories of your own childhood summers and the meaning of family and rituals in your lives.

Listen to what's between the lines and hear your own stories flooding back. But listen closely, for as the composer Igor Stravinsky once said: "To listen is an effort, and just to hear is no merit. A duck hears also."

Even a big white duck.

The Big Duck, Flanders (Southampton), New York

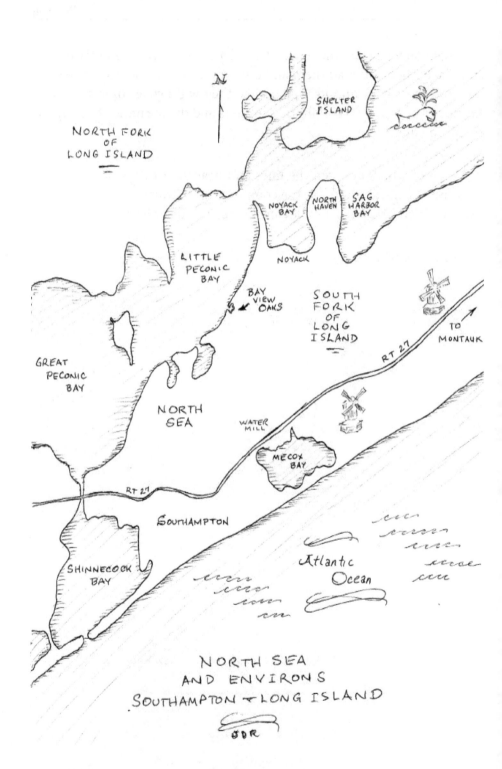

NORTH SEA
AND ENVIRONS
SOUTHAMPTON ~ LONG ISLAND

INTRODUCTION:
Everybody's Got a Story

I t's true. Everybody's got a story!

Well, it seems so at least.

It really does seem like everybody's got a story to tell, something interesting that's worth sharing. And if that's true, then it might also be true that every family has a lot of stories to tell. We've captured several of one family's stories in this book, a series of recollections of six decades of summers in Southampton, Long Island. The stories, as told by 15 different authors, were written by members of three generations of the extended Marra-Maffei-Saracino family.

The family's stories are, first of all, fun; they're straightforward, simple and easy to read.

Perhaps even more importantly, they're all true. Okay, so there's probably been some embellishment thrown in here and there. What hyperbole may have been included serves to jazz things up just a bit, but the stories are still true. And if one can believe the words of the English writer C.S. Lewis, that there are no ordinary people, then these are no ordinary stories.

What's more, all the stories are interrelated. They revolve around simple (but not ordinary) folks who came from three branches of the same extended family and who share a common heritage. The family, whose

1

first generation of Americans left their Italian homeland early in the 20th century, did what many similar immigrant families did: they worked hard, saved their money, and focused on giving their children and grandchildren a better life.

That included buying wooded building lots in the North Sea hamlet of the Town of Southampton in 1951 from Peconic Shores, Inc. The lots were located just two blocks from a quiet, no-name beach on Long Island's Little Peconic Bay. And beginning in the mid-1950s, three of the five siblings put in motion plans to build simple bungalows on their lots. Those three little bungalows have witnessed five generations spending 60 years of summer vacations. Clearly those vacations have provided abundant raw materials from which these family stories arise.

The family's stories are not only fun, simple and true, but they all take place in and around the Hamptons and have much to do with the area's famous beaches and attractions.

So let's go there; let's go to the beach. But not to any of the many famous Hamptons beaches. No, let's go to a no-name beach on Long Island's Little Peconic Bay, east of Roses Grove, at the end of Oak Grove Road and across a narrow channel from the Noyac Road community of Bay View Oaks. At that little beach the usual "beachy" scenes of sand dunes with sea oats

The entrance to our little "no-name beach"

waving in the breeze or broad vistas of pounding surf are nowhere to be found. The beach boasts few remarkable features, besides the ever present moss- and algae-covered rocks and a thin strip of sandy pebbles that shift wildly with the tides. That beach has been like this for as long as anyone can remember and possibly will be for centuries to come.

The beach never attracts anything resembling a typical Hamptons crowd, which is good. Maybe because it's more than a bit out of the way, you won't find any New York or Hollywood celebs or wannabees there. Likewise, there are no paparazzi or any of the typical Hamptons illuminati who grace the covers of the local society papers. All of that's good too!

What the beach does have, besides its ubiquitous rocks (yes, remember the rocks!) are regular, everyday people from regular middle class families, that is, families very much like the Marra's, the Maffei's and the Saracino's, the subjects (and authors) of these stories.

Our family crowd at our "little beach"

For those three families, what many people might consider negative factors about the area and its beach may ironically have turned out just the opposite. Those "negative" factors may well have motivated the family's first generation to build on their lots near that quiet little beach. Nobody ever said; and for all we know, nobody ever asked. And then as well as now, having similarly minded people at the beach makes everyone feel, well, at ease.

And sixty years ago, as today, feeling at ease and restful in a quiet summer beach setting with similar folks may be all the motivation any of the family members ever needed.

Southampton Beginnings

James A. Michener, setting the locale for his 1974 novel, *Centennial*, carries the reader back three billion years ago to the cooling of the earth's crust. He does that before introducing the dinosaur diplodocus from 160 million years ago or the Arapaho brave Lame Beaver, who doesn't come on the scene until the year 1747.

For our stories to make sense, there's no need to examine colonial times in Southampton, much less its geological history. However, it will be most beneficial to review briefly what brought the family to the Southampton area in the first place. Further, it will also help to take a general look at the surrounding area, its land and its people.

Unlike Michener's story, the family's stories begin a few years after World War II and about fifty years after the first generation of immigrants came to America. Our family physician, who was the youngest of the family born in Italy, Great Uncle Alfred Marra, and his wife, Aunt Anna, vacationed in the late 1940s in Southampton Shores. In that community, near the store known for years as Garamone's, Dr. Marra rented a summer home from Fred S., a physician colleague he befriended in World War II. (Note: for privacy, non-family members, other than public figures, will not be fully identified.) In that cottage Alfred and Anna Marra spent several

4

thoroughly enjoyable summers with their children, Judy and Anthony, as well as the brother and sister-in-law of Dr. Marra, Arthur and Mary Marra, the grandparents of this book's main author.

Before the decade of the 1940s ran its course, other family members, from both the first and second generation, visited the summer rental cottage at Southampton Shores as well. Among the visitors was the family of Savino and Sylvia Saracino. As the family's original visitors to Southampton Shores continued renting, still other family units added their names to the guest list. Word was now spreading throughout the family about the pleasantly inviting beaches of Southampton. That enthusiasm reached a crescendo with a major milestone in the early 1950s.

With Southampton now the family's preferred destination, when land nearby became available, it didn't take long for four sisters and one brother from the family's first generation to jump on the idea of starting their own "Long Island Lido." They came, they saw and they bought five contiguous lots on Noyac[1] Road (a major road between Southampton and Sag Harbor) just a mile east of their Southampton Shores rental. For a few hundred dollars each (paid in cash), the four sisters (Elena Saracino, Silvia Maffei, Filomena Manzo, and Adelina Tamborino) joined their one brother (Arturo Marra) as landowners in the Town of Southampton. The rest, as they say, is history. And of course, it's our story and the material for the stories in this book.

Southampton: Beaches and Bungalows, Villages and Villas

Before describing the building and development of the family's three beach bungalows, it would be useful to explore the Town of Southampton and environs, including area beaches. After all, the beach is what attracted the family in the first place.

The Town of Southampton consists of 16 hamlets extending from

---

[1]   Throughout this book we use this spelling of the word Noyac, recognizing that there is an alternate spelling—Noyack—both may be used interchangeably.

Westhampton on the west, through its epicenter in Southampton Village, then east to East Hampton and northeast to Sag Harbor. According to the 2010 US census, Southampton has 55,000 year-round residents. But from Memorial Day through Labor Day, the population swells to double that figure. Driving east from New York City on Route 27, Montauk Highway, Southampton would welcome you with several historical markers on the side of the road. One of the signs that for many years greeted visitors and residents alike—and delighted us as kids—featured a guy in a Pilgrim hat. Yes, it was a guy in a Pilgrim hat, looking just like in your history books.

Of course you realize that's not exactly beach wear, so you try to avoid shifting from summer to fall and the first Thanksgiving, which, as any third-grader knows, didn't happen *here*. Then you get their message: you're entering New York's first permanent English settlement, founded in 1640 by Kentish Puritans who sailed from Lynn in the Massachusetts Bay Colony and landed at Conscience Point. That outcropping in North Sea Harbor lies just minutes away from the family's three bungalows and the site of many of the stories that follow.

Imagine! The first European settlers landed four miles from the family's settlement, in land originally occupied by bands of Shinnecock Indians. And 300 years after the Puritans, a new crop of "settlers," looking to escape the city, arrived at nearly the same spot on Long Island. Were the family members attracted to Southampton for its place in colonial history? Not likely. Even in the 1950s some of our stalwart Italian immigrants still struggled with the vagaries of the English language, so who among them would have cared about Southampton's English history?

It's clear that the entire East End of Long Island boasts a long history and, given the restored windmills and villages of the South Fork, a picture-postcard one at that. Like everyone, the family's "pilgrims" were doubtless delighted by the area's man-made and natural beauty. So were

6

the five siblings attracted to the picturesque charm of the Hamptons? Still not likely. Instead, much like Indians, whalers of the 19th century, and vacationers from the late 19th through the mid-20th century, they too came for the sea.

From the 1930s through the mid-1950s, except for World War II, Southampton saw a gradual increase in home-building by "old money" families, who typically built houses in classic English or French country styles. Sometimes large but not outwardly opulent, and often called "cottages," these homes projected an air of understated style. Not that you could see them easily. In keeping with their penchant for privacy, owners often surrounded their houses with high hedgerows. Unlike the showy oceanfront mansions built after the 1960s, these older houses, which line the streets from the village center of Southampton south to Dune Road, recall an era of simple Hamptons

Houses hiding in the hedgerows

elegance. Westward along the dunes towards Shinnecock Bay, older homes give way to architecturally diverse dwellings built in the 1970s and 1980s and beyond. Many of these "Mac Mansions" greatly overshadow the classic Hamptons "cottage."

Regardless of dips in the economy from the 1980s to today, Southampton Village and most of the surrounding oceanfront have seen a seemingly unending influx of new-money home-buyers, many of them celebrities and Wall Street *wunderkinder*. They are drawn to trendy, contemporary mega-mansions-on-the-sea, so many locals may consider that Southampton homes have grown grandiose in scope while declining in elegance.

Even so, there are doubtless many among this new wave of homeowners who followed the same model the "old money" folks did: they built (or bought) their summer homes for their kids, their parents, and other family members to enjoy the beach. Hey, that's just like this family!

Beaches

The Hamptons in general, and the Town of Southampton in particular, according to the travel guides, boast some of the nation's best beaches. Usually when discussing Hamptons beaches, one usually is referring to the unspoiled Atlantic beaches. These beaches, such as on Dune Road west from Southampton Village towards the Shinnecock Inlet, or east towards Bridgehampton, Flying Point and East Hampton, provide the beachy feel travel gurus and cable TV producers love. They can't get enough of the unspoiled, natural splendor. Unlike the narrow, rocky beaches of Long Island's bays (such as the Little Peconic in North Sea), the Atlantic Ocean beaches—what most people call "the ocean"—appear broad and expansive, with undulating sand dunes and 180-degree views along the beach and over the water.

The sand at the Hamptons ocean beaches isn't the whitest white, but it's light, finer and more abundant than the stretches of sand at the area's bay beaches. It's great to lie on, play in, take walks along. On bright, sunny days, however, the sand could get hot. But the water? Usually a dark green, it's not at all like warm, turquoise Caribbean water; it never gets warm. In fact, the ocean water around Southampton rarely warms above 75 degrees, even at the end of July. And the waves on all of eastern Long Island, at three to four feet on a "calm" day, inspire awe even in good swimmers. But the wave action always proves fun to swim, surf, or boogie-board.

The Hamptons beaches have grown more popular over the years, but there's still plenty of room. It's never blanket-to-blanket crowding like at Long Island's Jones Beach. And the towns and villages have become more protective of their beaches over the years, with limited admission (by resident permit usually), no high-rises, no boardwalks or vendors. With their open vistas, anyone would love to enjoy these beaches. If you can get in, that is! Those beaches still open to the public such as Cooper's Beach, do not provide the precise kind of solitude and restfulness that drew many families to seek out homes in Southampton. But they will do in a pinch.

In the case of those who do seek a family style beach, many would usually gravitate towards Southampton's bay beaches, such as the town beach called Long Beach (where Noyack Bay meets Sag Harbor), Meschutt Beach in Hampton Bays, or any number of Peconic and Little Peconic Bay beaches in the North Sea area, from Towd Point to Roses Grove and Bay View Oaks. And that's just what the Saracino-Maffei-Marra family did in the mid-1950s.

BAY VIEW OAKS

NORTH SEA
SOUTHAMPTON ❧ LONG ISLAND

The Early Years: Three Little Houses in a Row

What's a nice Italian family like ours doing in a posh place like Southampton? Our first generation explorers had no desire to compete with the grand homes in Southampton in the early 1950s. They would never want anything resembling oceanfront mansions or cottages near area villages. No, the Marra-Saracino-Maffei families found that the small building lots on Noyac Road suited them perfectly. It was all to their liking. And what's not to like? They could build basic homes near a beach at just a mile from Southampton Shores, and all of this at just 85 miles from the city. It all seemed, in a word, well, perfect.

The community they found, Bay View Oaks was indeed perfect: thick woods surrounded them, farms were just up the road, and beaches were in walking distance. While all five siblings had formed perfect plans to build their perfect beach homes, one on each lot, only three families (the Saracino's, Maffei's, and Marra's, from west to east along Noyac Road) eventually did build.

The Saracino, Maffei and Marra lots extend between two dirt roads: Pine Tree Road on the west side, and Red Cedar Lane on the east. The lots weren't large, about a quarter acre each. But that was big enough—at least by Southampton's existing zoning ordinances and building codes—for very small houses with relatively generous front and back yards. Soon after buying, Helen and Joe Saracino began making plans to build the first of three small houses, or as the family called them, bungalows. The Saracino bungalow was finished and occupied in time for the family to enjoy the summer of 1955.

The Saracino's: The Family's First Bungalow

Ironically, the first generation passed up Bay View Oaks waterfront property; they bought lots on the two-lane main drag from North Sea to Sag Harbor. Perhaps they wanted to be *near* the water without being *on* the water and worrying about storms. So they bypassed waterfront lots (at only a few hundred dollars more) which today command a premium of at least $200,000. Of course, in 1951 a few hundred dollars meant a lot to working-class immigrants. Their Southampton property was not an investment, not something to sell, but a family resource. And it was still only a couple of blocks to the beach.

Just the Basics

Each of the three family houses was designed to be a small (at almost a thousand square feet) summer bungalow, all with the same basic floor plan: living room, cook's galley, two bedrooms (one barely fitting a double bed), one tiny bath, and a screened porch. While only two or three adults can eat comfortably in the small kitchen, large family groups of 20 at a time have dined al fresco for more than 60 years on the porch.

Construction at the Saracino house, spring 1955

All three houses followed a design that could have been drawn by kindergarteners: a rectangle for the house, a center door, one big square window and two skinny ones, and a triangle for the roof. Add a tree near the porch and there it is: any one of the three bungalows. And simple was good. Anything more complex would have meant extra cost and unnecessary complications. Take the electricity, for example. Instead of breakers, there were fuse boxes (the norm in the mid-1950s), and thus, minimal electric power. And instead of town or village water and sewers, each house came with a well and a cesspool, systems which functioned well enough, perhaps owing to the amply endowed Long Island aquifer.

For hot water, all three houses relied on bottled gas. Tanks were customarily delivered a day or two late by a local family-run gas company, the only game in town. That meant one house or another was always on the brink of running out. So as a conservation strategy, the families did a lot of cooking on charcoal grills—every house had one (in fact, Uncle Joe built his out of cinder blocks left over from his house foundation). Good thing everyone liked barbecued food.

There was no municipal trash collection, but there was a private company they used periodically in the early years. But they considered the carting service expensive at a dollar per can! So all three houses took care of the garbage themselves in two ways: paper, cardboard, and anything that burned went into a wire frame for weekly fires, all perfectly legal, albeit mostly ceremonial, back then. Everything else—bottles, cans, kitchen garbage, broken dishes—was bagged or boxed, put in the trunk and driven to "the dumps," as the grown-ups called the town landfill. That was a great adventure, real fun for the kids: parents piled us and the rubbish in the car, drove three miles down twisty, bumpy Major's Path (to us Southampton's *Schwarzwald*), and we all pitched trash with wild and reckless abandon into the open pit as complacent, well-fed gulls circled. The alternative to burning, paying to haul it at a dollar a can, or roller coaster trips to the dumps? Garbage soup. I'd swear at times I think they actually made that.

Due to design shortcomings, e.g., electricity issues, the houses had few amenities most Americans consider minimum, like phones (the Saracino house being the exception for several of the early years) or central heat, let alone air conditioning. These were summer houses, never built for harsh Long Island winters. Not that there wasn't any heat: each house had a gas unit with metal floor grate between the bedrooms to take the edge off chilly summer nights. But no one used them much. Air conditioning? The houses had windows. Those high, horizontal '50s ranch-style windows which were never well-suited to A/C units anyway.

What else didn't the houses have? The list is long: dishwashers, modern washing machines (the Saracino's had an old-fashioned portable wringer type), dryers (but there were miles of clotheslines spider-webbed throughout the back yard trees!), or the space for any of these or, as noted, necessary electric power.

Before the Saracino house underwent renovations, hardly any alterations had been made to any of the three family bungalows. Except for minor repairs, until 2009 (when Sylvia Saracino began working with a contractor), all three houses remained as built. Did builders build better houses in the 1950s, with better materials and craftsmen? Maybe. Or maybe the family luckily found a builder who did things right. Whatever the answer, it's amazing: for 60 years of summer use and unheated hibernation, the three little bungalows have withstood the worst that Mother Nature could dish out. Sure, the two un-renovated houses show their age, but the structures are sound. And thanks to the rebuilding of the Saracino house on its original 1954-55 foundation, one could assume that the integrity of the other two houses also remains fundamentally sound.

The Saracino's house was rebuilt in 2010-11. The living room and porch were reconfigured, and a back deck added. Everything new inside and out, including a more traditional exterior, brought what had been a mid-century bungalow into the 21st century. Except for family, nobody would have had a notion about this momentous achievement. But it *was* momentous to the family! It was all new and held the promise of summers (and generations!) to come, just as the original house did. In a sense, history had repeated itself: the first house, the Saracino's, had been built for the second time at the corner of Noyac Road and Pine Tree Road.

The Marra's: The Family's Second Bungalow

In the winter of 1955-56, following the lead of his sister (Great Aunt Helen Saracino and husband, Joe), Arthur and Mary Marra family from LaFontaine Avenue in the Bronx began making plans for putting up their own Southampton beach house. The second home was to be two lots down from the Saracino's and, using the same builder as the first (Ruscon), one of the three sons of Arthur and Mary, the author's father, Frank Marra, secured the mortgage to enable the family's project to proceed. Their arrangement went something like this: since he had obtained the funding, upon initiation of the project, the parents would cede him full title to their land. Their agreement further stipulated that the grandparents, as well as the families of the other two sons, could have the use of the house for vacations at mutually agreed upon times.

Site preparation for the second family bungalow began in the late winter of 1956. With melting snow still whitening adjacent woods, in early spring the builders laid the foundation for the house. Frank Marra's brother-in-law, Dom Genovese, applied his architecture's skill in overseeing the construction, as well as selecting materials and colors. From there, things moved quickly compared to the apparently lethargic pace of current homebuilding. In the mid-1950s, houses went up in no time. By mid-April, when the oak trees had barely begun to bud, the house was already under roof. The Marra family ended the school year in grand style, leaving the steamy Bronx for an endless summer in Southampton, the first of many Southampton summers.

The Maffei's: The Family's Third Bungalow

In 1963, Sylvia Maffei, from Yonkers, New York, built her summer bungalow on the lot she had purchased over ten years prior along with her brother and three other sisters. She built her home in partnership with her son, Gilbert Maffei, on the middle lot, between the Saracino and Marra houses, and by so doing, completed the family "compound." With her two sons, their spouses, and her grandchildren, she vacationed at her Southampton home into the 1970s. The house, which was built by the same builder using almost the same design as the first two family bungalows, passed on to Gilbert, upon Sylvia's passing, and later to his wife, Marion and daughter, Frances.

Following the construction of the Maffei house (sometimes called the "middle" house), the other two family properties, owned by the Manzo and Tamborino families, lay untouched for several years. They remained as vacant lots for years until they were sadly were sold off on the open market to non-family members.

Southampton Summers: The Exploring Years, Late 1940s to Early 1950s

CHAPTER ONE:
First Generation Stories: Explorers and Builders

Albert Marra

A mere seven miles from the Saracino-Marra-Maffei enclave of modest homes, a community of wealthy, elite and influential people had established itself a few decades before the family's arrival. These well-established groups of old Hamptons families resembled characters one reads about in novels (*The Great Gatsby* comes to mind) or sees in Depression-era movies (like *My Man Godfrey*).

In some ways (wealth aside), there's a parallel here, an enormous irony. But one could easily say that not one of the family's first generation—with minor exceptions all skilled craftsmen—ever gave this juxtaposition of cultures and classes a fleeting thought. They could not care less. Why? These family members had experienced such challenges, worked so hard, saved with such frugality, and had become so proud of their accomplishments that none of that could matter. More importantly, they were enjoying Southampton and the beach too much to care!

One's fascination with thinking about all those contrasts could go on and on. But rather than dwell on more of the same, presented in this chapter are sketches of the irrepressible members of the family's first generation. They are the principal family members who explored, built and vacationed at the family's three little bungalows in their senior years.

As children and young adults, the authors of the family's third generation, the "Baby Boomers," were fortunate enough to have spent many of their summers growing up with this special group of people. The images that follow are drawn from still quite vivid recollections of these wonderful

17

people, all of them truly the salt of the earth.

Aunt Helen Saracino

The first members of the family to build a house in Southampton were my father's Aunt Helen and Uncle Joe Saracino, who completed their bungalow in the summer of 1955. Great aunt Helen ("Aunt Helen" to us, "Mama" to her children and grandchildren), was born Elena Marra.

Aunt Helen reveled in her Neapolitan-Italian culture. She represented everything good about the Campania region of southern Italy, especially its culinary arts. And why not? After all, what most Americans consider Italian cuisine emanates from the working-class kitchens of Naples. So it's no surprise that Aunt Helen often treated the entire family, visitors and guests as well, to a number of Neapolitan specialties, which were everyday cooking to her. Among the dishes I remember best: her pizza (a thick, square, usually called Sicilian, often "white"), her linguine with clams, and her unique *scungilli* (conch) dishes.

Aunt Helen and Uncle Joe would spend hours chatting with her brother, Arturo (my paternal grandfather, or "Uncle Arthur" to the family). As he once explained, talking with Aunt Helen involved a linguistic minestrone of Italian, Neapolitan and English that carried him back to his youth in Salerno. Aunt Helen used that mix with her children and friends, sprinkling in enough English for her grandchildren and others of our generation to understand her.

How fortunate for anyone to hear her using colorful Neapolitan words and colloquialisms that you couldn't find in readily available Italian texts. Back then, without anything like Google translate, so much of her language remained strangely unfamiliar to the family's third generation, the born in America "Baby Boomers." Then again, some of Aunt Helen's Southern Italian dialect has crept into the vernacular via popular movies or TV shows like *The Godfather* and *The Sopranos*. The intensity with which she spoke, her hand gestures and body language, and her English and Italian vocabulary tested the PC bounds of her day. Strangely enough, her use of the language surfaces from time to time. A case in point: a few years ago we chuckled after seeing a car with a Virginia vanity license plate reading "SCUGNIZ." Thanks to Aunt Helen, a few *cognoscenti* among us knew that *scugniz* (pronounced skoon-yeetz), the shortened form of *scugnizzo*, meant something like "little street urchin." That's how, with a cheeky grin, Aunt Helen would say "you little rascal" to me or my brother.

Aunt Helen became more vivacious and talkative at the beach. For as many years as she went there, she would insert herself into the middle of things. Resembling a 1950s version of *Masaniello*, the legendary Italian rabble-rouser at the port of Naples, Aunt Helen seemed to lead many of the bayside discussions. She would flit around like a firefly from one group to another, involving everyone in her funny stories in Italian or English. A master conversationalist, no topic was beyond Aunt Helen.

As some would attest, Aunt Helen knew how to stir the pot, and not just on the stove! She immersed herself in everybody's personal matters. Her keen interest in the family extended beyond children and grandchildren to her nieces and nephews. Similar to others of her generation, such interest, welcome or not, came from genuine concern, never malice. Advice? Whether requested or not, it came, and with authority. Somehow she often found out other people's business before they did!

She was such a strong presence that my father always worked at staying on Aunt Helen's good side. For example, every time we arrived at our bungalow, before we unpacked, turned on the power, or hit the head, his standing orders were: drop everything and go directly to the Saracino house to greet (i.e., show respect) to Aunt Helen. She acted like the lady of the manor in returning our hugs and kisses three-fold. Then again, she didn't have to act it: she *was* the lady of the manor.

There were times at the beach when my maternal grandfather ambled by Aunt Helen on his way home from fishing. She would peer into his bucket and compliment his fishing prowess. Always ready to cook fresh seafood, she would volunteer to take any fish he didn't want. That enthusiasm for seafood drew her to the family's favorite Southampton beach game:

19

clamming. Aunt Helen's love of clamming made her legendary. She'd join the family at low tide and have at it with considerable success, gabbing it up the whole time. And then she'd cook them that evening or the next. I'd rate Aunt Helen's clam sauce right up there with my mother's, and that's saying a lot. I still give my mom's red (Manhattan) clam chowder the nod over Aunt Helen's. But nobody (since her passing in 1983) has been able to match Aunt Helen's world's best scungilli.

Uncle Joe Saracino

While Aunt Helen Saracino, my grandfather's sister, was a fun person who loved to talk to her grandchildren and grandnieces and nephews, Great Uncle Joe didn't. "Papa" to his children and most of his grandchildren, Giuseppe Saracino seemed to have little use for talk, at least with the younger generation. If one looks up the word "taciturn," you may easily conjure an image of Uncle Joe.

Maybe he had a reason for his silent demeanor; and maybe some of the kids, making noise and acting like jerks, played a big part in it. Admittedly, it was summer, so many of our generation played tricks on the older adults, and the kids may have upped the ante in Uncle Joe's case. In any event, whether he spoke broken English or his Barese Italian dialect, Uncle Joe's powerful baritone seemed to reverberate even after he stopped talking. That alone would scare anyone. And he *always* used that voice to chastise (and chase) us when we used his back yard as a shortcut to the beach.

I recall Uncle Joe patrolling his property like a veritable *signore*, the lord of the manor, with his dog, Prince, at his side. Prince seemed like the world's biggest, scariest, and smartest German Shepherd. Not only that: Prince was definitely the world's biggest, scariest German Shepherd that responded to his master's commands spoken in English or Italian or both!

War Games

What's hilarious now felt dead serious 60 years ago. Picture this: An old man stooped in an unsteady arthritic gait, approaching from a distance. He leans on a huge wooden shaft—just a sturdy cane, but one that looked like an Iroquois war club to us—with one hand, and restrains his attack dog with the other. We faced this on a daily basis as we tried to get down to the beach as fast as possible by crossing something like Southampton's Siegfried line. We knew what Uncle Joe knew, and he knew that we knew it too: that it was five minutes quicker to get to the beach across his back yard to Pine Tree Road, the dirt road leading to Lake Drive and the beach. Since Uncle Joe rarely went to the beach, he spent his afternoons at the house, often chatting or playing cards with his brothers-in-law. Back then most kids actually thought he stayed back to guard his property! In later years we realized that, like his contemporaries, he preferred his cool screened porch to the hot beach.

It was in the late 1950s and early 1960s when our dealings with Uncle Joe and Prince mimicked the deepest freeze of the Cold War. Patrolling his yard, he looked like an East German border guard on TV. This war of wills began to seem serious. It was as if our little game had become his *raison d'être*. When he wasn't engaged in conversation over espressos with my grandfather or other relatives, Uncle Joe seemed to turn our game into a serious mission. Our little cat-and-mouse (or dog-and-kid) game went something like this.

"Wha youz-a goin-a heah?" he'd shout, then he'd pause and, before we could answer, Uncle Joe would ask where we were going, in Italian: "*Beh, a do' vai?*"

And all through the not so pleasant exchange, Prince would be snarling and testing the limits of his leash and Uncle Joe's strength. After all these years I wonder why Prince, one smart German Shepherd, didn't recognize us. Maybe that dog was on to our game. But his loyalty was to Uncle Joe, and Uncle Joe was yelling at us. We were the invaders, the enemy.

"Youz-a gotta go 'roun-a otha way," he usually added, capping his command with a crisp-"*Capito?*" Got it?" We got it, but that didn't change anything.

"But Zio," we'd sometimes plead tongue-in-cheek, "we're only going to the beach. Can't we just pass through?" His now contorted face expressed loud and clear a definitive no.

Despite how angry Uncle Joe got, we often played dumb and said nothing. A few times we did turn back and go down Red Cedar Road, the dirt road on the other side of our property. But often we just kept talking while still taking the shortcut, thus exacerbating the old man's frustration. His mumbling in Italian and the dog's growling (in Italian, English, or German?) followed us in a crescendo. For years we played the same role in that one-act theatre of the absurd, forcing the old man to reprise his role. At times he'd fool us, planting himself in a chair on one end and tethering Prince on the other end, thus sealing up both ends. When that happened we had to navigate a steady course between our twin nemeses, like Odysseus passing through the Straits of Messina.

The game went on for years until first Prince passed on, followed in 1979 by Uncle Joe. Years later, recalling the game with cousins staying at the Marra and Maffei bungalows, we joked that it all ended upon the reunification of Germany. With peace, all borders disappeared. Guards were no longer needed in Germany, or at Uncle Joe's. Then again, I sometimes fantasize that the bilingual German Shepherd and his Italian master had been summoned to stand guard over a shortcut to an idyllic rocky beach in heaven.

Aunt Helen lived several years longer than Uncle Joe, enjoying fair health for much of that time. Her eldest daughter, Nancy (older by mere minutes than her twin sister Dina) and other relatives continued to take her to Southampton, and she was able to go down to the little beach to swim and chat. And we continued to enjoy talking with her for many summers.

In the years since, whenever we walked to the beach we would still cut across their lot, now owned by Uncle Joe's daughter-in-law, Sylvia Saracino. But under Sylvia's friendly watch, with no barking dogs or scary Italian uncles, the walk became ordinary, even boring: just a short, quiet walk down Pine Tree Road for at least the last 30 years. But to tell the truth, I think I'm not alone feeling like I miss them all: Aunt Helen, of course, but also Uncle Joe. And even Prince.

Grandpa Arthur Marra

When Arturo Marra came into the world in 1891, the Kingdom of Italy had completed its reunification, *Il Risorgimento,* only 20 years prior. For several decades after his birth, Italy continued to suffer political and economic distress, especially in the south. That's an oversimplified explanation, but it describes why the author's paternal grandfather and his brothers and sisters came to America.

Grandpa Marra's birth records and the family's Italian citizenship remain on file in Montesano sulla Marcellana, Province of Salerno. That speck of Google Earth barely houses 8,000 souls, down from when he left in 1906. With help from family members, the 16-year-old Arturo descended the rugged mountains to Naples, where he boarded a ship for New York City. After he arrived he worked as a tailor, married Carmelina (Mary) Marra, and raised three sons. And yes, the surnames are identical, as they were cousins, a not so rare thing back then in Europe.

Grandpa Marra was special to his seven grandchildren, several of whom got to know this well-mannered, soft-spoken man by spending summers in Southampton. With his riveting eyes, expressive smile and matinee-idol wavy hair, Grandpa looked the consummate Italian gentleman, even at the family bungalow. There, Grandpa the raconteur kept us spellbound retelling the story of the Marra family in particular and Italians in general. He shared one of many special "secrets" with us about our heritage: that there are just two kinds of people in the world, Italians, and those who wish they were!

Grandpa wore his Italian lineage like a badge of honor. He was so proud that he always reminded us that the world owed radio and television (like his big-box, small-screen Dumont) to an Italian, Guglielmo Marconi. He explained in great detail that were it not for the genius of Italian inventor Antonio Meucci, Alexander Bell could not have patented the telephone. (Ironic: we didn't *have* a phone at the bungalow; we used Aunt Helen's.) I didn't believe him about Meucci; I thought Grandpa's pride got the best

23

of him. But Congress (H Res 269, in 2002) recognized Meucci's lead in designing the telephone. Grandpa always said that like many immigrants, Meucci "was robbed."

A master tailor for Eagle Suits, my fashion-conscious grandfather always wore his own fine suits with Italian silk ties. Completing the look with a crisply starched shirt, he religiously followed the Italian custom of *fare la bella figura*, that is, to cut a fine figure, make a good impression. Thus attired, Grandpa would walk from his apartment on La Fontaine Ave. to Arthur Avenue (Little Italy in the Bronx) to buy bread, pastries and newspapers. In his heavily accented English he called newspapers "the papes," a malaprop we joked about but still use. And he called the big loaves of crusty Italian bread "sharp bread." Any crusty bread is still "sharp bread" to us.

Although he loved swimming in his earlier years, by the time the Southampton house was built in 1956, Grandpa rarely went to the beach, so no need for bathing suits. While on vacation he never looked "beachy," even on hot days. He didn't wear suits or ties in Southampton, but he did wear white shirts with rolled up sleeves, plus slacks, shoes and socks. On the rare days Grandpa ventured to the beach, he wore a sport shirt with khakis ("chinos"),  but no shorts or anything beach-casual. I can't even form a picture of him in shorts and a tee shirt, much less a swimsuit! Like Uncle Joe and the other traditional Italian-born men, in my more than 15 years of vacationing with him, he usually spent afternoons at the bungalow reading his "papes" or chatting and drinking iced espresso with Uncle Joe on the porch. When he did come down to the beach, it wasn't for the sun or the water: he came down to find Grandma and ask one of his best-known questions: *"Quando si mangia?"* When do we eat?

Grandpa worked in a far-off land called "Brook-a-leen" by the old Italians. He told us that it took him *only* an hour each way by subway from his Bronx home to the factory. He repeated the trip five days a week

24

for over 30 years with no complaints. So ingrained was his routine that when Eagle closed their factory for their July vacation and Grandpa went to Southampton, he couldn't sleep in. After dawn he'd quietly venture out, arms folded, for his first *passeggiatta* around the houses and down the dirt road. Besides taking in the milk and the fresh air, Grandpa had another reason to rise early: Dugan's bakery. Even in that countrified part of Long Island in the 1950s and '60s, with the nearest A&P and Bohack's seven miles away, there was home delivery of tasty American-style baked goods. And every morning, pacing like a sentry to greet Dugan's was Grandpa Marra. While Dugan's could never match Bronx sharp bread, Grandpa splurged on muffins, cakes and pies for all the family. Always generous, he'd tip the driver, as well as the milkman (Sherry's) and the garbage man, without fail.

When Grandpa stayed at the bungalow, he considered garbage disposal important enough to spend money on it, so he ordered weekly trash service. In fact, he disliked anything that wasn't squeaky-clean. He often warned us that something was "doity." The dirt thing—almost a phobia for him—carried over to his avoidance of domestic animals. His frequent warning, "Ats-a doity; no toucha da poozy," (i.e., the cat) struck his grandchildren as hilarious. It still does.

For Grandpa Marra, summers in Southampton usually meant good times for all. But when his grandchildren attained high-school age, it became increasingly challenging to stay with him. With his phobias on the rise, he became uneasy about us going off the property. Once the consummate gentleman on vacation, Grandpa had morphed into the consummate worrier as he entered his 80's. By then he obsessed and

kvetched about everything. Being in Southampton seemed to exacerbate things. Yes, there may have been more to worry about—the remote location, no phone or street lights, the distance from services. But he worried more and more about common things like people going swimming. Thank God he never found out that when we were teenagers we went out on boats!

Left to Right:
Diane, Albert and Eugene Marra

25

In our later teens, we went out with friends at night, and in their cars! Grandpa, who never got a driver's license, couldn't imagine us doing this. So unless my parents ran interference, he forced my brother and me to stay home, play cards or board games, and practice the accordion (me) and the clarinet (my brother). When we were younger, to keep the peace, we did; when we were older, we didn't. Whenever he agreed to let us leave the house, we always carried Grandpa's worries and his parting words with us: "*Stai atento.*" Be on guard, he would always say.

On the other hand, Grandpa found it a bit less worrisome if we went out with relatives, such as the Saracino cousins. Nor did he have a problem with us visiting the aunts and uncles at Aunt Helen's, where Grandpa usually stayed after supper, playing cards (poker, pinochle or "brisc") and drinking wine or strong espresso with anisette or grappa. Despite his quirks, anxieties and strict routines, especially in his later years, he nevertheless holds a special place in the hearts of all. Grandpa Marra was a good man, a well-dressed man, who enjoyed a good life up until his death in 1973 at age 83.

Grandma Mary Marra

Carmelina "Mary" Marra, grandma to us and Aunt Mary to the family, loved the beach. Her positive feelings about that alone would have motivated her to buy land to build a house in Southampton. Born in 1891, the same year as Grandpa, she also hails from the Province of Salerno. They share the same surname as first cousins. In early 20th century Europe, marrying cousins, although not a common custom, did not draw the attention it might today.

Their marriage lasted 60 years. As was the case with many couples of their generation and background, Grandma and Grandpa likely viewed marriage through a different lens than today. Maybe they followed the Italian proverb, "*Moglie e buoi dei paesi tuoi,*" meaning something like "Choose your wife and your cattle from your home town," and all that implies. Grandpa did, and he chose well. He chose Grandma. And she chose him. And it all worked out fine.

Grandma came to America at a young age and attended school here, so she spoke English with no Italian accent, but with some "New Yorkese" common among working-class folks of her age group. For example, an "oi" sound became "er." Thus Grandma said "terlet" for "toilet" and called mischievous kids "sperled" brats. She said it in reverse: an "er" sound often became "oi," thus the sound "thoisty" for "thirsty." And words ending in a vowel often added an "r" sound at the end, so with Grandma, "idea" was "i-*dear*." But we had no trouble understanding her, and found nothing funny when she pronounced the names of our favorite snacks and drinks when we came in hungry or *thoisty*.

For example, she'd always bring out chocolates, cookies and cakes, and chocolate milk or sweet drinks like Yoo-hoo and Hi-C punch. Judging by my memory and photos of her, Grandma helped herself to some of the Oreos or Sunshine Hydrox cookies as well. If we really lucked out, she spread out some Mallomars. And if the weather wasn't too hot (with no danger of melting), she'd sometimes give each of us a Chunky. I can almost taste one and hear the TV commercial with goofy actor Arnold Stang lisping: "Chunkies—what a chunk of chocolate." How odd that these all-American treats came to us compliments of our Italian-born Grandma!

Grandma really loved the little beach near our family bungalows. Anytime the weather was good, she'd go swimming. Try as I might, I can't remember Grandma ever complaining about the rocks at the beach. She always wore clunky old sneakers or old shoes so that the big, slippery rocks wouldn't bother her. Of course, as she got older she would regularly ask one of her grandchildren or other relative to take her arm to help her cross the great divide of moss-covered rocks to get into the water. But those requests were never a complaint or a requirement.

And when Grandma made her way to a waist-high "swimmable" depth, her unsteady gait would easily give way to a very methodical and graceful (albeit slow) form of the doggie paddle. By using that stroke she was able

27

to move well through the water in all but the roughest waves. After all, for a woman in her late70s/early 80s, why move any faster?

Grandma also loved socializing at the beach. I can't remember a decent summer day in Southampton when Grandma didn't enjoy a long afternoon at the beach. She took her time getting there, often walking arm in arm with Aunt Helen. Once they arrived, the two sisters-in-law, like sidekicks, stuck close to each other for their gab sessions. They'd stay together for hours, sometimes taking two or three good dips in the bay with no regard to how cold the water or air. Given what in the 1950s and '60s was considered an average day's exercise for seniors, their frequent swims might seem somewhat ambitious for women their age even now.

One of my most memorable stories about Grandma occurred during one of our earliest summers. One morning Grandma had just gone to the bathroom and I went into her bedroom to get my clothes from the shared dresser and to look for some misplaced baseball cards. While looking for the cards on top of the dresser I noticed something. It looked like a little toy, like a vending machine prize. But it was no toy: it was an eye! Right there on the dresser! Sitting in a tiny cup filled with a clear liquid. And it was looking right back at me, eye to eye!

I nearly jumped out of my skin, barely suppressing a shriek. Just then Grandma came in and, seeing the look on my face, she sat me down for a talk. I tried to look away from the top of the dresser and that slight void on the side of her face as she told me the story of her eyes—the one she lost, and the one still floating in the cup.

As the story goes, one day in her 50s she had a headache and her vision blurred. The blurred vision, resulting from a hemorrhage, caused the eye to become infected and it had to be removed. For years Grandma had been looking at us with a glass eye which she took out at night for cleaning and reinserted the next day, like many grandmothers do with dentures. Well, that seemed reasonable. But from that day on, I noticed a change in my behavior toward Grandma. Actually, two changes: I usually averted my eyes when I talked to her, afraid I might stare at her prosthetic eye. And I never again looked at Grandma's personal stuff, living in mortal fear that her eye—or a worse body part—might appear.

Grandma came to the family's Southampton house every summer except her last four. She was wonderful, and we loved her dearly. She died in 1983 at age 92.

Aunt Sylvia Maffei

On the lot between Aunt Helen and Uncle Joe Saracino and the Marra house, the Maffei branch of the family built the third and last of the family houses a few years after us. Aunt Sylvia Maffei, another of Grandpa Marra's younger sisters, had bought her property with the other Marra siblings at the same time. In the early 1960s she arranged plans with the same contractor, Ruscon Construction, to build a similar bungalow, right down to the exterior trim and the knotty pine kitchen cabinets. The Maffei branch of the family seemed happy enough to replicate the prototype, and whether coincidental or calculated, the uniform three-house design worked out fine for all. In fact, it looked kind of cute.

Aunt Sylvia was a strong but easygoing person. She was admired by most, usually showing a pleasant, friendly, generous demeanor to young and old. For example, on most of trips to Southampton, she brought along a good supply of fresh Italian breads, pastries, cheeses and cold cuts—purchased from specialty stores in the city—to be shared with the other two bungalows. What makes this generosity more impressive is that Aunt Sylvia didn't drive. She bought those specialties in different stores and schlepped them out to Southampton via public transit.

I knew Aunt Sylvia only as a widow. Her sons Richard and Gilbert were always attentive to her, but Gilbert assumed a more active role in building the Maffei family bungalow with her. A few years younger than her siblings, Aunt Sylvia grew up in the United States, spoke perfect English, but kept herself fluent in Italian. Like Grandma Marra, she retained only the slightest vestiges of an Italian accent, and lived a totally assimilated life. As a younger member of her generation, she bridged the old and the new worlds.

I distinctly recall one episode that clearly illustrates the depth of Aunt Sylvia's wisdom, strong but serene nature, and her positive outlook. It happened in the summer of 1966, after my freshman year in college. It was my first weekend off from my summer job, and I had made plans to drive out to Southampton for a weekend with my parents. That Friday evening Aunt Sylvia phoned me at home to ask if I could pick her up (we lived close by in Yonkers) and take her with me to Southampton. Of course I would. I picked her up early the next day.

We cruised along for the first hour with average Long Island traffic in my not so new, but smartly two-toned red on white, hand-me-down '61 Chevy Impala coupe. Twenty minutes after the Long Island Expressway ended, we headed north, and got on Route 25 East, a rural two-lane road on the north shore, and unfortunately encountered what we now call in PC terms an "aggressive driver." They were really just called jerks (or worse!) back then.

I remember that driver vividly. The guy was bad news, a total menace. His banged-up jalopy was swerving all over the road. I first noticed him in my left side view mirror, a few cars behind us, weaving in and out. Then passing three cars at once over a double line he came right behind us, tailgating dangerously close. Finally, it seemed like he was dying to pass not only us but several of the line of cars ahead of us. We were now just about in Rocky Point, approaching Port Jefferson, which in many stretches was still only a two lane (but very busy) country road.

That nut job of a driver finally did pass us, crossing over another double line and cutting in front of us to avoid a head-on collision. By so doing he came much too close to my beloved Impala. In order to get back into our line of traffic and avoid colliding with several cars in the oncoming traffic, he nearly ran us off the road. That last move infuriated young, macho me to the point where of course I wanted to return the "favor." I wanted to pass and cut in front of him and run him into the ditch. Dumb but true.

Older and certainly much wiser, Aunt Sylvia came to my rescue. In fact, she saved the day for all. She saw what I was about to do and calmed me down, speaking in her usual mature, deliberate tone.

"Albert," she said, after getting my full attention, "you must know how stupid he is for doing that." She added, "Why would you want to behave like him? He'll eventually get into enough trouble all by himself."

It took just five minutes to see how prophetic her words were. Call it karma, payback, or whatever, but that jerk sure got his.

He apparently had passed several cars in like manner and then disappeared from sight for those five minutes. Then we saw him on the side of the road. Right behind him was a black and white Suffolk County cop car with its big dome light revolving and flashing red all around. With a knowing smile on her cherubic face, Aunt Sylvia turned and whispered two little Italian words she knew I'd understand: "*Hai visto?*" ("Did you see that?") That's how she ended the lesson. And yes I saw.

Aunt Sylvia spent a few more summers enjoying the little beach with her sisters and brother. She left this world in 1971, just a few years after that incident. Her bungalow, the "newest" of the family compound, looks much the same now as when it was built over 55 years ago. It remained in the hands of her son, Gilbert, until his untimely death in 2013, passing then to his wife, Marion, and Aunt Sylvia's grandchildren, Frances and Louis.

Grandpa Antonio Genovese ("Nonnon")

My maternal grandparents, Antonio and Rosa Genovese, while not blood relatives of any of the Saracino-Marra-Maffei clan, nevertheless spent many summers at our bungalow. During the early years the family spent in Southampton, they got so close to everyone in the other two bungalows that they became part of the extended Marra family. They had become especially close to the other members of the family's first generation, those born in Italy.

We called my grandfather Nonnon, a form of *Nonno* ("Grandpa") whose suffix (*-one*) means "big" and "impressive." Thus, loosely translated, he became "Big Grandpa," as a term of endearment. While physically diminutive, Antonio Genovese embodied everything in the name "Nonnon." At five-foot-five and of slight build, he carried himself like a man twice his size. Whether hauling lumber, crushing grapes, or sporting his fishing pole like Don Quixote carrying his lance, he cut an impressive figure. We could never have used the Italian word "Nonn*ino*," or "*Little Grandpa*," for this larger-than-life character. And if you got to know him, you'd begin to understand the dead-on accuracy of his name.

Nonnon came from Palizzi, a small town in Calabria, the "toe" of Italy's "boot." He and his older brother, the curmudgeonly Zi' Cheech ("Uncle Frankie"), found their way to New York in 1908. Rumor has it that they left a sister behind, but nobody ever looked into it. Neither brother talked about having any family members other than the children who were born in America. And nobody ever asked.

Nonnon practiced the art and craft of cabinet-making and he maintained his little carpentry shop in the Bronx (near Zerega Avenue and Santa Maria Church) well into his 80s. All of his grandchildren still treasure the objects he crafted from raw wood into works of art using just hand tools. He could make anything out of wood and similar materials, and to support his wife and seven children he built room additions and even entire houses. He also left his mark on our Southampton bungalow.

For example, the cement patios he put in during the early years are still in fine condition, without a crack or other sign of their 60 years. He also finished the floor, walls and ceiling of our screened porch. Maybe it's something passed down by tradition, for it seems that from the ancient Romans to today, Italians like Nonnon can claim the title "World's Greatest Builders."

Nonnon was also a great fisherman. He caught fish when nobody else did, in places said to be "fished out." Locals told him that in 1956 when he first visited Southampton. Whenever he came, he spent most of his days fishing at the end of our beach, close to the end of a bulkhead where a narrow channel had been dredged into the salt pond. People often chuckled when they caught a glimpse of this solitary old man fishing near the channel. I'm sure they were thinking, "How cute; how quaint."

For as long as I can remember, with his shock of close-cropped white hair and day-old stubble sprouting from his wrinkles, Nonnon looked and acted old. Some of us joked that he may have been born old. We began to believe that after seeing the movie about Benjamin Button, born as an old man who grew younger as he "aged." Tongue in cheek, we convinced ourselves that Nonnon had inspired the film. We recognized deep-down that Nonnon, with his ruddy face, weathered skin and worn-out looks from his tough life, could never be a comic figure or the butt of a joke. With one look, anyone could see that life had challenged him. But he accepted and overcame whatever life threw at him.

Nonnon was a dead ringer for Feodor Chaliapin, Jr., the actor who played the grizzled grandfather in the movie, *Moonstruck*. And like that stereotypical Italian-American, Nonnon became a sympathetic figure to us too. Instead of walking dogs in Brooklyn Heights as in the movie, Nonnon, with forearms as big as Popeye's, portaged his gear along the dirt roads leading to the beach. His tackle accoutrement consisted of at least two high-end poles, a bucket, and a hand-made wood box filled with hooks, lures and sinkers made from lead he had molded the prior winter. He got up each day at first light and left without waking a soul. Our family fisherman knew the proverb, *"Chi dorme non piglia pesci,"* that is, he who sleeps catches no fish. Before the first boatload of would-be fishermen left the local salt pond, Nonnon had already cast two lines out into the smooth green-black surface of the bay. He then fixed his rods to a high post along the rip-rap, the row of large concrete chunks, where he patiently waited for a bite. His presence at the end of the beach stood in stark contrast to the gaggle of vacationers he had to run through as he left the narrow beach each day on the way home.

I frequently accompanied Nonnon to the beach and helped carry his things. At times I'd bring his favorite breakfast, Mom's made-from-scratch biscuits with jelly and a thermos of midnight-black coffee. He seemed to relish standing out in the damp, foggy morning chill. The heat of the peak summer sun never crept far enough under his hat to bother him, but he usually tried to get home by 3:00 p.m. after he had finished his breakfast, lunch, or snacks and before too many beach-goers showed up to annoy him, not so much by spoiling his fishing but his solitude. On the hottest days he might return before lunchtime, then spend a lazy afternoon reading the papers or nodding off in our cool, shady yard.

33

My earliest memory of fishing with Nonnon in Southampton was just after our house went up. In 1956 there were very few houses on the marshes around the salt pond. Nonnon and I were circling the brackish pond towards the channel when an old guy on his morning rounds stopped us.

"Whadderya goin' fer around here?" the old man asked. "Ya know it's all been fished out."

Nonnon, having heard this before, nodded at him politely, then looked quizzically at me and hid his annoyance well, but then directed two little Italian words to me.

"*Che dice?*" I understood, and explained in my best Italian that the guy said there were no fish left around here.

Nonnon smiled at the man, and deferentially tipped his hat, saying, "Wellatza' kay." He then mumbled some words in my direction. "*Ma che sa quello la?*" "So, what does that guy there know?"

I don't remember what the bag limits were or what was in season, but I do recall with my sense of pride or gloating when Nonnon caught several fish that day. Too bad, mister know-it-all, I said to myself with a smile. I helped Nonnon carry home a bucket with two nice eels, a flounder and a couple of blowfish (AKA sea squab or puffers, not the poisonous ones prized by the Japanese). So while that guy may have known the local waters, what did he know about Nonnon and his fishing prowess?

According to a proverb attributed to the poet Khalil Gibran, days spent fishing will not be subtracted from one's days on earth. The proverb may have been true for Nonnon. He lived until age 94, and experienced a peaceful departure he seemed to have willed himself. We consoled ourselves with the knowledge that he loved fishing, especially at the little beach in Southampton, almost to the end. And true to his convictions, in later years Nonnon never said good-bye when we were about to part company. Instead he'd shake his head and somberly utter two prophetic words: *sotto terra*—under the earth. In effect he was saying, "The next time you come will be to bury me." Of course, to be proven correct, Nonnon needed to make good on his prediction only once. He did that in 1978.

Grandma Genovese

You won't find any reference to the world's greatest Italian cook, my maternal grandmother, Rosa Genovese, in any gourmet guide or fine-living magazine. There are no books (except this one) by or about her. And forget whatever you may know about other famous chefs. While my family considers Lidia Bastianich among the most authentic of popular Italian cooks, she comes in second to the one we consider *the best* Italian cook: Grandma Genovese.

Born Rosa Maria Colitti in the province of Campobasso, Grandma came to America at a young age, and for years her life resembled that of an indentured servant. The relatives who had sponsored her trip made her work for them. Not knowing English or the ways of her new country, she spent years cooking and cleaning with little compensation. Eager to move on, she married Antonio Genovese at age 20, and together they raised four sons and three daughters, after losing one daughter, Irene, as an infant.

Grandma was endowed with many positive traits, but most memorable were her down-to-earth culinary talents. Our skillful Grandma's produced meals that were nothing short of heavenly, without equal. She cooked all kinds of food well, and her Italian cooking was not only authentic but out-of-this-world *saporito*. That's Italian for yummy, Giada. And she made every dish the old–fashioned way: from scratch, and with only the freshest ingredients.

In Southampton, where she spent over 20 summers, Grandma cooked anything bought, caught or gathered, whether groceries from store or stand or something from woods or water. She even made weeds taste great, like the dandelions growing around the bungalows. And she always found a time-tested way to turn anything into treats for the table. Grandma encouraged us to do things like pick wild blueberries and blackberries along the dirt roads, and buy strawberries and other fresh fruits and vegetables at area farms. She also encouraged us to catch fish and shell fish at the beach, and even to hunt small game in the surrounding woods.

And we did all that, some things more than others. For example, from an early age, my brother, Eugene, hunted. Yes, that boy really did hunt in Southampton! And he pursued all kinds of prey, using stones, a homemade slingshot, or bow and arrow. He later graduated to a pellet gun. He bagged anything with fur or feathers, from rabbits and squirrels to pheasants and partridge. And we all became skilled at catching fish and gathering shellfish alone or on frequent outings with Nonnon. And at low tide, Mom and I frequently dug for clams and scungilli (conch or whelks) in the waters off our rocky little beach. True to form, Grandma stood ready to clean and cook our catch. Thanks to Grandma's encouragement, our family became an unlikely, but successful, hunter-gatherer clan. We were apartment-dwellers spending summers at the beach, but we wanted and got fresh foods for the table, beating the whole-foods craze by decades.

Grandma had the knack to clean all kinds of fish, including tough-skinned eels. I was eight when I first saw Nonnon catch those amazing creatures at our beach. He told me that *anguilla* was their true Italian name, but that the larger females (at three feet long) were known as *capitone* in southern Italy. Eels put up a great fight and are very hard to catch; they're so tough that they can survive out of water for more than a day. But landing them isn't half the battle; cleaning them is the real challenge. Plus, the eels we got in Southampton, while not the electric kind, never stopped squirming and writhing. They're such marvelous survivors that it's easy to believe the tall tales about their ancestors slithering from water to mud to evolve into snakes. Plus, eel skin is as tough as leather and twice as slippery.

So to the rescue comes our four-foot-eleven Grandma. She explained in her best Italian-English mix that the sure way to skin an eel was by "the rag method." She gathered some rags, which I later had to bury with the stinky eel skins and guts using Dad's World *Al and the eel family* War II US Army shovel. With the skill of a surgeon, Grandma's arthritic but agile hands made careful incisions. Cut one carved out the guts; cut two encircled the ugly head, nearly severing it, leaving skin and connective tissue intact. Then with both hands wrapped in dry rags, she gripped the dangling head with one hand and the body with the other, pulled back the partially decapitated head along the length of the body in one swift move, deftly turning it inside-out. What was left was just the meat, a still-writhing piece of delectable white flesh, with hardly an errant bone anywhere. She had made the eel ready to grill, fry or pickle.

Far less ghastly a treat had to be Grandma's signature dish: *maccheroni alla chitarra* (guitar-pressed egg noodles), a specialty of her Molise region that she often made in Southampton. It consisted of hand-rolled dough pressed through metal wires strung on a wooden apparatus much like a guitar or an Appalachian zither. The result: tasty long noodles similar to fettucine. Rumor has it that Grandma's lost "guitar" is buried somewhere in somebody's attic. Assuming we find it intact, we can only dream of replicating Grandma's skill. Maybe only *she* could make those divine, cook-in-a-flash, light-as-air noodles that tasted like al dente confetti from heaven. She teamed them with a variety of sauces, like fresh marinara or meat ragu, in soups, or with lentils or chick peas. For some reason, her fresh macaroni tasted much better at the bungalow. Was it the iron-rich well water? Salt air? Farm-fresh eggs? Or maybe it had something to do with how nice it was for family to work together at the beach house.

After Nonnon died in 1978, Grandma lived on for over ten years, and she spent several of those summers in Southampton. In her final years, her advanced age prevented her from making the trip while she was in the care of the good sisters at the Providence Rest nursing home in the Throggs Neck section of the Bronx. Ironic, but the home backed up to the Long Island Sound, near where Nonnon took me fishing as a young boy. When Grandma died in 1991, she was more than six months into her 100th year. A devout Catholic, she surely earned a special place in heaven. The world lost a top-notch cook, but we have a feeling that not only is she close to God, but that God now can enjoy something we sorely miss: Grandma's heavenly *maccheroni alla chitarra*.

Uncle Domenico (Zi' Mimi)

He was neither a Marra, nor a Saracino or a Maffei, but Uncle Domenico

37

Colitti—our Italian uncle, Zi' Mimi—should be included here, since he travelled all the way from Italy to spend three summer vacations with the Marra family in Southampton. He is called our "Italian uncle," and although all of our first generation family members were born in Italy, this uncle was special. Zi' Mimi belonged to a rare breed, as one of only very few of my grandparents' siblings on either side who never left Italy. So in his case, "Italian" really means "from Italy," to distinguish him from the Italian aunts and uncles born in Italy who emigrated from their native land to spend their lives in America.

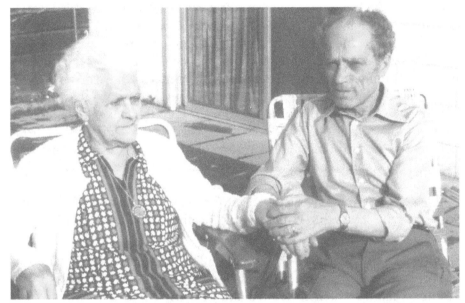

Grandma Rosa and Zi' Mimi, circa 1979

Zi' Mimi was my maternal grandmother's younger brother. He was a baby when she set sail for America and he stayed behind in Campobasso. As a result, Grandma didn't really get to know her brother until she visited Italy and stayed with him in the 1950s and 1960s. We got to know him when he visited the family in the New York area in the 1960s and 1970s.

Zi' Mimi reveled in his three visits to Southampton. He did go down to the beach a few times, but like other males of his generation, he hardly ever put on a bathing suit or went swimming, no matter how hot. He enjoyed visiting local tourist spots like Sag Harbor's Whaling Museum and the Shinnecock Canal. As the head of his provincial elections board (a big deal in Italy), Zi' Mimi showed keen interest visiting historic places in America, including many Civil War and Revolutionary War sites in Virginia and the DC area. But his main reason for coming here became obvious when he spent time with his sister, Rosa, and when he chatted with her and the Italian-born Marra, Saracino and Maffei relatives from the other two bungalows.

Being with his sister meant a great deal to him—to both of them—because they didn't really know each other well until they almost entered their golden years. Their separation as children endured all the longer thanks to Italy's problems of the early 1900s, then World War I and World War II (during which, as a soldier in Mussolini's army, Zi' Mimi spent time as a "guest" of the British in South Africa). Brother and sister could never make up for so much lost time, of course, but these Southampton visits helped them solidify their relationship in their later years.

One small, everyday interaction between Grandma and Zi' Mimi illustrates the different directions their lives had taken. The setting, the screen porch; the time, breakfast.

Now it should be noted that Zi' Mimi, fully educated in Italy, spoke mostly standard Italian, while Grandma spoke the south-central Molise dialect she had learned as a child. She also functioned well in English, but with a heavy accent.

On several occasions, Grandma offered to cook breakfast for Zi' Mimi at the bungalow. Usually she offered her signature—and wonderful—eggs fried in olive oil.

One day she asked her stunned brother, "You wanna hegga?" (Well, that's how Grandma always asked us, and we always understood, so that's how she would ask her brother too.) The poor fellow had no earthly idea what she was saying, or to whom.

Hearing no reply, Grandma repeated the question several times, each time more emphatically: *"You wanna hegga?"*

Now totally bewildered, Zi' Mimi asked everyone what she was saying. We tried to explain that she was using the word "egg" in English because that's what she always said, and that it didn't occur to her that he needed to hear the word in Italian. Also, maybe she had forgotten the word *ouvo*, Italian for egg. We never succeeded in explaining the dilemma to him, but no matter. The fact is, most Italians, Zi' Mimi included, don't eat eggs for breakfast. But he did have another cup of her rich coffee, perfect for double-dunking his toasted Italian bread.

We last visited Zi' Mimi in Campobasso in late 1998, a year before his death at age 95. While there we looked through some photo albums with him, his sons and grandchildren, and found several photos taken in Southampton, including several of Grandma with her brother, our Zi' Mimi. All of the photos in those albums seemed to glow with warmth and love. But the ones of Grandma and our Italian uncle seemed to jump off the page.

"Heggas" anyone?

Messages from Our First Generation

They were old fashioned and they were Italians. Not only were they all old fashioned Italians, but they were all from the South of Italy, all *meridionali, terroni,* that is, your garden variety, red wine and red sauce, pasta-eating types who incessantly talked to each other but seemed to erect barriers to strangers, rarely expressing their true feelings outside the family. Yet, they enjoyed opening themselves with the rest of the family at their rocky Riviera on the bay. To them, that all constituted proof positive that they had fulfilled the American dream.

Some first generation members who did not have their own place would visit the family compound of their siblings for what usually meant short stays of two or three days at most. These included my grandfather's brother, Zi' Pep (Uncle Joe), Aunt Phil (Filomena) and Uncle Mike, Aunt Adelina, Aunt Lidia, and others. They usually bunked at Aunt Helen's or Aunt Sylvia's. Unfortunately, the two other property-owning sisters, Aunt Phil and Aunt Adeline, never built on their lots and ended up selling their properties.

The explorers and builders of the family's first generation in Southampton left few tangible assets to their heirs other than their houses. But they left an even greater, more important legacy, albeit in a totally intangible form: that relying on one's own hard work, dedication to family, and careful husbanding of resources, anything is possible, even a home in Southampton.

Cousin Gilbert Maffei, second generation owner of one of the bungalows, pulled no punches in assessing the accomplishments of the family's first American generation in these words of praise: "For a family that came to this country with virtually nothing, I think that the three bungalows represented a tremendous achievement ... a dream many immigrants have, but few could ever achieve."

Southampton Summers: The Building Years, Mid 1950s to Early 1960s

CHAPTER TWO:
Second Generation Stories: "*Our* Greatest Generation"

Albert Marra

By the mid-1970s, the steady stream of visitors to Southampton from the "old guard," that is, first generation family members born in Italy, slowed to a trickle. By the early 1980s, with most of the original settlers and builders deceased or in declining health, the stream of visitors had already shifted to another group of owners and their families. These were the members of the family's second generation at the beach. They are the family's first native born Americans, and they belong to "The Greatest Generation," the term author Tom Brokaw used in his book of that name.

My parents, their siblings, and their cousins also belong to an important sub-group of that generation: the children of immigrants—and not just Italian immigrants. They and their peers, especially those raised in bi-lingual, bi-cultural communities, insulated themselves to some extent by language, traditions, and mores. A smaller, though not insignificant number of their sub-group also experienced subtle bias and episodes of mistrust by the dominant culture. Throughout their lives people like our parents underwent tremendous pressures to "Americanize" and to assimilate into the dominant culture. And assimilate they did. They did that for the sake of their families. Fortunately for those of us who followed, they did so without compromising the best features of their Italian heritage.

The Great Depression, which had influenced this generation greatly during their childhood or adolescence, shaped their adult world view. So a few years later, almost all of them helped their country fight in World War II because it was "the right thing to do." And in the post-war years of the late 1940s through the 1950s, these family members joined fellow

Americans to share in the fruits of peace and prosperity: they found good jobs, got married, started families, and bought homes, many of these in the suburbs. They enjoyed successful, satisfying, American lifestyles. Their 1950s lifestyle included vacations with the family at the Southampton bungalows. While there they passed down the Italian traditions that nourished them as children to the generations that followed. Through these stories about the second generation it is possible to shine a light on the second group of owners of the Saracino-Marra-Maffei family bungalows and their Southampton summers.

Memories of Cecile Marra

My mother, Cecilia Pasqua Genovese (Cecile or Celia to many family members), was born in New York City, the fourth of Rosa and Antonio's seven children. Mom worked as a seamstress before and during World War II, and later in small union shops in Yonkers. She stopped working when the children came, then went back to work when her second son, Eugene, hit third grade; she finally retired from her active life as a seamstress when in her mid-70s. My children still remember attending union events with their grandmother and singing along with her "Look for the Union Label," the popular 1970s-1980s jingle promoted by ILGWU in their TV spots.

We lived in a small apartment off Gun Hill Road in the East Bronx until I reached 13, when Dad bought a home in Yonkers. I don't remember my mother complaining, and I don't know how she managed things before that move, but our Bronx flat had little space and few conveniences. Nor do I know how my parents, both of modest means, managed to swing a Southampton vacation home for 60 years along with the house. But they did! Although Mom liked the break from the city, she developed a love-hate relationship with the bungalow. As enjoyable as the beach became, perhaps she didn't relish packing up her household in June, unloading it 85 miles away, and reversing things two months later.

Each summer Dad packed the car, did all the driving and, with our help, unloaded the car into the bungalow. After that, Dad, my brother, Eugene, and I gravitated toward the beach, thus leaving poor Mom to get the house in order. Sometimes we helped collect the smelly moth balls she had tossed around the prior year; but Mom often did that alone. And,

44

yes, the moth balls worked. Consider: we never had many critters, just occasional attic mice, a family of chipmunks, and an errant raccoon who billeted himself in the crawl space. Not bad, considering that the land really belonged to them.

Mom's conflicted attitude towards the bungalow might be attributed to its very basic conditions and her workload there. Still, she always tried to have a good time. And Eugene and I had lots of good times with her, especially in the earliest years when Dad had left the three of us to return to work in the city. I have fond memories of Mom playing with us at the beach, walking along the beach to collect rocks, shells or tide-tossed flotsam. We had fun gathering clams and other shellfish at low tide. In fact, Great Aunt Helen's clam digging prowess aside, Mom should have been crowned family "clamming queen." And after she caught them, she cooked them. Her seafood dishes included baked clams with homemade bread crumbs, linguine with white clam sauce (still my favorite) and Manhattan (red) clam chowder, the best ever. She also performed culinary magic with my grandfather's catch of the day. And to this day, nothing compares to breakfasts with Mom's made-from-scratch biscuits or waffles.

From the earliest years, Mom had a lot on her plate every day: she waged a constant battle to keep our beach house free of sand, dirt and

bugs. She also did almost all the cooking, three great meals a day (we are, after all, Italian) with no respite, and without a grocery for miles. Every afternoon, Mom rushed home from the beach to start cooking dinner, following which she washed the dishes (we helped dry them) and cleaned up. It wasn't until close to dark that she got to finish the things she

L-R: Cecile Marra, Grandma Rosa Genovese, Nonnon, Aunt Lena Genovese, Frank Marra. circa 1975

didn't get to in the morning. To that frenetic pace just add a liberal dose of visiting relatives!

From the mid-1950s to the mid-1960s, it seemed we had a red neon sign in front of our bungalow that flashed "Vacancy." This may be one of the downsides of a large Italian-American family, that is, relatives tend to stay close, sometimes too close. We tend to get together frequently, and at times we run the risk that we glom on to each other, like what sometimes happened in Southampton.

No surprise then that so many relations visited, some just "passing by" on Noyac Road. And no surprise that the real burden fell on my mother, adding to her ambivalence toward the place. Visitors like hers or my father's brothers, sisters and children, my cousins, meant continuous work: entertaining, cooking and cleaning. All of that plus catering to the needs of our aging grandparents could have been a recipe for disaster. Yet, to her credit, Mom always averted that seemingly inevitable explosion, always trying to make things pleasant. She took pride in how the house looked, periodically redecorating with new bedspreads and wall hangings; she spent winters sewing new curtains; she insisted that the walls look freshly painted; and she planted flowers every spring, usually bought from farmers on the drive out, always after some skillful haggling on her part.

We enjoyed helping Mom plant the spring flowers (with pansies being her favorite), rake the abundant leaves and trim the bushes. In the 1970s and beyond, after both of her sons had married and moved away, she took on the yard work herself and did a great job. The whole property looked neat and clean and welcoming to visitors of her generation and ours. It continued that way when my brother and I visited with our own children, whom we often left in her care for days or even weeks. In her declining years, Mom told us how she and Dad enjoyed their quiet "empty-nester" years in Southampton and the many things they did alone or with their four grandchildren—Andrew, Alex, Clara and Gabe.

After making many great summers possible for her immediate and extended family through the summer of 2013, her last at the beach, Mom passed away in late 2016. Since then, things have never been the same at the Marra bungalow. Well, at least we can dedicate this book to her. She *earned* it!

Frank Marra in Southampton

Frank Marra is my larger-than-life 100-year-old father. He's "Dad" to me and my brother, Eugene, and Grandpa or Pop-Pop to his grandchildren. But to many people, inside or outside the family, he's Frank *E.* Marra, accenting the "E," to distinguish him from his first cousin, also a Marra and also named Frank—Frank *M.* Marra. Why two Franks? And with the same last name. "Frankly," nobody really knows for sure. But somehow the US Army found a way to keep the identity of the two Frank Marra cousins straight throughout World War II combat, while they both served in the same field artillery unit in the UK, France, Belgium and even into Germany.

Our Dad, "Frank E," has always prized our bungalow and the nearby no-name beach. That beach is Dad's favorite part of his favorite place in the world. He has always relished that first swim of the summer. Okay, he has always loved swimming, at any body of water or pool: in-ground, above-ground, or hole-in-the-ground. But it's only at the rocky beach where he would seem totally at ease. The last time I saw him spend a full day at his little preserve he followed the same rituals: after unloading the car, he sat in a beach chair to put on his rubber shoes to protect against rocks and shells; then he carefully navigated his way over the slippery rocks. After washing away his worldly woes he would emerge renewed from the water with a look of contentment only to be found at that beach. It's been like that from our earliest days there until about five years ago. Since then, on his last (no-swim) visits, even with help, he struggled to make it down the dune and across the rocks to chat briefly with good friends like Margaret and Pat C.

But let's get back to the beginning, the summer of 1955, with building at the Saracino bungalow winding down. My father, then a management trainee at Chemical Bank, hatched a plan with my grandparents, who owned property two lots away from the Saracino's. It went something like this: whoever among the three sons could finance a house would get title to the land. Neither his brother Joseph nor Edward stepped up, so Dad put in his bid. Realizing that he'd have to work harder at his job at the bank by day and at Yonkers Raceway by night, he obtained a $5,000 mortgage to build our bungalow. In today's dollars, that 1955 mortgage would be a tidy sum for many, but it would pale in comparison to the loans in place in the Hamptons today. Dad paid off the mortgage 60 years ago (see Appendix Three, page 245), thus permanently securing the bungalow for our family.

Dad mastered the beach vs. career challenge many years ago. When you love the water as much as Dad, you find time for the beach. When we were kids, he split his three weeks of summer vacation into one- or two-week periods. For the rest of the summer he'd come to Southampton only on weekends. Like many other dads, he'd leave Mom, Eugene and me at the bungalow during the week with grandparents or other relatives. He could hardly wait for Fridays to drive back to Southampton.

So what did we do with Dad in Southampton? Well, we didn't go fishing much. No, he left that to Nonnon, our family's great fisherman. Mostly we went to the beach, provided we had finished doing daily chores such as making the beds, sweeping the porch, and picking up twigs and leaves around the bungalow. Dad also took us almost every summer to one or two special events such as the carnivals put on by the Fire Department or Elks, and the Pow-Wows held by the Shinnecock Indians. While we didn't visit many local tourist sites, he did take us to the Long Beach town beach near Sag Harbor often enough, and to Montauk once, but I had to discover other local attractions such as Shelter Island and Orient Point later in life. Maybe he was tired of driving; maybe he just loved the local beach more.

Who wouldn't treasure the good times we had in Southampton, which I know we owe to my father's hard work at two jobs. Dad taught us a great deal about life, especially about dedication to work, to family, and to friends and community, as well as the importance of spending summers with family at the beach. Thus, to him as well this book is dedicated.

Cousins Savy and Sylvia Saracino

I remember my father's friend and close cousin, Savy, and his wife, Sylvia, very well. And my memories apply to them both not only at Southampton, but also back home in the city. Why? Simple: Savy served as the Marra family dentist for many years.

Dr. Saracino treated me well as his special patient, taking great care of my teeth, almost throughout my childhood. As soon as I hit fourth or fifth grade, I would periodically walk from my school, St. Ann's on Bainbridge Avenue and Gun Hill Road, the few short blocks to Savy's dental office. If I had to see "my dentist" other than when school was in session, I just hopped on the number 15 bus up Gun Hill Road to his office. I remember Savy as a kind, gentle person, who always treated me with a great amount of caring attention, both inside the dentist's office or beyond. He often drove a bunch of us kids to the movies and other special attractions in the Southampton area.

Savy's wife, Sylvia, remains a favorite of kids, no matter what age. As a youngster, I remember how kindly she related to all the cousins at the three bungalows, often treating us to sweets and cold drinks, both down at the beach and at the house. While we were little she often invited us to join her three children, Linda, Ellen and Raymond, on visits to "town," that is, Southampton village. She also included us in many outings to the movies or the drive-in theater. There always seemed to be room for many more kids in Sylvia's growing family brood.

Upon the passing of Aunt Helen Saracino, one of the last surviving members of the family's first generation, ownership of the Saracino bungalow passed on to the second generation of the family. Decades old rumors about the details of that matter notwithstanding, the Saracino property legally transferred to Savy Saracino in 1983. After Savy's unfortunate losing battle with cancer, the first family bungalow built in Southampton became the property of his widow, Sylvia, who has lovingly cared for the family's legacy property for over three decades. Any account of the process of how those two transfers occurred remains well beyond both the scope and certainly the premise of this book.

How ironic, or maybe fitting, that Sylvia Saracino has become the owner and trustee of the family's legacy property in Southampton. After all, she formed part of the nucleus of vacationers who first visited the area when they rented a Southampton Shores cottage in the late 1940s and early 1950s.

Cousins Gilbert and Marion Maffei

In 1962-63, a little more than five years after we built our home, my father's Aunt Sylvia Maffei, one of the family's first generation, began to build her home. She did that together with her son, Gilbert, and her daughter-in-law, Marion. The Maffei house was right next to ours, in the middle lot between our bungalow and the Saracino clan. Of course, the family went with the same Riverhead-based builder, using almost the identical design, materials, and even color, not that there ever was anything wrong with those similarities. With all three little houses in a row looking very much the same from the outside, it seemed to unify our little family enclave in another important way. That lasted for about 50 years, until 2010, when Sylvia Saracino remodeled their family's home.

Marion and Gilbert, my father's first cousins, spent most of their lives in Yonkers; in fact, they lived not at all far away from where my parents lived. In Yonkers the couple raised their two children, daughter Frances and her younger brother, Louis. As mentioned elsewhere in this book, due to the age difference (I was more than ten years older than Frances, and thus even a few years older than Louis), we did not do much together in Southampton during our childhood years. Well, at least we were able to observe our two neighboring second cousins a "half-generation" behind us, as they grew up, got married, and had children of their own: Selena, Victoria, and Anthony to cousin Frances; John and Joseph to cousins Louis and Bianca.

Marion was always a delight to be around; she was usually happy, easy going and very positive about most things. Marion always offered to help any of the older generation and it should be noted that she rarely entered any of the family—well, with discretion and for the sake of family peace—it may be best to just use the term "family discussions" in lieu of a more precise but possibly pejorative term.

Gilbert, on the other hand, who never seemed to me to be a shrinking violet, seemed to be a realist or maybe a pragmatist. He saw things as they were. That meant that he often took positions on things quite diametrically opposed to my father. The two first cousins debated, discussed, and yes, they argued, on anything and everything from current events and politics to where the boundary lines between their two adjoining properties could be found. Without ordering a surveyor or pulling out copies of the plats, let's just say that they had to agree to disagree about which tree belonged to whom, which bushes hung over whose property line, and who should be responsible for cutting which piece of lawn. For what seemed like years and years (decades?), the two cousins never seemed to get beyond mere tolerance or maybe a peaceful coexistence with each other. Gilbert loved to rib my father about things that obviously needed to be done on my father's property. For example, Gilbert would say things like, "Frank, didn't you notice that branch is falling down, that it's nearly hitting your roof?"

Not ever to be outdone by his younger cousin, my father would likewise never pass up an opportunity to give Gilbert "the business" on any similar shortcomings on the other side, the "Maffei side" of the (non-existent, but imagined) fence separating the two bungalows.

Gilbert Maffei, working in his back yard, circa 1965

On reflection, one can surmise that the cousins did not really dislike each other; rather, they each wanted to see who could get the other guy's goat by the constant poking and prodding. Why? To this day I can't figure precisely what caused their usually good-natured animus, except to note that Gilbert was about 20 years younger than my dad. That put him closer in age (by a separation of just over ten years) to me and my cousins, the family's third generation at the beach. Gilbert's proximity to me and my generation, and his separation from my father and his generation, very likely accounted for much of the testy relationship between the two first cousins.

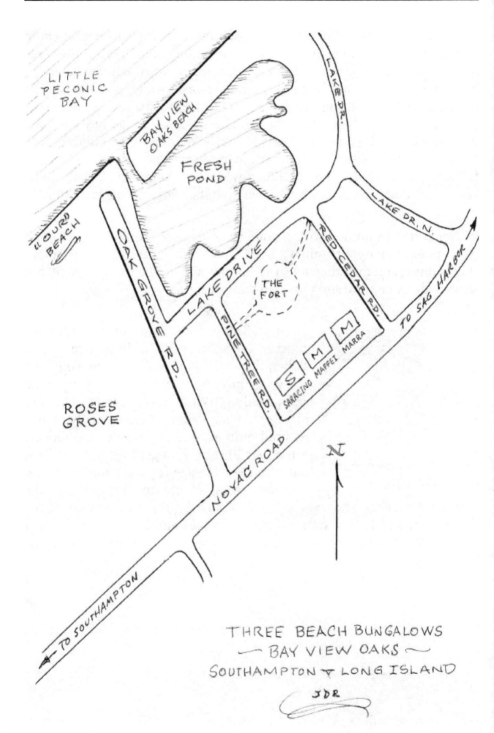

LITTLE
PECONIC
BAY

BAY VIEW OAKS BEACH

FRESH POND

LAKE DR.

LAKE DR. N.

"LOURD BEACH"

OAK GROVE RD.

LAKE DRIVE

THE FORT

RED CEDAR RD.

TO SAG HARBOR

PINE TREE RD.

S   M   M
SARACINO MAFFEI MARRA

ROSES GROVE

N

NOYAC ROAD

TO SOUTHAMPTON

THREE BEACH BUNGALOWS
~ BAY VIEW OAKS ~
SOUTHAMPTON ⳨ LONG ISLAND

JDR

Southampton: Our First Years

Judith Marra Scott

The landscape of my young life was never brighter than in the summer months we spent at the Southampton community of Southampton Shores. The vast cloud of World War II had cleared, albeit slowly, and days were bright with renewed promise.

By 1948, my father had been discharged from duty as an Army physician and my mother's summer vacations from teaching held the prospect of true leisure. They learned of this idyllic community on Little Peconic Bay from a decorated war hero and an Army buddy of my father's, Fred S., who had owned a summer place there for many years. So in August of 1948 we rented a pretty hillside cottage from a family. It overlooked its own pond and was just a block from the beach. I was almost nine years old; my brother, Anthony, was just five.

What was unusual, to us, about Southampton Shores was that each cottage was unique. Although they weren't very large, each one was set into its surroundings with plenty of space between houses and plenty of old trees for privacy. In 1949 and 1950 we rented a cottage, owned by another family, that was set in a clearing beside a forest. In 1951, my father's friend Fred offered us their place, which sat in a clearing at the top of a hill, and was invisible from the road.

During our summers there, we eventually saw that the interior of every cottage was paneled with knotty pine, that some walls didn't join the ceilings; that loft space surrounded the living room in many of the houses, and that they all had a screened-in porch for dining.

My Uncle Arthur and Aunt Mary Marra accompanied my mother, Anthony and me every summer. They were our grandparents in every way imaginable, despite the fact that Uncle Arthur was one of my father's older brothers. There would be visitors, too, from the Bronx: relatives, friends, and a few who didn't seem to fit into either category.

On the day of our arrival each summer, we headed to the beach as soon as we located and changed into our swimsuits. (The Marra family is famous for not wasting time.) Aunt Mary, who loved to swim, put on what she called her "bathing shoes"—funny-looking white rubber things—to protect her feet from the rocks, and led my brother and me into the water. Uncle Arthur marched resolutely  into the bay and began a beautiful, perfect Australian crawl parallel to the shoreline, back and forth for an impressively long time.

Idyllic days melted one into the other, with a sweet sameness that gave us the security of the predictable, a true blessing after the anxieties of wartime. We swam. We occasionally picnicked on the beach. My brother liked collecting crabs from the pond below the cottage. Not having any playmates there, Anthony and I spent a lot of time together, especially on rainy days, when Uncle Arthur taught us to play poker and *scopa* (an Italian card game similar to casino). He also taught us card tricks, which we found magical.

We also welcomed rainy-day adventures. My mother loved to explore new surroundings (a trait I inherited), so on cloudy or rainy days she would load us into the car and just drive. One day we went all the way to the lighthouse on Montauk Point (which was relatively undeveloped then); the lighthouse set upon an empty field of uncut grass and wildflowers. I thought it looked like the most breathtaking place I'd ever seen.

On another excursion we discovered the ocean beach along the heart of the village of Southampton, the "real" Southampton, the old and old-moneyed bastion by the sea. This was the famous side of Southampton where weathered siding wrapped enormous, many-storied homes on huge grass lawns. These homes were set back from the beach and were surrounded by high walls, tall hedges or towering cypress trees. And we had never seen anything like it.

But the Atlantic was calling loudly, thunderously, and despite clouds and wind, we walked on that glorious beach. My mother promised to bring us back for a day of swimming. She did, and one "ocean day" every summer became a tradition. At the time there were no fees, permits or restrictions for using any of the ocean beaches near Southampton village: just park, walk a very short distance, and jump in! The sea was thunderous and challenging. There were heavy ropes tied to pilings in the sand and stretching out to pilings in the water protect swimmers from being swept away by the powerful currents. Fearless as only a kid can be, I was overcome with pure delight.

All through those summers we went into town to stroll past the amazingly elegant shops, but mostly to buy fluke from the one and only fishmonger. (Fluke is an eastern Long Island fish we didn't know much about in the Bronx.) And on many evenings we went to the movies, a love we all shared.

I loved the two summers we spent renting the family cottage, which was inland and a bit of a walk to the bay. It sat at the edge of the woods, and the huge backyard had a hammock and a badminton net. My mother, a college tennis champ, taught us badminton, and we played daily. We also recruited all visiting adults to play, too, ignoring their inevitable protests of their incompetence.

The woods were right out the back door. As we listened to the radio one dark night, Uncle Arthur bolted upright and cried out, "There's a bat in the house!" I was too scared to scream. Anthony thought it was one terrific adventure watching Uncle Arthur sweeping the ceilings and eaves with a broom until the poor creature emerged. I have no idea how Uncle Arthur coaxed it out the door without injuring it, but I recall that someone had turned on all the indoor lights, sending the nocturnal beast away.

Uncle Arthur taught us how to go clamming—how to find clam beds at low tide and dig with our hands to find these tasty treasures. Anthony loved helping fill the buckets with clams, but he wouldn't eat them after seeing what they looked like shucked.

Anthony and I didn't know that the summer of 1951 would be our last at Southampton Shores. That cottage was the largest we had ever rented, and it provided the luxury of separate bedrooms for my brother and me. It could also accommodate more visitors.

Upon reflection later, I concluded that my mother had probably tired of the housekeeping and cooking that occupied so much of her time. And since my father joined us only for the last few days of vacation, she didn't have his companionship, nor the company of their lively and interesting friends and colleagues.

And so for the next several summers we took take many road trips instead: three cross-country trips and several forays into Canada, among others. The road trips meant having my father with us for our entire vacation—along with the luxurious bonus of hotel/motel stays and restaurant services. But part of me missed the freedom of our summers in Southampton Shores, so many days of doing just what we wanted to do.

Sometimes the past is recollected within the softly lit mist of wishes— that it had all seemed so because it should have been so. Perhaps there's a bit of that here. More likely, those brightly innocent Southampton days reflect time clearly etched in the solid gold of happiness remembered.

The Second Generation, In Their Own Words

Note: Five years before finalizing this book, each of the principal owners of the three family bungalows—first cousins Sylvia Saracino, Frank Marra, and Gilbert Maffei—were interviewed by the author. They were tasked with providing key background information about their generation as well as the generations of the family that both preceded and succeeded theirs in Southampton. They were also asked to share briefly their personal impressions about Southampton, as well as their most vivid memories of the summers they experienced there. The narrated stories they provided were faithfully transcribed and are presented in the following pages.

Frank Marra, In His Own Words

Being able to experience a different lifestyle and a slower pace really motivated me to cooperate with grandpa and make plans to build our bungalow a year after the Saracino's built their house. After plans were in place, I remember all of us becoming a bit anxious during the months when construction started. It got even more tense when the house was getting close to completion.

We could hardly wait to get established in Southampton. We were looking forward to a different way of life and to make a break from our routines in the city. The whole set-up there was so different. It was so quiet and yet it wasn't that far away, only about 85 miles.

And there were a number of things we liked about the beach. I loved seeing all the old folks at the beach. I remember that they enjoyed the water so much. They also loved spending hours there each day talking among themselves and with their many friends and neighbors. It [the beach] was so close to our house and yet so quiet and secluded. And you know, in many ways it's still kind of like that.

One strong memory revolves around [my father-in-law] Nonnon, who spent most of his days in Southampton fishing down at the beach, even on cloudy or chilly days. I often brought his lunch to him. It was his special place too, especially when there was nobody swimming. I think he enjoyed it even more those times.

I recall spending summers with our family, and with all the other members of the family, like all the aunts, uncles and cousins who went to the other two bungalows.

Can you imagine, here we all were, in three houses full of Marra family members and other relatives. All the people there got to relate to each other closely. We all got closer, and we didn't seem to need anyone outside the family to have fun. That made every day a happy occasion.

It was like having a big family reunion every day we spent out there.

Sylvia Saracino, In Her Own Words

Note: With her husband, Savino/Savy, Sylvia became one of the family's "pioneers" by spending several summers renting a cottage in Southampton Shores before Savy's parents, Helen and Joe Saracino, built the first bungalow in 1955. As an "ML-LD" [Memorial Day to Labor Day] regular, after Savy died in 1985, Sylvia drove to and from Southampton several times each season by herself. In more recent years, her daughter, Ellen, does most of the driving, with periodic assists from her son and daughter-in-law, Ray and Mary Ann, and her grandsons Greg and Mark and their families. Sylvia spent most of her interview talking about razing and rebuilding the Saracino bungalow in 2010-2011.

I had to recognize facts: after 55 years that house needed some major repairs! And so I had to invest a great deal of time and money in the reconstruction. The bungalow needed to be brought up to current standards: to be sound and secure, and also modern and comfortable. It's still a smallish structure. We basically just rebuilt it, using the original 1955 foundation. And so it still looks like a bungalow.

I wanted to keep it [the house] and eventually pass it on to my children in good condition. I hope that soon maybe all three [houses] can be fixed up. It would be nice if all of our family's houses could continue on the way they always were, you know, the way they always looked very much alike.

Yes, I have fond memories of Southampton. I remember the old times, those were really magical times at the bungalow, when I was there with my husband, our children, and members of the extended family. And sometimes there were quite a few of them, but you know, somehow we were able to get along so well out there, regardless of how many people came. Yes, it did get crowded at times, but that also made it more enjoyable. I remember the fun we had taking out all the sleeping materials at night— the beds, sheets, pillows . . .

I can't really remember what had originally attracted the family to that part of Southampton. Maybe it was because it was just such a simple place at the time.

I recall how all of us, especially the old folks. well, except for my father-in-law [Joe], how we enjoyed going down to that beach, the place my mother-in-law [Helen] called in her heavily accented English "ooh beach." Somehow it brought all of us together, including people from our extended family you might not see that often, like Aunt Mary [Marra]. I remember that she really enjoyed herself there. And I remember her special laugh. Oh, that Aunt Mary, she had the most infectious laugh!

Gilbert Maffei, In His Own Words

Note: Unfortunately, the youngest of this trio of second generation owners, Gilbert Maffei, succumbed to chronic illness in late 2013. But before his passing he too had a chance to share with the author the following thoughts and observations about his time in Southampton at the family bungalows.

My earliest memory of Southampton involved driving my mother [Sylvia] out to see her lot and visit relatives who were already staying at the other two family bungalows. We stayed at Aunt Helen and Uncle Joe Saracino's house during those visits, and again when my mother and I were planning to build the house in 1962-63.

I had to take my mother to Riverhead, the biggest so-called city in Suffolk County. It was about a 20-mile drive west of our area. There we had to meet with the bankers to get the mortgage arranged and later to talk things over with the builder.

It was hard for her, as a widow of limited means. You know, things were tight, but we put our heads and our hearts together and built the place for $15,500. I also picked up some of the bills just to help her out at first.

Somehow those three bungalows had the effect of bringing several separate family groups together. With all the aunts and uncles going out there, that kept all us cousins close together, and of course we enjoyed seeing each other too. But in later years, when those I called the 'kings and queens' [the family's first generation] started dying off, we also started drifting apart a little bit. I guess that's sort of natural.

You know, for a family that came to this country with virtually nothing, I think that the three bungalows represented a tremendous achievement; it was a great success. And you know, it's something I hope the family would continue to recognize for many generations. It was a dream many immigrants have, but few could ever achieve. But our family did it, somehow they did it.

It was a struggle for them [the three families], but they made that place into something of a symbol of the permanent impression they had made in the new world.

Notes: Second generation family members, in addition to those profiled above, regularly visited the bungalows with spouses and children. At the Saracino's, this included (in two-week rotations): Nancy Saracino and son, Sal Anselmo; Dina and Willie Cioffi and children, Lorraine, William, Maria and Joseph; Savy and Sylvia Saracino and children, Linda, Raymond and Ellen; Alfred and Vera Saracino and children, Mary Ellen, Jennifer, Adele, Jolaine and Jospeh; Elaine and Ed Launzel and daughters, Margaret, Elena, Francine, Suzanne and Danielle. At the Marra's, there were brief visits by Frank Marra's brother, Joseph and wife, Anne, and sons, Arthur, Ronald and Joseph. There were more frequent stays by his brother, Edward, first wife Mary, and, following her passing, his second wife, Helen, and daughters, Diane and Marie. Visitors from the Marra's maternal side (the Genovese's) are addressed at greater length in other sections of this book. Finally, at the Maffei bungalow, Gilbert and wife, Marion, spent every summer with children, Frances and Louis, while Gilbert's brother, Richard, and wife, Nettie, and children, Richard and Paula, visited periodically, mainly in the early years.

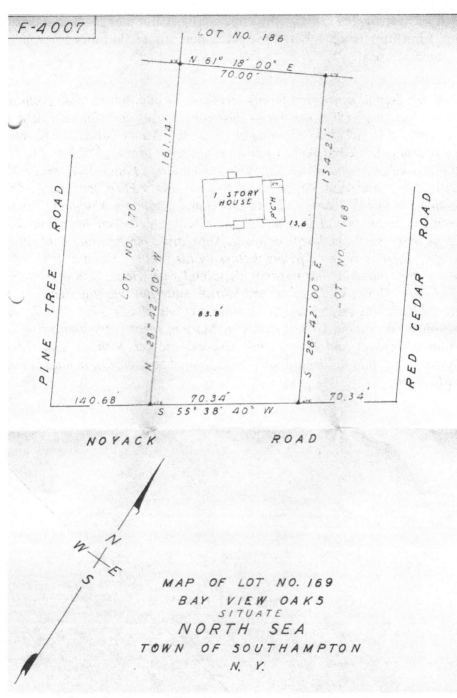

LOT NO. 186

N 61° 18' 00" E
70.00'

161.14'

154.21'

PINE TREE ROAD

LOT NO. 170

N 28° 42' 00" W

1 STORY HOUSE

P'CH

13.6'

83.8'

S 28° 42' 00" E

LOT NO. 168

RED CEDAR ROAD

140.68'

70.34'

70.34'

S 55° 38' 40" W

NOYACK   ROAD

N
W ⊕ E
S

MAP OF LOT NO. 169
BAY VIEW OAKS
SITUATE
NORTH SEA
TOWN OF SOUTHAMPTON
N. Y.

The First Generation's Dreams Became Plans for Generations

Chapter Three:
Third Generation Stories: Boomers and Beach Bums

Albert Marra

M y earliest memory of Southampton dates back to 1954 after a three-hour drive with my parents and grandparents. We went to look at the property I heard that my grandparents had bought with other aunts and uncles three years before. When they told me we were finally there, I became disappointed. I didn't know what to expect, and all I saw were thick woods and some fields as we slowly chugged around the winding roads in our clunky 1951 Dodge sedan. So this was Southampton? Well, yes, it was. But we were nowhere near the place people think of as Southampton; we had entered the undeveloped North Sea part of the town, specifically the part between Southampton Shores and Sag Harbor. It all looked rural, desolate and very scrubby.

When we arrived at the part of the woods they said marked our property, it still looked much the same. Driving the two blocks to the beach we saw nothing but more woods and dirt roads with large, swampy puddles. It gave me the feeling of a no-man's land. Our car could barely fit down the narrow dusty lanes of Pine Tree Road and Red Cedar Road. We had to slog our way through thick bushes that scratched the sides of the car like nails on a chalkboard. Funny how 60 years later one can experience almost the same on both of those roads, still unpaved and still under siege by briars and tall weeds. I remember sticking my arm out to catch some leaves as a souvenir, only to have my fingers splintered bloody by thorns. Why I would want thorny vines as a souvenir I don't know, but I never forgot that dense and pervasive underbrush.

The next steps were more exciting. Not only had my apartment-dwelling grandparents bought a piece of this landscape, I heard they were considering putting a house on it! They were following the Saracino's lead. Dad's Aunt Helen and Uncle Joe Saracino had already started building their bungalow two lots away. My grandparents considered several alternatives, so I've been told. They settled on a plan to give the land to one of their sons, the one who could obtain the funding to build a house. Since neither of Dad's two brothers seemed so inclined, my Dad stepped forward, applied and got a mortgage, and began the project. My grandparents further agreed that they would transfer full title to my father, and he would assume all responsibility for the house. Their agreement also provided for my grandparents and Dad's two brothers to use the house on mutually acceptable schedules. Nice all around!

On land that still resembled a Walden-like wilderness, in the fall-winter of 1955-56, my parents contracted with a builder who would turn the family dream into reality. The bulldozers began clearing the land in late winter, and in the spring of 1956, the builders laid the foundation. Mom's brother, Dom Genovese, lent his artistic and architectural skills to the project by communicating special design wishes to the builder, a pleasant gentleman from Riverhead whom everyone in the family called "Mr. K." Uncle Dom also helped my parents choose coordinating colors and some materials, both inside and out.

Things moved quickly that spring of 1956 and our house began to take shape in no time flat. After our first visit in March, the building progressed even faster. By the time we visited in mid-April, when the oak trees just started to bud, the house looked already framed. Our dream bungalow began taking on reality right before our eyes. All of us were optimistic that we would end that school year trading our steamy Bouck Avenue apartment for this tiny bit of beachy heaven. We would be spending a glorious, uninterrupted summer, the first of many, at our beach house. And that's just how it turned out for this lucky eight-year-old Bronx boy.

"Baby" Willy

Our first overnight stay at the bungalow dates to late June of 1956. On that virgin visit we took our first visitor: cousin William Genovese, AKA "Baby Willy." Only seven months younger than I, we were always close as kids, although I can't remember his sister, Linda Jean, or his parents, Aunt Lena or Uncle Willy, ever spending overnight visits with us in Southampton. But back to my cousin's name, the term "Baby" distinguished William from his father, Mom's brother, also a William. Who knows why Italian American families resort to those kinds of nicknames, pejorative as they seem, but they did. So instead of calling him "Junior" or "Young William," to many in the Genovese family, he became and remains Baby Willy, even as a septuagenarian grandfather.

I lucked out in the Italian name-game. First, everyone usually called me Albert, or the elders, Alberto. By my teens I had to act cool, thus "Al" to friends. The only ones who used a differing form of my name were, ironically, Uncle Willy and Baby Willy, who called me Albie.

Baby Willy and I reached the bungalow on a chilly day. With construction winding down, some finishing work lagged, such as missing screens on the porch, at that time still open to the elements and the critters. So it came as no surprise that a pair of nesting robins staked a claim between two beams. We loved seeing the chicks hatch and beg their mama for lunch while we ate ours mere feet away. By the sixth or seventh day, some chicks flew away, leaving their safe nest to strike out on their own. Their flight created a great metaphor for us, soon to gain our own liberties. On our third day my parents let us go to the beach alone. This was huge! Easily construed as child neglect today, back then it seemed normal. We now had the freedom to walk alone down two uninhabited dirt roads, around Lake Drive and the pond, then to Oak Grove Road and the beach. But that freedom came with a catch. Freedom isn't free, as they say.

That's because my father imposed this rule: we had to sit quietly for 30 minutes after each meal before going to the beach or even playing. That same rule applied to every child who visited—even mine years later! He ordered us to "relax" after eating for what seemed like an eternity. How interesting that the rule didn't apply absolutely. Sometimes after supper

Dad would muster his best drill sergeant's voice to order us to "police the area." We had to pick up leaves, sticks and any remaining construction debris. Fun.

That first summer trip gave William and me the opportunity to take a big bite out of life. And how delicious it was! We savored flirting with danger and tasting freedom by walking to the beach alone and swimming unsupervised. We were good swimmers, actually, and always used the "buddy system." No doubt that's why my parents allowed it. All we knew: we were free!

William and I spent a couple more summers at the beach, and we saw each other often growing up in the Bronx. We also spent two weeks together at the Salesian Camp near the Catskills. But besides weddings and funerals, we haven't gotten together enough as adults. It would be great to reunite, reminisce and plan a return visit to the bungalow after 60 years!

Sleeping at the Bungalows

From day one, sleeping at our Southampton bungalow usually seemed like an adventure, or a complex, complicated affair, because of two main factors: one, the place was small; and two, we always seemed to have visitors. With a challenging layout—one small bedroom, one smaller bedroom—common to all of the family bungalows, things got very complicated very fast. And the more visitors, the more complicated. Add to the mix a small kitchen and a tiny bath, and the challenges could have turned insurmountable.

But the fact is, that never happened. For by some magic, the three bungalows would sleep as many relatives who were there on any given day, expected or not, even if they arrived late and with no plans to spend the night. It didn't matter. They were always invited to sleep over. Most did, either because it was getting late and they were tired, or to keep the party going, or both. Somehow all hands found a bed. Sometimes nearly a dozen relatives (or so it seems!) slept at our house. And I often observed that Aunt Helen's house managed to accommodate even more than that! She would never dream of turning anyone away.

An old Italian saying goes, *Chi tardi arriva, male aloggia,* that is, he who arrives late gets the worst lodging. How true, and in the case of our bungalows, the least comfy/least private of the beds—if any real beds were actually left. "Beds" for us meant sofas, rollaway beds, convertibles, US Army cots, sleeping bags, even a hammock. And at times the cars outside.

Cousin Sal Anselmo recalls that at the Saracino house, sometimes overflow visitors ended up sleeping on the floor—wherever there *was* open floor—including the kitchen, the screened porch, and outside. Another Saracino cousin, Linda Saracino, recalls the so-called "pillow parade" when piles of pillows, sheets, and blankets were carried to bedrooms and elsewhere to make up beds in early evening, and then carried back to the minuscule linen closet or at the foot of a bed in the morning. Linda also recalls how the younger kids were marched to the bedrooms to be tucked in at bedtime, doubled up in twin beds or tripled up in the one double bed. They were later carried, sound asleep, to the made-up couch or makeshift beds in the living room to free up space for adults. It was confusing and yet somehow magical to wake up in a different place, she recalls. It was always noisy, with people talking, moving around, clanking in the kitchen, getting ready to start the day, and lining up near the one tiny bathroom.

We came close but never quite reached that point at the Marra house. We too had people sleeping on the porch (not bad, if you prefer it cool). Our house had a few beds in the two bedrooms, a sleeper sofa in the living room and a platoon's supply of army cots. My personal favorite was the one and only "sleeper chair" I've ever seen. Yes, it really was a sleeper *chair*, and it was all mine for years. It wasn't a Castro Convertible, that mainstay of the mid-20th century, and little Bernadette Castro, the star of the TV ads, never demonstrated anything like my chair. It was mossy brown, with a lot of elongated leg space; kind of plushy by day and when folded out—a process that required two grown men—it was big enough to hold me into my teen years. It wasn't the widest "bed" I ever slept in, but then again, I never fell off. I don't remember where it came from or what ever happened to it, but it was definitely my "bed" when we had visitors, especially in the early years. I miss my chair. They don't make them like that anymore.

Our families definitely showed creativity in supplying everyone with a place to sleep. On the downside, they couldn't guarantee a good night's sleep (that plus we had Noyac Road getting noisier with increasing traffic over the years). But nobody seemed to mind that they were roughing it. They were all in Southampton, all together, and summer after summer they came back for more. And it was great fun for everyone.

A Day in the Life

From the late 1950s into the early 1960s, a typical day at the bungalows started bright and early. We never wasted a moment of daylight; we only slept when dark. In those long summer days, the sun nudged my parents awake early, around 6:30 a.m. and, once up and around, they made enough noise to get everyone going. My brother and I and any visitors had no alternative, as sleeping past 8:00 a.m. would never be part of anyone's daily routine.

And so, at what seemed like the crack of dawn to me and Eugene, we washed and got dressed for breakfast and the day, which was easier said than done, taking turns in that one tiny bathroom. And there would be no shower to slow us down. That would use up all of the available hot water. Much as we would have liked a morning shower, it wasn't crucial: there were sweaty chores yet to do, and usually afternoon dips in cool bay waters!

We ate hearty breakfasts on the screen porch, often featuring Mom's made-from-scratch biscuits, or the crispy, flaky waffles she made on a press she got for her wedding in 1946. We also enjoyed "al fresco" dining for most other meals too. Eating on the porch meant breathing that unique fresh air and the sweet fragrance of the dewy Southampton grass. I'm convinced that something in that clean, salty air stimulated our appetites. Why else would we always be hungry enough to put away not only a big breakfast, but a hearty lunch and dinner too?

But first, each day we had to help clean house: make the beds, tidy up and (unless I had gone fishing with my grandfather) do an outdoor chore or two. There were always bushes to trim, plants to plant, grass to cut, leaves to rake—and all before lunch or going out to play for the rest of the morning (if there was anything left of the morning) with my cousins or friends.

After two-three years at the bungalow, some mornings friends would come over to see if I could go to the beach or somewhere else. Mom and Dad might approve going out to play but usually not to swim: they didn't guarantee Eugene and me a swim until after lunch, and even then after a 30-minute rest. If we were lucky, and if all of our chores were done, they allowed us some play time, about two hours at most, with our Saracino cousins, either at Aunt Helen's or at our secret fort in the woods down the road. Then home for lunch, and then the beach!

Even in our early years at the bungalow, everything focused on the beach. The beach was the reason we were in Southampton in the first place, and right after lunch was our regular beach time. Spending all afternoon at our little beach became standard operating procedure. As a young child we swam, played in the coarse, rocky sand with family and friends, learned fishing and clamming. We took long walks along the shore and collected all kinds of good stuff, from water sculpted driftwood to shells and pieces of "beach glass" (bottles worn smooth by the waves). In our teen years, those quiet afternoon routines changed dramatically, especially when our friends got cars. We cruised all over, especially to the ocean beaches. But more about that later.

As kids, when weather didn't cooperate, we made the best of it. During rare rain-outs, there wasn't much to do. Watching TV was hopeless, so we'd play cards or board games like Monopoly or Clue on our porch or the cousins' or at friends' houses. Sometimes our folks took us to the movies in Southampton or Sag Harbor; or we borrowed books at the library. One cool, cloudy day we visited the Sag Harbor Whaling Museum; another time we went to Montauk. Since there wasn't anything vaguely resembling a shopping center, we never faced the danger of becoming mall rats. On other cloudy days we'd cajole our parents into taking us to the miniature golf in Southampton on Montauk Highway. Viewing the Shinnecock Hills Country Club across the road presented a study in contrasts and our first glimpse of lifestyles of the rich and famous.

Weekends at the Bungalows

We counted every summer day at the bungalows as a special day. And weekend days turned out to be extra special. What made them so? Well, during the early years, at our house as well as the other two family houses, weekends brought the most guests. That was special enough, but there was another difference on Saturdays: right after an early breakfast we usually headed "to town" (i.e., Southampton Village) to help our parents with the weekly shopping. It was an end-to-end adventure, going from the woods to civilization—to grocery stores, drugstore, hardware store, five and dime, post office and other businesses, such as the laundromat. That meant no time for sightseeing, casual walks or soda or ice cream breaks. Well, if we had behaved during the week, and if the A & P didn't take too long, rewards came our way in the form of comic books like Superman, Batman, Archie and Beetle Bailey. Extra good behavior added a pack of Topps baseball cards, complete with a rock-hard stick of stale pink bubble gum.

Sundays brought other specials to our everyday beach routines. And that also meant rising early, maybe even a bit earlier than on the weekdays, but with us never needing any alarm clocks. That's because Mom had already worked her magic: she had set a wonderful Sunday red gravy (tomato sauce) simmering on the stove. Along with the coffee-enhanced vapors spewing forth from Grandma's old percolator pot, you know, the kind you can't find any more, those twin aromas would wake a sleeping beauty quicker than any prince charming could. Yes, everyone knew when Sunday rolled around. We knew that the midday macaroni fest would come in just a few scant hours.

But first, anther iron clad, non-negotiable requirement had to be met: mass. So up we'd spring, slicking down cow licks or crew cuts, donning clean summer shirts with what passed for "dress" slacks or shorts (matching or not) and off we'd go. But first we had to consider to which church? With two Catholic parishes in Southampton, the larger Sacred Heart or the smaller Our Lady of Poland, that left a lot to be determined, not only schedules. No there was more at stake.

Our Lady of Poland attracted its usual core of year-round residents, many of whom (like Bridgehampton resident and Major Leaguer Carl Yastrzemski) claimed Polish ancestry. Some of these Polish families had descended from the original Long Island potato farmers. Most of the summer visitors in their congregation, of Polish origin or not, seemed to come from similar middle class or working class families as ours.

Sacred Heart attracted a congregation that certainly seemed to look like groups of Southampton's elite. The church filled quickly with what appeared to us to be well-heeled, well-dressed, perfectly coiffed (both males and females!) families of Kennedy clan look-alikes. The men sported loafers with tassels or shiny pennies, perfectly creased khakis, crisp shirts, natty blazers; the women, the real fashion plates, wore flowered, full-skirted dresses or brightly hued A-lines, high heels and matching purses. The kids? They looked much the same. We had to check ourselves—was this really a Catholic church? It got to be a challenge to tell the Sacred Heart congregation apart from the Episcopal or other nearby Protestant congregations. So on Sundays, for church services, our family always opted for Polish, not posh.

Church wars aside, the ride home, usually a thrill-seekers delight through the wilds of Major's Path, ended quietly buying the Sunday papers at Garamone's on Noyac Road, right outside Southampton Shores. And that began the countdown to Sunday's main event: the huge mid-day repast, always featuring some form of macaroni products, gravy meats, often grilled meats, vegetables, salads, and desserts. That big meal alone would make anyone's Sunday special, but it always seemed to cut into prime beach time. Life's a compromise, isn't it?

Chi Mangia Bene . . .

One way or another, interwoven through most of my Southampton memories is the topic of food. It will come as no surprise that the importance of food—acquiring, cooking, eating, and just talking about it—is central to the Italian culture. And our patch of Southampton was nothing if not rife with Italian culture, and thus Italian cooking.

As in any culture, language reflects values, which explains why Italian includes many proverbs about food. Thus: *Chi mangia bene, vive bene,* "One who eats well, lives well," as the saying goes. But it's more than just eating. It gets to the heart of what it is to be Italian: that much of the richness and joy of life emanates from the traditions surrounding food.

As "everyone knows," Italians taught the world (including the French) how to cook. How do we know? My Grandpa Marra told me! And he also told me that the Romans perfected a form of dried pasta a millenium before Marco Polo took it with him to show the Chinese, which is true as well. Well, truth be known, Grandpa didn't tell me that Columbus brought tomatoes back to Europe from natives in the New World, and that Italy went crazy over them.

Needless to say, food was central to our life at the Southampton bungalows. No matter the day of the week or the number of visitors, we ate well, as well as, if not better in some ways, than we did at home. In Southampton we had access to fresh seafood from our beaches, fresh produce from our gardens, and fresh eggs and dairy from farms down the road. There were stores for everything else—Garamone's, the small general store a mile down Noyac Road, and a couple of chain grocery stores in town. But all of them were quite limited early on, and none of them carried much if any Italian food or ingredients for many years. Also, there were no authentic, neighborhood-style Italian specialty stores anywhere. In fact, there still aren't any that we would call legit. So how do Italian Americans meet that challenge in Southampton? We "imported" them, that is, we brought everything in from the city.

Along with the suitcases, beach chairs, swim tubes, towels and other sundries, we loaded our Dodge sedan with the important stuff: *food.* Boxes, bags and coolers of *food.* There were: meats and cold cuts; boxes of macaroni in various shapes and sizes; large cans of imported plum tomatoes; little cans of golden Italian tuna in oil; 16-oz. cans of Medaglia d'Oro coffee; some fresh vegetables and fruit to get us started; and several gallon jugs of red wine, both Nonnon's homemade and California's "best" from the likes of Ernest and Julio or Charles Krug (known as "CK," as if a member of the family). We filled every available cubic millimeter of that car, and surely pushed it way beyond its tested weight limits.

Is it called gravy or sauce? It's an endless Italian American dilemma.

As mentioned, all three bungalows have small (albeit eat-in) kitchens. They had all the necessities, but the stoves were tiny, the fridges bulky on the outside but small inside, a single-bowl sink with an attached drain board, and a few knotty pine cabinets. (Did the house have a dishwasher? Sure: one person wielded a sponge and another a *moppine!*) An adequate kitchen for some, e.g., NYC apartment dwellers, but a challenge for cooking Italian meals, especially dinners. And that brings up another Italian saying: *La cucina piccola fa la casa grande.* "The tiny kitchen makes the house big"—in other words, a little kitchen can still make for a grand home. Our little bungalow kitchens did exactly that, especially for our big mid-day Sunday Italian style dinners, and they still do.

Mealtime was always filled with talk, laughter and general merriment. It was also an opportunity for more of my grandfather's culture lessons. Grandpa Marra taught me how to twirl spaghetti with a fork and spoon, and how to use both knife and fork for eating meat without shifting the silverware back and forth. He called it "continental style." I called it two-fisted or "overhand" eating because you see the back of your hands. I'm grateful to him for showing me a neater, more efficient and (in most of Europe) a more acceptable way of using flatware.

And my parents required that all meals were to be unhurried events. The concept of "eat and run" didn't exist in our house. After the main part of the meal was over and the table partly cleared, we lingered over dessert, which sometimes included cheeses, but usually just fruit and espresso. The lingering and time-consuming aspect of our meals became especially annoying to us as kids on Sundays, when Italians eat that big, pasta-rich dinner in the middle of the day. That killed some of our best afternoon beach time and played havoc with our mornings, since we had already needed to push ourselves to make it to church for mass, always a *de jure* requirement at our bungalow. There's at least one takeaway from our multi-cource meals: we can remind ourselves of our fellow Italian, Sophia Loren, who extoled the virtues of our obvious obsession with macaroni with her words of wisdom: "Everything you see I owe to spaghetti."

At many evening meals, our "American" friends came by while we were still at the table. They'd marvel at the vast variety of dishes and, if we had company, the number of people sitting on our porch. This wasn't a typical tableau at their houses. They'd be anxious to leave at first, but after we'd invited them to join us, not only did they stay but, despite having just had lunch or dinner, they jumped at the chance to eat Italian, especially macaroni. As soon as we all left, they'd say how lucky we were to have such good food, except if we were having something unfamiliar to them, like clams, calamari, scungilli, or eels. Then they'd make faces and ask how we could eat that stuff. Some of those foods have become mainstream, e.g., calamari, and for all I know, they eat them now. But I was lucky: I tasted them years ago as a kid at the bungalow.

But no matter who was there, after every meal and before anyone left the table, the very same topic came up: the *next* meal. I can see and hear my mother saying, "So, what are we going to eat for ... (fill in the blank with whichever came next, lunch or dinner). That gives an idea of how important (and how enjoyable) food and mealtimes were in Southampton.

Clam Wars

The Little Peconic Bay doesn't have lobsters or shrimp. As far as we know, it never did. There were a few blue crabs in the ponds and inlets, and in some years, little bay scallops bloomed in late summer. But until the mid-1960s, at low tide, the sand bar just off our beach teemed with what seemed like an inexhaustible bounty of clams and scungilli. My mom became our family's undisputed "clamming champ." If Mom went looking for clams at low tide, too bad for a lot of those clams. They came home with Mom.

Given our competitive nature and a never-ending taste for seafood, we found ourselves engaging in periodic clam wars and scungilli skirmishes with our relatives, the Saracino's. These weren't serious, just friendly competitions, fun contests. Mom, with her ability to dig up more clams than anyone around most of the time, constantly challenged Aunt Helen for the title of senior clammer of the family. Mom attacked her task with the enthusiasm of a forty-niner panning for that elusive placer. Aunt Helen, the undisputed champ from the Saracino bungalow, always wanted to take home at least as big a haul. So whenever Mom moved to mine a more productive colony, Aunt Helen followed close behind.

As they say, "war is hell."

When Mom found what turned out to be a "good spot," she'd have me turn my back to everyone's view, and with a quick sleight of hand, palm some clams from our bucket and stick them down my bathing suit. Then I made a quick run (or swim) to the beach to hide them in the cool pebbly sand under our blanket. So if Aunt Helen or anyone came near Mom's bucket, they'd only see half our take. Not able to tell how good our spot was, they'd then move on to an area of their own, far away from ours. Mom and I worked this "clams-down-the-swimsuit" maneuver (down hers and mine!) frequently. It's a good thing clams don't bite. Or do they?

No need to feel sorry for Aunt Helen because she had her own tricks. She'd slide clams down her own bathing suit, purportedly just to stow them, as all the old Italian women did; but soon enough she'd take them to her blanket, also hide them, and go back into the water for more. No one kept track of how many times she did this (we were too busy clamming!), so no way to know just how many clams she had.

By the late 1970s, when the older relatives were no longer spry enough for clamming, we always shared our catch with them, which they greatly appreciated. But it was also getting harder to find clams, and by 1990, the clam population had just about disappeared, owing more to overall environmental degradation (changing conditions in the bay) than to any over-harvesting. (We didn't overindulge; and we always threw the babies back.) So the clam wars ended. But they provided fun and fine eating for many summers. Most of the Marra's and Saracino's remember the "clam wars" and all those wonderful clam dishes with humor and affection. And we still talk and joke about it. Good thing the clam wars never turned into "clan" wars.

Scungilli

And then there were scungilli, which also figured in the families' shellfish-gathering exploits. Pronounced "skoon-*jeel*" by the family, the word is the Neapolitan version of *scuncigli,* Italian for whelks. Scungilli are a large snail-like mollusk (common name: channel whelk or conch) with a long, spiral shell that looks like a big, grayish-white periwinkle. It's the shell children hold up to their ears to hear (what sounds like) the sea. Prevalent in New England and eastern Long Island, scungilli shells on our beach typically ranged from six to eight inches long.

My family had an advantage over the others in scungilli hunts. From age 10 on, I wore fins, mask and snorkel to dive and scan the sea floor for scungilli. Although their shells attract brown algae camouflage, scungilli lie on the surface of the sea bottom, and with a decent mask, they're easy to spot. I would reach down, pick one up and put it in a plastic bucket or nets used for oranges. Since we got so good at scungilli, we never had to resort to any trickery. When my brother, Eugene turned seven he'd scungilli scrounge too, scoring five or six per hour on a good day. We soon took things to the next level: diving with no gear and scooping up almost as many. We fancied ourselves the Italians' answer to the Greek sponge divers of Tarpon Springs, Florida.

The only thing more fun than gathering scungilli and clams is eating them. I learned to love both at an early age, even clams on the half-shell. How many non-bungalow kids can make that claim? Scungilli taste wonderful simmered in thin slices in a spicy, non-viscous tomato sauce. Because they're tough and rubbery, it takes hours of cooking to tenderize them. Mom was great at cooking all kinds of seafood, including scungilli, but let's give credit where it's due: Aunt Helen's scungilli beat all. Lucky for us, she always sent some over to our house when she made it. And so the story goes that the Marra bungalow brought in the most scungilli; the Saracino bungalow took the culinary prize for dishing them up.

And we all lived happily ever after. Or was that "happy as a clam?"

The Agony of the Feet

Oh, how we all loved that little beach, even with its countless rocks. It seems only the Dead Sea might have a rockier sea bed than the Little Peconic. Add to that the innumerable sharp shells, which, in sum, present all kinds of hazards to heel and toe at our beach.

The members of our first and second generations got smart fast and took no chances. I can't remember any of them venturing onto the beach without protection, including old shoes, old sneakers and, later, special swim shoes (derided by our children as "beach booties"). It seems the first and even the second generation wore them as a badge of honor.

As very young kids, we wore some kind of foot protection too. Much as we may have considered them lame, we all learned their value— usually after the first cut. But by the time I was about 10, I felt weird and embarrassed. So I rebelled, deciding never to go to that beach—or any beach for that matter—with anything on my feet except skin. After all, I had to look good, with an image to uphold. Image vs. common sense? This 10-year-old always picked image!

And so I ventured out to the beach, but not totally shoe-less. Truth be told, I wore sneakers or sandals to and from—but I took them off as soon as I hit the dunes. I did a shuck-the-shoes barefoot routine day after day, refusing to wear any kind of footwear on the beach or in the water. I even became expert at walking along the beach at low tide among those big brown rocks. I was a tough kid, a beach kid, would-be beach bum. And I could beat those rocks.

Of course the beach beat me. Who on earth could confront those rocks and shells barefooted and win? Nobody, not even me. So my poor little 10-year-old feet ended up paying a steep price. At first I noticed a few little cuts and superficial scratches, just an "ouch" here and there going to and from the water or walking along the beach with my cousins or my friends. But I was tough. I was no pansy; no, not me. I was a beach kid and I knew I could take it.

A few days passed, but the little cuts didn't heal. Then the grains of sand that had ground their way into the skin of my soles and between my toes turned kind of black, then became swollen mounds with glistening shades of green and yellow. The rocks and shells exercised their power over this "tough" 10-year-old with a show of multiple pustules on my feet. Yuck.

Applying liberal doses of bubbling hydrogen peroxide followed by immersing my feet in hot water and a colorful merthiolate solution sometimes worked. That could stave off a bigger infection, at least for some of the cuts, some of the time, if applied right away. With limited success I concealed the results of my beach bum bravado from my parents. That didn't stop me, though: I continued to hit the beach barefooted, and continued to minister to my wounds. But it wasn't always successful. On those occasions, I had to give up, "man up" and tell my parents—which meant having to endure something worse than any physical pain—their yelling. Then I'd hope they'd get me some actual medical attention. They did, and that involved a lengthy visit to Southampton Hospital's emergency room (where our family had already or would soon become "regulars") and taking antibiotics, all at a hefty, pre-Obamacare, out-of-pocket cost.

The next summer, at the sadder but wiser age of 11, did I put my hard-earned lesson into practice? Did I wear shoes? No, that would have been too simple. Barefoot boy hit the beach again. I kept up the façade, skipped over the rocks to go swimming, checked my feet when I got home, washed and soaked them in hot water and, having learned that peroxide is antibacterial, dabbed my soles with it as a preventive measure every night before going to bed. So I guess I did learn something: keeping up appearances is okay, but it comes at a high price.

On further consideration, I guess I'd rather wear booties.

Friends

My Southampton friends spun Southampton summers into lifelong memories. They had much in common with us, especially those who came from a handful of Italian American families or other similar families who had homes near our beach. The downside: with few exceptions, these were almost all summer friends, because distance, among other obstacles, prevented most of us from communicating or being together on a regular basis. But we were glad to see each other, summer after summer, and pick up where we had left off.

I developed good friendships with many more kids from Bay View Oaks and Roses Grove during high school. We were all typical middle-class American kids, and that made us more alike than different. We spent a lot of fun times growing up in those mid-'60s summers. Our looks and activities put us somewhere between *Beach Blanket Bingo* and *Happy Days.* Most of us were clean-cut (maybe even "preppy cute") in those pre-hippie days. We'd go swimming, boating, dancing, and, if we could get a ride, to the movies or bowling. And we often paired off from the group as boy-girl friendships developed. Yes, it was our time for exploring opposite sex relationships.

My best Southampton friend was Robert, later called Rob, then Bob. In 1957, my second beach summer, Bob and I became good friends after swimming together a few times at the little beach. We started going to each other's houses. Both sets of parents didn't really know each other, so they felt better at first driving us back and forth, but they soon let us walk the three blocks by ourselves—another early taste of Southampton freedom!

The first time I went to Bob's house he mentioned that his father's family traced their heritage to the *Mayflower*. It sounded so amazing I could hardly wait to tell my parents about his roots. Dad seemed totally unmoved, but what he said next explained his blasé reaction. He told me when I next saw Bob to tell him that one of our Italian ancestors, Columbus, had come to America a hundred and thirty years before the *Mayflower*, and that he not only made the trip in half the time, but did it four times! I felt so proud about our heritage that I decided not to revisit the *Mayflower* matter or Columbus with Bob. I still keep that retort about

Columbus in my back pocket for when October 12 rolls around each year and people start playing up the Indians or the Vikings.

Family origins aside, Bob and I became good friends and stayed good friends into our 20s. In our high school years, we developed close ties with kids all over Bay View Oaks, Roses Grove and other North Sea communities. Our "gang" of regulars included (remember, outside the family, it's first names only!) Paul, Roger, Ralph, Charlie, Jimmy, Eddie, Alfred, Janet, Mary Alice, Grace, Denise, Stephanie, Mae, Joyce, Joan and others. There were also the neighbors' kids from the house behind ours: Catherine, Walter, Jimmy and Tommy, whose family remains friendly with ours.

Our closeness, and my memories of friends, owed more to the quality than the quantity of time we spent together during our summers. In many ways, we grew up together. We became good friends because we shared many of life's "firsts" together: that first pairing off from the crowd at the beach bonfire . . . the clumsy attempt at clasping hands while walking the beach with a new love interest, then that first awkward kiss . . . that first night cruising to town with no adult in the car . . . and, best of all, the first night your father hands you the keys to the family car and says, "Be careful." Count here, too, the first night of missing curfew, putting our heads together to come up with a "good" excuse and hoping not to be grounded or even yelled at. And the first drink in a teens-only setting—a landmark moment.

As much fun as we all had for several summers, the same beach that brought us together most likely set us apart too. Come each September, we all had to go home: to the city, to the suburbs of Long Island and Westchester, or New Jersey and Connecticut. "Home" meant school and other aspects of "real life" for nine months until the next June rolled around and we got together again. But as we grew older things began to change too. Some of us moved on, ties loosened, and we slowly drifted apart.

We became distant because it wasn't as easy to stay in touch then as it is in today's world of Facebook, What's App, and the internet. In those summers, our mode of communication was face-to-face; rarely did we use the telephone to talk to each other. And remember, my family didn't even have a phone! Back home for the rest of the year, all anyone had was a telephone, but long distance calls then would break anyone's budget. Letters and cards worked, but some of the kids were not the best at written correspondence. In-person visits (if you could get a ride) were limited. And so our lives and lifestyles eventually started to change as we moved into adulthood.

Apart from several of my cousins, the one notable exception to drifting apart after summer was Robert/Rob/Bob. We became "year-round" friends, helped by the fact that he and his family lived in the Parkchester section of the Bronx, a 20-minute walk from my grandparents' house on Zerega Avenue. He and I got together during some of our weekly visits to Grandma and Nonnon. Sometimes it was just an afternoon visit; sometimes a sleepover. I'd call Bob just before we left for Grandma's. Then I'd walk to his family's apartment, and he and I would go play basketball or touch football at one of the playgrounds. Or we'd go to the matinee movie on Castle Hill Avenue. We often ended our visits with a slice and a soda, or an Italian ice. We grew close and stayed close into our early twenties. I miss the guy. I miss our friendship, and the summers of youthful, innocent fun we had swimming and playing near our beach. My memories of Bob and all of my Southampton friends are as warm and clear as a sun-filled summer day.

Cousins

Southampton summers meant a world full of cousins at our bungalow and the two other family houses. Some cousins on my mother's side were regulars at our bungalow, and some came only occasionally—including two who traveled to Southampton all the way from Italy!

The 13 Genovese family cousins (including me and my brother) comprised a group of eight females and five males. The range in our ages covers an amazing 30 years, extending from the World War II-era to Generation X, but most are Baby Boomers.

I recall that my cousin "Cookie," Elaine Mauro, spent more time with me at our Southampton house than any other cousin. At three years older,

Southampton Summers: Aunts, Uncles, Cousins at the Beach (Early 1970s)

Cookie got her nickname it would seem not from Italian traditions but Native Americans ones. She was given her nickname soon after birth to reflect her calm demeanor and her sweet facial expression. Sweet Cookie and I got along great, due mainly to my parents spending a lot of time with hers. Cookie's mother, Aunt Vinnie, my mother's sister, and her father, Uncle Leonard, were perennial favorites. For three or four summers in the mid-1960s, our teen years, Cookie's parents stayed at the bungalow for several days and they often left Cookie with us when they went home to the Bronx.

Cookie and I spent afternoons at the beach, swimming and walking to gather rocks, shells and whatever the storms had washed up. Sometimes we went boating with friends, weather and gas money permitting. Other times we'd bum a ride to one of the ocean beaches in the Village, Flying Point or East Hampton. At night we went to the Sag Harbor or Southampton movies, or we'd go singing and dancing with friends around a beach bonfire, often passing around bottles of Miller's or Schlitz, Mateus or Lancers, to lighten the mood.

Almost all of the cousins on my mother's side spent at least some time with us at the beach. Tina Silvestri, Aunt Fran and Uncle Dom's daughter, was also one of our earliest guests. Our two families also spent many special occasions together. In her later teens, Tina, who lived in New Hyde Park, Long Island, came to Southampton on several on day trips with her future husband, John, often driving one of Uncle Dom's sports cars: first a Fiat, later an Alfa Romeo, and then one of the original Ford Mustangs. I took several cool top-down rides with them, jammed into one of the Italian two-seaters or the Mustang's shelf of a back seat.

My cousins Rosemarie, Lorraine and Anthony Genovese, children of Aunt Betty and Uncle Joe, my mother's oldest brother, lived an hour away in Rocky Point, then a small town on the Long Island Sound. Over the years I spent some of the most pleasant days, dinners and evenings with these cousins, including Rosemarie's husband, Johnny Halama (AKA "the Drac," due to his nighttime antics). Rosemarie and Lorraine were a few years older, but Anthony was only a couple of years ahead of me. He visited Southampton on his own, driving out in his gold 1964 Pontiac GTO, several times when I was still in high school. I thought I had died and gone to heaven cruising around Bay View Oaks and Southampton Village.

Rosemarie and John continued as frequent guests for 30 years, often making the one-hour drive from their home just to spend a quiet afternoon or evening with my parents. Although I wasn't there for most of those visits, they always enjoyed my parents' company a great deal.

Other cousins on my mother's side included the children of her younger sister, Aunt Bella, and her husband Uncle Conrad. Although Doreen, Barbara, Roseanne and Phillip visited frequently, the difference between us in age (at ten years and more) accounted for a certain distance between us coming together for fun in Southampton until well into adulthood. Nevertheless, I know that they all enjoyed their trips from their home in Queens to Southampton.

In a similar way, my "upstate" Genovese cousins, Jeanie and Irene, daughters of my mother's brother, Uncle Alfred and Aunt Connie, were infrequent visitors at the Southampton bungalow. We probably went to visit their home in (then rural) Dutchess County, New York, much more often than they ever came to Southampton.

Visitors to our bungalow from my father's side, the Marra's, included all of my first cousins: Arthur, Ronald, and Joseph, sons of Dad's brother, Uncle Joe, and Aunt Anna; as well as my female Marra cousins, Diane and Marie, daughters of my father's brother, Uncle Eddie, and Aunt Mary (and following her passing, Aunt Helen). While Diane and Marie spent considerable vacation time at the Marra family bungalow, my male Marra cousins usually only came once a year on a day trip. That visit always included a barbeque, complete with hot dogs and hamburgers

Marra family: Uncle Eddie and Aunt Mary at the little beach; daughters Diane and (camera-shy) Marie, circa 1959

that Uncle Joe had brought from the city. We often cooked the meat over a blazing wood fire, and, with a great deal of help from the kids, it sometimes (usually?) grew into a raging inferno, or, what I might call a bonfire of the insanities. When the flames died down to a roar, we would proceed to cook, roast and toast marshmallows. At dark, if the adults did

not pay careful attention to our horseplay, it became fun for us to set the sugary cushions fully aflame and catapult them at each other like ancient Romans hurling hot bundles of flaming pitch. Fortunately, as much as we tried, I can't remember anyone getting hit. Thank God.

Diane and Marie, on the other hand, not only stayed with us often at the bungalow, they frequently stayed with their parents for one or two-week vacations. Sometimes our bungalow time overlapped. I also recall the several times

Beach Buddies: sisters Diane and Marie Marra (L and R), Mary Ellen Saracino (center), circa 1961

that the girls stayed in Southampton with our grandparents while I was there with them. It was always a delight. We were over five years apart, but we found ways to have fun together, often mocking our grandparents and their Italian accent or their special Italian way of viewing the world.

Saracino Cousins

Among all of my many cousins on both sides of my family, and whether at our bungalow or the other two family houses, my best friends among the cousins were Sal ("Sonny" to us in those years) and my "girl cousins" Lorraine and Linda. Sal, who was one of our "leaders" early on at the Southampton fort, has become a person quite dear to me and my entire family over the past two decades. We live sort of close to each other, well, a hundred miles does not usually constitute an insurmountable obstacle. Linda's younger sister, Ellen, who matched up nicely in age and personality with my brother, Eugene, has also evolved into a dear friend and confidant. Their brother, Ray, also befriended Eugene for many years in Southampton.

It was in my teen years in Southampton that I developed (and still enjoy today) a special relationship with my cousins Lorraine and Linda. Those two girls became my "kissin' cousins." We became very close, just as close as brothers and sisters, and as close as boys and girls could get without ever crossing over any boundaries of what might be considered unacceptable behavioral norms. How sad that in many families, people don't even know their second cousins, much less have a chance to become dear life-long friends. We have our Southampton bungalows to "thank" for that example of serendipity.

While Aunt Helen and Uncle Joe Saracino's five children (Nancy and Dina, Savy, Alfred and Elaine) produced over a dozen offspring, I only became friendly with a few of them, mostly due to our differences in age. On the other hand, Lorraine and Linda, both of whom share birthdays within a year of mine, hit it off like gangbusters with me from the onset. We played together at the fort, at the beach, and in our teen years, all over Southampton. We shared our love interests, secrets about those on whom we had a "crush," and gossiped about who among the large group of girls and boys from Bay View Oaks or Roses Grove would make a good catch for each of us. We must have looked like an odd "pair" as we headed out each evening after supper, ready for "action," such as it was, but we proved that blood is thicker than water, as we always looked out for each other. Nobody was going to take advantage of my "sisters." We were forced by our families, not that they had to at all, to watch out that nobody got into any trouble, or not one of the cousin's feelings could be hurt by anyone.

Fortunately for us, the three cousins lived rather close to each other (North Bronx, Yonkers, and Mount Vernon), so we saw each other often and went out together many weekends in the city long after our summer vacations had passed into Southampton memories. We went out on double dates through high school and into our college years. Sometimes we even helped each other to find dates, always selecting only the best possible match-ups for each other.

We got married, had children, and two of us (Linda and I) moved away from the New York city area, so we don't get many chances to buddy up again in Southampton. But we can always hold on to our memories of that special "cousins" bond we developed there and hope for a cousins' reunion soon.

86

Again possibly attributed to age differences (over ten in this case), until a few years ago, I did not develop a close relationship with the Maffei cousins of my generation, Frances and Louis. Thankfully, we have seen each other and communicated in the past few years and all is well. Frances even contributed a wonderful set of stories to this book. Cousins are great!

A Pack of Winstons

 They say every boy tries a cigarette at least once. A rite of passage, it took place easier in those years (in my case, six years) before the Surgeon General's warning appeared on cigarette packs and before you had to show proof of majority age, legal immigration status, your credit-worthiness, etc. I tried smoking, too, of course. With a little "help" from my good friend Bob. It was in the spring of 1958. We were both 10.

Bob and I got together that Saturday afternoon and walked from his house through the woods on the dirt road that parallels the houses along the Roses Grove beach. We knew that the road ended near Cunningham's bar, a half mile from my home. (Note: the bar has undergone multiple changes, including Pellegrino's, Armand's, and, as I heard, even a Thai restaurant.) Bob and I used to visit Cunningham's on a regular basis. Lots of locals did. It was the closest place to buy snacks, sodas or ice cream; and for the adults to hoist a few "*poynts.*"

With little more than a few coins in our pockets, Bob and I swaggered into Cunningham's like Friday-night pay-day regulars. We went in to listen to the juke box and buy snacks, but the cigarette machine started beckoning. First we dared and double dared and then formulated a basic plan, with some built-in precautions. Next we confidently bellied up to the bar and casually ordered two icy bottles of Coke. We retreated to a booth near the cigarette machine to effect our plan. We scoped out the place to see if there were any potential problems, like the remote possibility of bumping into family members or neighbors or nosy adults who might cause us trouble. We were ready at a moment's notice to give each other the standard high sign—two fingers across the Adam's apple—if we needed to abort the mission and bail.

We also discussed what brand we'd buy. We decided against the more popular and significantly more macho Marlboros, a decision based solely on Marlboros' higher price: they cost a nickel more. (Here the author offers belated apologies to his Uncle Dom, who, with his Madison Avenue graphic-arts firm, designed the iconic red and white Marlboro packaging now known world-wide.) But hey, a nickel's a nickel to a couple of mischievous 10-year-olds.

With the coast apparently clear, we dug out another batch of coins, about 50 cents' worth, inched our way toward the nearby cigarette machine which was near the service area at the back of the bar. We reached that metal monument to "King Tobacco" without incident and proceeded to the second part of our plan. Back then, cigarette machines were fairly large glass and metal structures, often a dull green with some red and white lettering and chrome trim, often sporting an Art Deco graphic element on the front. Ironically, they now evoke in me the image of an adult coffin in size and shape.

Their operation was purely mechanical, not electric, as the lights were just for show. So coins go in, handle is pulled, and presto, a pack of cigarettes delivered. And they took anyone's change, no questions asked. They held a wide assortment of popular brands, from soft packs of unfiltered, old-school Lucky Strikes, Chesterfields and Camels to the more modern flip-top boxes of Kents, Parliaments, and mentholated Kools and Newports. Just drop your quarters, dimes and/or nickels in the slot, pull the handle under your carcinogen of choice and down tumbles the pack into the knee-level tray. Decisions, decisions.

We fed the coins into the slot and gave its cold, smooth-as-glass, stainless steel handle a firm, quick tug. With an equally quick release of the handle, just as we heard the distinct clatter of the coins reaching bottom, *bam!* Out flew our red-and-white pack of Winstons and a book of matches (you always got matches with your ciggies) with a classic "Can you draw this?" correspondence school ad inside the cover. Bob reached for our pack of trouble and quickly hid it inside his windbreaker as I grabbed the matches and tucked them deep in my pants pocket.

Quietly, and avoiding eye contact with anyone, we sashayed toward the door as if nothing out of the ordinary happened. We slipped out of Cunningham's, looked at each other with a knowing smile, and silently spoke the same thought: So far, so good. Mission accomplished! Well, phase one, anyway. All that remained was the main act: smoking.

With that pack of Winstons firmly in our possession, Rob and I turned downhill towards the beach and away from Noyac Road and civilization. After a few steps we turned right onto the same dirt road (really just a path through the woods) heading toward home. A few more steps and we felt sufficiently obscured by the dense trees and underbrush. We took our time looking up and down the path to make absolutely sure no one was around. Then we lit up.

Sure, we were somewhat clumsy at first. Somewhat? Ha! It took two or three matches per cigarette and many awkward puffs to get the cigarettes to burn. At that point we egged each other on to see who could advance from a quick mouthful to inhaling fully. Bob paved the way but I managed to overcome the initial burning sensation and inhale. By our second cigarette we were both casually filling our lungs—and the still air of the Roses Grove woods—with copious amounts of acrid smoke. Oblivious to the toxic fumes, we continued slowly down the road, although we were chatting nervously, puffing awkwardly, and coughing like typical smokers. We were *trying* to be cool. Of course, we weren't. I remember desperately trying to put out of my mind the scary cigar smoking scene from Disney's *Pinocchio,* and I wondered if my asthma, while not active in those years, would make me as sick as my little wooden Italian friend. It didn't, so we smoked another cigarette, getting better with each drag. But we knew we had to go home eventually. And that there might be trouble.

Non-smokers can smell cigarette smoke a mile away. Non-smokers who abhor smoking can detect cigarette smoke within a five-mile radius and a 30-day time frame. That day, my father was on it, like, well, use your own analogy. The minute I got home Dad took one look at me as I quickly passed by him, then with what seemed like an unsuspecting sniff, he smelled smoke. He looked in my direction, told me to come back, and fixed his laser gaze on me. He eyed me up and down without forming a word. I felt his dark eyes burning deep holes in me, slicing through to my very soul. With his eyes open twice their normal size, he finally spoke.

"What's that I smell? Have you been smoking, or what?"

If only I could answer the "or what" part, I would have gladly given it. Like maybe I was at a party where many people older than 10 were smoking? No, that wouldn't work. Maybe we just lost track of time at Cunningham's, then it got crowded with smokers, and then the smoke stuck to us? Nix that too. I couldn't conjure up a decent, plausible answer to his questions.

I stammered a mealie-mouthed, "Uh, yes, Dad." And he blew his stack. Completely.

He grimaced, his face contorting in all possible hues of red, and let fly a few choice words. Some he directed to me, some to himself and some to the creatures of the forest. Then he screamed out a litany of questions, starting with a string of purely rhetorical ones, like, "What the hell were you trying to prove anyway? What are you stupid or something? Didn't you know what you were doing to yourself? What are you supposed to be, a big shot?"

And then the clincher: "You didn't think you'd get away with this, did you?"

It was as if his head had erupted with the fury of Krakatoa and Mount Vesuvius combined. I still remember the fear that traveled up and down my spine as he promised abundant medieval-style forms of corporal punishment. He swore he was going to whip my ass with his belt and that it would hurt so bad that I would never be tempted . . . and on and on.

I took him at his word.

But he never touched me. Then again, somehow the punishment he dished out was worse. Yes, he dished out many forms of mental punishment, which began immediately with his next line of seemingly endless questions. He conducted an interrogation worthy of Torquemada's best during the Spanish Inquisition. This was the Marra Inquisition, a combination of badgering and leading questions. Perry Mason wanted details here, all the lurid facts and factoids.

"Whose stupid idea was this? Why did you go along with it? How did you get the cigarettes? And with what money? How many did you smoke? Where did you smoke them? When do you plan to do this again?" etc., etc.

His questions went on and on from there, without a peep out of me. He then expanded his line of attack and took his inquisitorial tribunal on the road. The grilling that began with just me at our house was soon moving to Bob's house, and he took me on that road trip. That ride, usually only five minutes by car, this time took mere seconds. But at the same time, somehow those seconds felt like hours or days to me.

So now poor Bob's mother and father, both smokers (Old Gold brand, if I remember, if only for the coupons), were forced into the fray. But he was lucky. Things at his house had been a lot more tranquil than at ours. His parents apparently hadn't noticed anything out of the ordinary when he got home. In fact, while I was being reamed out at my house, he was watching TV with his mom and dad. My father, still smoldering, carefully laid out the details of our misadventure. Bob's parents took it seriously and then pondered a moment or two. Then his father broke the silence. He apologized for his son's poor judgment and said he'd have "a good long talk with Bob."

What? That was the worst he planned to do? Talk? Maybe it was different in a house full of smokers. To me, their reaction was a stark contrast to my dad's. Bob told me later that they did give him a lecture but he shrugged it off as nothing. I on the other hand didn't know which was worse: my father yelling at me for being stupid; or yelling at me in front of my best friend and his parents. Probably the latter, as I think back. But at that point, the only thing I knew for sure was fear: not of the health hazards of smoking (which we were just beginning to learn then), but of the physical health hazards my father threatened if I ever again smoked just one cigarette.

I never became a smoker, not even a casual one. In fact, it was years before I took a drag on another cigarette. It tasted lousy. Likewise, I have no interest in vaping or hookahs. Okay, permit me a cigar and cognac for male bonding once or twice a year, but please don't tell Dad.

A Fishing Expedition with Nonnon

I often went fishing with Nonnon at our Southampton beach. One fishing trip turned out especially memorable. It was an outing one morning right after a late-night storm. I remember that I was about ten, which would have made it late in the summer of 1958.

Southampton's summer seemed to go on hiatus that year, and the bay seemed to dare anyone to swim. After one gruesome thunderstorm, a chill northwest wind blasted over 30mph while Mother Nature pounded the Roses Grove and Bay View Oaks beaches with angry three-foot waves. You could almost feel the ocean-sized waves tearing at the rocks and sand. It was too cold to leave the house early that morning, so we ventured out just before noon, loaded down like sherpas leaving a Himalayan base camp: three rods, two tackle boxes and lots of bait. We also packed an Italian-size lunch. In other words, we carried food for four adults for two days.

With nobody swimming and only a few sweatshirt-clad sunbathers on the beach, I tried casting into those northwest winds. I managed to reach barely 20 feet, so I took on the role of bait boy, deferring to Nonnon's superior casting skill. I always responded quickly to his call for bait: *"Alberto, piglia u suidi,"* he shouted, using his dialect-rich Italian-ish, tongue, and words which sounded like peelya oouh sweedie). Simple translation: Albert, go get the squid.

We had been braving the winds for about two hours with no luck, except for not slipping on the mossy rocks and falling into the chop. Even Nonnon showed signs of frustration. He told me to get the bucket and put fresh bait on each hook. Then he cast the three lines into the fierce wind for one last try. That done, for the next ten minutes we stood mesmerized by the lines bobbing up and down with each wave. Nonnon began packing, when suddenly I called out for him to check one rod, which seemed to bob in an erratic way. Like a knight deftly drawing his sword from its scabbard, Nonnon slid that rod from its sand-support tube and in one smooth action, set the hook, all with no expression at all.

"Hee-ah id iss," he shouted (here it is), with no small amount of satisfaction. But we weren't done. Nonnon struggled, for the first time ever. He had to summon a vast reserve of Popeye-like arm strength for this fish. Without speaking, he handed me the rod, told me to reel in steadily as he calmly proceeded down the row to the next rod, also bobbing and bending out of synch with the rhythm of the waves. And before I could land the first fish, Nonnon went to the third rod, also bending with some salty monster. With considerable effort I managed to drag the first one near the beach. When its rubbery, silver-gray body slid among the brown rocks on the beach, there was no mistaking it.

It was a shark.

Okay, it wasn't Jaws, not even one of his little cousins. But I was a kid, and that sand shark, dorsal fin and all, looked like a real shark to me. Nonnon, now busy with rods two and three, explained that we had found an actively feeding school, which the storm and the current had blown in from points north; and that these fish were very good eating—*molto buoni*. The first one turned out to be a nice four-five pounds, strong enough to give us both a good fight. It kept us tugging and reeling for what seemed like an eternity in three to four minutes.

Somehow Nonnon managed to keep the fishes hooked on the other rods, each still bending and testing the elasticity of the fiberglass composite. But he prevailed, capturing the second of those voracious sand sharks. He handed me the nearly complete second catch and went to finish the third. By the time it was over, we had landed three nice sand sharks, with the second clearly coming in first in class at nearly seven pounds. The sharks were still very much alive even after we brought them back to the house. Amazingly, that takes into account several blows to their heads with a rusty hammer, each blow administered by Nonnon, the master carpenter-fisherman, before he removed the hooks.

Back home, Grandma got to clean the monsters, so she'd decide how to cook them. For her, cooking fish, shark or minnow, is what fishing was all about. For us, it was the eating.

A Smash Movie

We clearly favored the Bridgehampton Drive-in, but we also frequented the old time picture shows in both Sag Harbor and Southampton, especially on rainy afternoons. When my friend, Robert and I got bored by board games, and with no good beach weather, we asked my Dad to take us to a movie in town. The year 1960 featured a blockbuster epic "Exodus" and lucky for us it would play in Southampton that cloudy afternoon. He agreed, but with a catch.

We had to take my brother, Eugene (then seven). Although we hated tag-along friends, we agreed. During the long movie they planned an intermission. Did they just want to sell more refreshments, or did the moviegoers really need a rest? Probably the former.

Not wanting to share either our refreshments or the rest of our money with the little bugger, Bob and I ran away and hid in the men's room. That worked for a few minutes, even though we had to share the room with a dodgy old bugger, an older "gentleman" hanging around, for what purpose God only knows, we thought. While he started asking us a set of inane questions, we heard Eugene's voice from outside the door, loudly calling our names. We could not suppress our laughter and the little guy obviously heard us, so he yelled for us to open the heavy door. We wouldn't, of course, but just then the old guy started approaching the door. As the stranger released the weight of the door, Eugene summoned all his strength and flung it wide open, smashing it into the face of the old man. Unable to speak, and unsure of what had just happened, the guy turned to us with a stunned look on his face.

But that was not the only thing on his face.

The cigarette he had been smoking, burning tobacco embers and all, became plastered all over his mouth, nose and cheeks. Before he could react, the three of us bolted out, headed for the exits, and ran outside at top speed. I've never seen the ending of that movie, but I know it was a smash. Yes, in more ways than at the box office.

My Long Island Nemesis

Not counting the soles of my feet scourged by rocks and shells, I had one other health issue that perennially plagued me in Southampton: the terrible skin rash caused by a plant that thrives all over Long Island: Rhus toxicodendron. Translation: it's that toxic red plant, known by most everyone as poison ivy. Ironically, neither "poison" nor "ivy," the plant is certainly toxic, especially to me. For decades, poison ivy was my personal Southampton nemesis.

Everyone in scouting learns the catch phrase "leaves of three, let it be," and can identify poison ivy before his/her first foray into the woods. Before going to Southampton I too could identify that nasty plant with its toxic, oily compound known as urushiol. My problem was that I never learned how to avoid it in the woods. I knew what it looked like, but I don't remember ever touching the evil stuff. I'm not sure if I didn't see it among the foliage or if I wasn't looking in the right direction. One sure thing: I got poison ivy a lot. Every time I did, the rash grew more intense than the time before.

When I was 12, I suffered a poison ivy episode in late July. It affected my hands, face and my eyes, which swelled shut by inflammation and oozing fluids. It was so bad that when my parents took me to the Southampton Hospital the ER staff took one look and told them to take me back to the city for specialized treatment immediately. They did; we went to Misericordia Hospital in the Bronx, where I was admitted. It took more than a week as an inpatient before the dermatologists and infectious disease specialists could get my bodily fluids under control. Not fun. Not only that, but it ended Southampton for me in the summer of 1960.

I had another bad bout the end of August 1964, and the problems lingered into the fall. I kept fighting that outbreak for almost a month. Finally, except for a few blisters around one of my ankles, the late-summer rash seemed to have finally disappeared. Or so I thought. On the last weekend in September while I was visiting Lorraine Cioffi (one of my Saracino Southampton "kissin' cousins"), things got much worse. That Friday night Lorraine and I went out to a dance, and dance we did. When we got home I realized I couldn't remove my shoes without a great deal of pain. The cause: swelling from that late August bout of poison ivy. The next day it got worse, and I was taken to our family doctor, my great-uncle Alfred Marra. By that afternoon I was an inpatient again, this time at Pelham Bay General, under the watchful eye of my uncle and his physician colleagues. Again it took two weeks for a team of specialists to get the infection and swelling under control and my body back to normal.

I continued to get poison ivy poisoning every so often. I've tried just about everything, even taking part in a nationwide protocol sponsored by the US Army to test an immunotherapy anti-ivy drug. The drug was a total bust for me: I got poison ivy. After that, my only recourse was to stay away from the woods when in Southampton. Not easy; woods are everywhere. But I'm happy and relieved to say I must have finally mastered the challenge of my Long Island nemesis somehow: I've been poison ivy-free for 30 years or more. I don't know if I'm "out of the woods" for good. But I'm not taking any chances. I still stay far away from the woods.

All's Fair

In 60 years and five generations in Southampton, I can't remember any family member ever going to the famed polo matches, or any equestrian events that took place throughout "the season." We were by no means the horsey set; the word "posh" did not exist for us.

Not that anyone in the family felt deprived. For us, the "ponies" didn't mean polo or the races. No, it just meant, well, *ponies*. It meant going with our parents to local fairs and carnivals and riding a semi-retired old pony round and round. How long before that gets boring? And then you outgrow it. So except for occasional outings to the track for amusement (or for Dad, for his job at Yonkers Raceway), that was it for us and horses. But not for fairs and carnivals!

Church bazaars . . . the North Sea Volunteer FD July 4th carnival . . . the

Elks fair . . . and my favorite, the Shinnecock Indians' pow-wow. These had become some of the highlights of Southampton summers. And not just for kids; generations of adults loved them, too.

We're not talking sophisticated venues here, like Six Flags, Hershey Park or Disneyland. No, not even the old-time New York area amusement parks, e.g., Coney Island, Palisades Park or Rye Beach. These were small four-five day events, moveable feasts. These type of Hamptons events (not to be confused with the polo matches or benefit galas) resembled those summertime fairs held on muddy fields on the outskirts of towns across America. And we didn't find out about them on TV, but by two-color posters nailed to roadside trees or telephone poles.

In the early years, going to fairs was a family affair. Members of two or three generations often attended, and that was a big deal. It meant having dinner earlier, packing six or more into each car for the ten-minute ride to North Sea, Southampton, or Sag Harbor after sunset. Then a couple of hours of fun at the fair. The adults probably reached other conclusions as to what was fun, but we loved these fairs for the games, the food, and especially the rides. The elders usually spent time at the games of chance, wheels and such (not exactly real gambling). They kept the younger children with them, but they always sent us older kids off on our own with a couple of bucks each and these instructions: don't eat too much junk and don't fall off the rides.

Freedom and a few bucks—what a deal! So off we went to test our skill at midway games like balloons and darts, baseballs and milk bottles, dunk tank, ring toss, shooting gallery. I couldn't care less about winning a stuffed animal, the usual primo prize. I went right for the ping-pong-ball-in-the-fish-bowl booth. That prize? A goldfish! It took me several years, but my skills improved and I won gold fish. Twice. One of them survived the trip to the bungalow and lived out the rest of the summer there. But poor "Goldie" didn't make it back home to the Bronx. Remember, nobody's car had air conditioning. Enough said?

At the fairs, we didn't need to try carnival staples like pizza, burgers and fries. We had eaten a complete dinner at home. But we were typical kids: we *had* to sample the cotton candy, candied peanuts and popcorn, and hot dogs. And I could never get enough lemonade. And I remember always bypassing the sorry-looking pizza and funnel cakes/fried dough (*zeppole* to us), none of which ever looked as good as what our parents and grandparents made at home.

And then there were rides. How we loved those rides. Like the rest of the fair, the rides were small-scale, transportable, and unsophisticated. There wasn't much beyond a basic Ferris wheel, a tame little roller coaster, bumper cars, carrousel, tilt-a-whirl, fighter planes. We'd see them at church bazaars, too. But no matter how simple, for us kids, they were still fun. I loved the Ferris wheel and more than that, I loved getting stuck at the top. Here again I discovered the two kinds of people in the world: those who rocked the cars (or gondolas); and those who didn't. I was in the first group, a "rocker." Another observation: girls usually weren't.

As kids we loved the fairs. The second time around, as teens, we loved the fairs even more. Those same fun, familiar events drew us in, with the added attraction of having a good place to go *at night*. With *friends* (girls, too!). *Without parents.* Freedom! Sheer joy!

The simple joys of Southampton's fairs became more pleasurable the third time, when we took our own children. Attending the same Elks and Fire Department carnivals several times with my kids when they were young, "doing" the fair and going on rides with them, eating the fun junk food. All of that beat anything from my childhood or teen years. Being there with my two boys made much sweeter memories. I hope that one day my kids will take *their* kids to one of the Hamptons carnivals or country fairs. And I especially hope that I can be there with them.

Walking on Water

One time in Southampton we walked on water! We did that at our little beach about five years after our bungalow was built. It happened during the brutally cold winter of 1960-61, a couple of weeks after President Kennedy's inauguration. Those who watched the inauguration on TV may remember the words of the young president freezing in the brisk northwest wind as soon as they left his mouth during his speech. The weeks following

Little Peconic Bay—completely frozen over

the inauguration day snowstorm allowed no break in the intense cold.

But the intense February cold that year didn't stop my family from driving to Southampton one Saturday. Although snow still whitened the ground, as long as there wasn't any on the roads, they were game. Mom and Dad wanted to bring some furniture and boxes of "summer stuff" out to the beach. Great news for me: they'd let me bring a friend, and I chose my classmate, Brian. With almost no traffic, we arrived at the bungalow in record time, less than two hours. We quickly unloaded the car and before heading to town for lunch, Dad drove us all down to the little beach to see if it looked different in winter.

The sight would have taken our breath away, but the biting cold had already done that.

And just like our breath, the Little Peconic Bay was frozen. It was frozen solid.

The bay looked like it had frozen all the way across to the North Fork of Long Island. We could not hear a sound except for the relentless wind piercing our ears through our woolen watch caps. Brian and I carefully crunched our way over the top layer of crusted snow and ice along the now unmarked path from the road down to the beach, and then across the shards of snow and ice covering the rocky beach.

We thought we had found the high-tide mark, that nearly invisible confluence where bay water begins and sand and rocks end. We continued. Now we gingerly made our way over the tiny mounds of uneven ice, step after tenuous step, expecting at any second to hear cracking and crumbling of the iced over bay water under our feet as it gave way with our weight. We easily imagined falling into the bitterly cold water.

But nothing happened. No cracking. In fact, there was hardly a sound at all, but for the relentless wind and the occasional crunch of our black rubber goulashes on the now solid ice wavelets dusted in powdery new snow. So we kept moving out over the ridged ice, 100 yards past the invisible shore line, as we tested the limits of the frozen waves with each step.

We didn't keep track, but I'd say we spent nearly five minutes walking until we heard my parents yell for us to come back. We almost thought we could ignore them and keep going, but even at 13 we had enough sense to know that we might be pushing our luck with the ice, if not with that, certainly with my father. So we beat a hasty retreat to the relative safety of the snow-covered beach, then still a football field away. It felt good finally to get off the bay ice, to climb over the dune to the heated car. After that, a quick lunch in town, and then home to the city. We were all glad to call it a day—a very special one—for two adventurous 8th-graders.

Years later on a blustery, early spring drive into Sag Harbor, I came upon some locals fishing off the main pier. I told them my story, that it got so cold out there that the bay could freeze so hard you could walk on it. They chuckled a little and then shrugged off my frozen bay story as no big deal. Taking my story down a notch, they told me they had seen the bay freeze several times over the years. And here I thought I had something over the townies.

I don't know how many times the Little Peconic has frozen over since 1961. It probably happened during the "Arctic winters" of the late 1970s or at other times too, but no one ever mentioned it. Global warming aside, it might happen again—and I'm not going back to look for it. All I know is, I'm lucky I got a chance to experience and share such an unforgettable thrill.

Entrance to the Bay View Oaks community

When We Marched on Bay View Oaks

In late August of 1963, at a time when several friends owned boats, but before any buddies had graduated to cars, a not so momentous event (or non-event) took place in Southampton. It happened, or really didn't happen, at the Bay View Oaks beach. That day, we "marched" on Bay View Oaks. Well, not exactly, so some explanation is in order.

A bunch of the local kids had gathered to have fun at the BVO beach, while something truly significant would soon take place elsewhere. After our water skiing at the beach, we anchored the boats, went swimming, and tuned in one of our rudimentary portable AM transistor radios to some tinny, scratchy pre-British invasion tunes beamed across the Long Island Sound in Connecticut. After a few songs the deejay interrupted the music and our afternoon of dancing came to an end due to a special bulletin out of Washington, DC. The other crappy stations turned out to be no help either; everybody had joined the same broadcast.

We found out that a quarter million people had assembled at the base of the Lincoln Memorial to protest discrimination and to advance racial equality. We could barely make out the words of the main speaker, but we later came to know that a certain southern preacher, Dr. Martin Luther King, had already begun to deliver what would be hailed as a landmark

101

speech, perhaps the most eloquent speech in American history.

That happened on August 28, 1963, while we went swimming in Southampton, 300 geographic miles and thousands of socio-political miles away from our fun activities. Mentally, culturally, and all other ways, we may as well have been a million miles away, it mattered so little to us. Reflecting on that day now, we must have settled deep into a bubble of sorts, into our own little world, lost in the exuberant naivety of our youth. We had missed something special; we had missed America turning an important page in its history. That would all soon change; for in three months, the innocence of our teen years would be erased by the assassination of our president and the years of violence and unrest that followed. The times, they were a-changin' and we would be changing too.

Endless Summer

All of my Southampton summers were great but for two things: they were too short and they ended by Labor Day. Plus, after Labor Day the Hamptons get great beach weather.

But the summer 1963, after my second year of high school, turned out differently for Bob and me. Labor Day fell on September 2 and our Catholic high schools (All Hallows for me; Saint Raymond's for Bob) had delayed their usual opening, giving us off the week right after Labor Day. But it didn't matter. My family already had plans to head home on Labor Day. Worse yet, to avoid the Hamptons exodus, my father planned on leaving right after breakfast on Monday. So Sunday after lunch I took a quick dip in the bay and said my good-byes to Bob and other friends.

Sunday afternoon, while carrying boxes to the car, Bob came barreling over by bike. His big toothy grin signaled good news. No, with that face it had to be *great* news. The good news: Bob was staying in Southampton with his mom that week and going home the next weekend. The great news: he had asked his mother if I could spend the week with them, and she agreed, if my parents approved. That left one, no, two obstacles: Mom and my Dad.

I had to convince my parents to see only the good in all this. What could be negative? They'd be getting rid of me for a week and I'd still be home before school. Bob's father would take us all back to their apartment in Parkchester, four miles from our home, and my folks could get me there next Sunday, so what could be bad? In we went to finesse our plan wrapping it in glowing positives. I was nervous asking Dad's permission, but he offered no resistance, just indifference. "Talk to your mother," he mumbled. One obstacle down!

My mother surprised me too. She couldn't care less, but rolled out her "mom-isms."

"Be on your best behavior ... Don't make work for Robert's mom ... Remember, say thank you." She went on and on, ending her motherly litany with "And don't get in trouble!"

Nodding my head, I kept thinking, "Trouble? Pinch me, I'm in Southampton heaven!"

I packed the barest essentials—two bathing suits topped the list—into a gym bag; retrieved my bike from its short-lived storage; and Bob and I drew a bee-line down Noyac Road towards Roses Grove and his house, ready to start our post-season bonus week.

Bob's mom and dad couldn't have been nicer hosts. His mom handed me fresh towels and told me to take my time putting my things away in his room. I'd be sleeping next to his bed. This was heaven. Robert, an only child, had a whole room to himself. I could only dream of that. I rarely slept in a bedroom at our bungalow; I usually slept on the convertible sofa or my sleeper chair. And in the city, I shared a room with my brother.

Yes, things were certainly different. All of their furnishings seemed perfectly arranged, with nothing out of place inside or in the yard. And unlike my family's place or the other two bungalows, nothing looked overcrowded. For example, the lounge chairs Bob's parents used looked new and quite stylish, with a little café table between them.

But I noticed other subtle differences too. Both his parents smoked and alongside their separate packs of smokes and matching ashtrays they had carefully placed their cocktails, in matching highball glasses. I couldn't remember seeing my parents or relatives with a cocktail. The only alcohol they consumed was beer with sandwiches at lunch, red wine at dinner, and a generous anisette pour with after-dinner espresso or while playing cards at night.

The differences extended to food, too. At our family bungalows, good things to eat were visible all over; in Bob's house, food was never in sight. It was kept neatly organized in the kitchen, mainly in the fridge. At our place, the tables on the porch and kitchen were overflowing with all kinds of fruits, counters cluttered with Italian bread and cookies, and cupboards stuffed with boxes of macaroni products and cans and jars of plum tomatoes.

But I reveled in some of the differences. Maybe because he was an only child, or that his family wasn't restricted to Italian food, but it seemed that whatever foods he wanted, his mother prepared. The first night we had hot dogs and hamburgers that we helped his father cook on the grill, with a choice of sodas too! In my family, soda meant special occasions. Also, Bob's family bought *name brand sodas*, proving again that I had ascended to heaven.

There were other obvious pluses at Bob's house. It was much quieter, almost eerily so, than at our bungalow, and I don't mean just in the woods. It was quiet because unlike at our bungalow, there were no relatives or other visitors walking in and out or around the yards hanging laundry, tending the garden, prepping the grill, checking the propane tanks, etc. And I didn't miss all the noise and confusion one bit. I literally basked in their tranquility.

Bob's mom took great care of us each morning. She made breakfasts that teenage boys love: pancakes, waffles, bacon and eggs, and cereals—the brand-name sugary cereals with prizes, the ones that my Mom didn't buy. Those breakfasts fueled us for the beach.

The first day or two we tried the private Bay View Oaks beach, which was off limits to us as non-members. We liked that beach because they had a raft in the deep water and when we could sneak in we had a ball diving, jumping and pushing each other in. Through each summer the BVO association had an attendant checking members' ID cards; after Labor Day, the beach was open. So we left our bikes near the fence and went in. But not having to sneak by a guard took the fun out of it. Also there was almost no one around, certainly nobody our age. On the second day there they took the raft out of the water, so with no raft, the beach got totally boring. We had to find something exciting to do to maximize our bonus week.

We found it: Bob's boat, moored at the North Sea marina (Peconic Marina), just 10 minutes down Noyac Road by bike. That summer and the one before, Bob's parents gave him carte blanche to use the boat, and we sure did that week. We went out several times, enjoying a few good runs before gas and money ran out. We went fishing twice, but Bob wasn't too patient, and neither of us had half the patience of Nonnon the fisherman, so we quit before catching any fish. We had better luck with the floating beds of bay scallops in Wooley Pond, Turtle Cove, and Towd Point. Scooping them up with a small net, we caught a half bucket of scallops before figuring out what to do with them. Bob wouldn't eat any and his mother would not know how to cook them. But we took them home anyway.

My simple solution to the cooking dilemma: stick them in a pot and throw in some butter, salt and pepper. I had remembered seeing my grandmother cook all kinds of seafood in a simple blend of garlic, olive oil, and Italian herbs, but those ingredients one wouldn't find in Bob's family kitchen. Still, my substitute recipe worked fine and I had more than my fill. They were a bit chewy, but sweet and still tasting of the briny bay. Bob's mother ate a couple, just to be nice, but he didn't touch a single scallop.

For the first days of our bonus week we had no luck finding anyone our age, let alone girls. Seeking greener pastures than Roses Grove and Bay View Oaks, we headed to the freshwater lake at Elliston Park. The three-mile bike ride seemed fine, and a dip in the lake waters always refreshed. We had the place to ourselves, except for mothers with young children, so the park got boring too. At least we treated ourselves to ice cream and sodas at Garamone's general store on the way back home.

Most evenings flowed by pleasantly uneventful. After supper we rode bikes to the local beaches to see what was going on. Although we promised to get home soon after sunset, we always underestimated the dwindling September daylight and seemed to arrive when it was pitch black. We had to explain each night that we weren't doing anything but looking for fun. Then back at the house we either played board games or watched TV. If there was a choice of shows, Bob's mom let us pick. Their antenna, stronger than at our house, got good reception on two channels beamed in from Connecticut. After lights out (not counting the flashlights for reading comics in bed), we had debates on important topics such as which character had more power: Batman or Superman. We never determined who would win if they fought.

We finally found new friends Friday. On our last run to the Bay View Oaks beach we happened upon two girls: townies cutting class. The two lovelies provided some female companionship, but it didn't make up for the whole week. We Romeos tried to be irresistible and we managed to get the girls to join us the next day. We didn't have wheels until next year, but we had a boat, and Saturday we took them for a nice ride (they brought lunch), followed by a walk and a fire on the beach that night. Too bad we had to head home the next day.

Bob and I had visions of running amok like wild young bucks that week of endless summer. That never happened. Our post-Labor Day bonus vacation turned out to be a quiet, peaceful time, and a calming transition between summer and the serious work of our junior year in high school. We didn't tell our folks much, and they didn't really ask. My mom was especially happy though. Robert and I may have bent a few rules about how far we ventured and what we did in that week, but in the final analysis, we kept my promise to my mother. We didn't get into any trouble.

Round, Round, Get Around

The first generation chose land far from any of Southampton's development. We were, in a word, isolated, far from anything interesting or fun. Even Southampton Village ("town" to the family) was seven miles away, accessible only by car. As kids, except for the little beach, we had to stay close to home, with nowhere fun to go, unless someone drove us. The exceptions: the "fort;" the rocky beach; the other family bungalows, or a nearby friend's house. Sooner or later we would run out of fun things to do within those areas. Thank God my parents came to the rescue when I was 11, just in time to save our summers. They bought, found or were given (I never did find out) second-hand bicycles, to our grandparents' dismay. The grandparents carried on about the dangers of bikes on the main roads, and they had a point. Noyac Road, even in the late 1950s, was the main drag for folks in a hurry to get to Noyac, Sag Harbor, or Shelter Island. But we couldn't have cared less. Those hand-me-down bikes were *wheels* which expanded our travel and social capabilities dramatically. Our bikes meant freedom!

With our bikes, we had Bay View Oaks, Roses Grove and Southampton Shores in reach. In fact, we could go just about anywhere within a five-mile radius. We never chanced biking to town, but in a few minutes we could leisurely ride about half a mile down Noyac Road to Cunningham's bar and grill, a true oasis for young and old. There we could buy sodas, chips, hot dogs and ice cream. More pedaling got us half a mile farther to the main outpost and our true mecca, Garramone's general

107

store, now called a more upscale name, "The Country Deli."

We loved Garramone's. That place carried all kinds of wonderful things that Cunningham's didn't: comic books, magazines, games, toys, candy, gum and baseball cards. In short, it was a veritable cornucopia of the sundries that boys treasured. And as long as we had money, we could buy with no parental interference! And if we didn't have money, we could linger and browse, often without anyone telling us to move on. With bikes, the world—at least a one-mile stretch of Noyac Road—was now our Long Island oyster.

Bikes were our only mode of transport for three-four years. But we soon grew into an infinitely more exciting way of getting around on our own. Many of the houses in Bay View Oaks and Roses Grove had boat slips, and several friends got boats. My good pal Bob got his first boat at about age 14, a couple of years before we could get a driver's license. And in 1960s New York, you weren't required to have special training, much less a license, to skipper a boat.

Bob's Boat

I recall that Bob's first boat, *Rebel,* was a 14-foot runabout, with a 25 horsepower two stroke outboard, but it greatly widened the scope of our travels. A common engine back then, the two-stroke required hand-mixing of oil and gasoline. We kind of liked that. It required a hand crank to start, but it was a real boat nonetheless. And with only a rare breakdown, it took us many places, some reachable only by water, and all of them new to this city boy. So to load up on as much summer fun as possible, all we had to do now was ride our bikes about five minutes down Noyac Road to the North Sea marina on Wooley's Pond. We would literally drop our bikes at the marina, row a dinghy to the mooring, and ready the boat for a fun afternoon.

With Bob as coach, I quickly learned how to mix the right amount of oil with the gas. We primed the engine and took turns pulling the cord— sometimes a dozen times before it caught. After belching out blue smoke, the *Rebel* would spring to life and take us all over. We traveled the Little

Peconic Bay from Towd Point to points as far away as Jessup's Neck. With gas at about 25 cents a gallon, we could fill two portable tanks for an afternoon of cruising with money from our weekly allowances or odd jobs. Getting from the marina to our little beach took 15 minutes, most of which we spent getting out of the no-wake zone.

After two summers with the first *Rebel*, Bob's parents bought him a new boat. I soon learned that that's not unusual: nearly everyone who's bitten by the boating bug "needs" a bigger, more powerful boat every two or three years. That was true of Bob and his parents, which meant he was on track to keep getting newer and better boats. Those bigger, better boats also made us more daring. On some afternoons, we'd challenge the mid-bay waves and cross-currents in a northwesterly direction heading for Cutchogue or Mattituck on the North Fork. Round trips usually took about three hours—a little longer than it would take by car, but a lot more fun.

Bob's Car

Soon after he turned 16, Bob's parents went many steps beyond getting bigger and better boats. They got him a car. It's sometimes good to be an only child!

I found out about the car one Saturday in May of 1964 when Bob went cruising the neighborhood looking for friends. That wasn't unusual, only this time instead of a bike he was at the wheel of his car. He surprised the heck out of me when he pulled into our driveway in that sweet 1956 two-tone, green and white Ford Fairlane Victoria. Okay, the car had nearly 10 years on an underpowered six. But it had some goodies, not least of which was a Hurst floor-mounted stick shift, so he was able to maximize that baby's power. Best of all, it was *Bob's*, his alone, not his parents' car. He didn't have to share it with anyone, but he shared it with me. Because I was his very good friend, the car was mine to enjoy too, that summer and the next few. We finally had real wheels, and they were wheels of our own. We could now cruise all of eastern Long Island, and cruise we did, in either Bob's car or boat. That doubled our possible fun times.

Three Deuces and a Four-Speed, and a 389

In 1964, AM radio stations nationwide could hardly muster enough open air time to meet teenagers' demand for the hit song, "Little GTO," by Ronny and the Daytonas (and later covered by The Beach Boys). The song had that fun "surfer" vibe that was becoming one of the signature sounds of the mid-'60s. And who could forget those lyrics? Words like "three deuces and a four-speed" were simple. Sure the words paid tribute to the new General Motors muscle car, a machine that was not only captivating Americans, but are said to have helped "drive" the GTO phenom. Almost every testosterone-laden teen could immediately start singing along as soon as that song came on the transistor. "Wind it up, blow it out, GTO!"

"Muscle cars"—a class of autos undergoing a renaissance (note the many cable-TV car auction shows and the popularity of current models like the "new" Dodge Charger and Chevy Camaro)—can be defined as Detroit-made, two-door sports coupes, with high-performance V-8 engines. "GTO" (in Italian, *Gran Turismo Omologato*), means Grand Touring Homologated (i.e., officially certified), as designated by the creative and later infamous John DeLorean. He was the GTO's chief engineer at GM. And it was indeed grand. For of all the muscle cars Detroit was turning out, including such models as GM's Chevy Chevelle Malibu SS, Ford's Torino Cobra 428, and Chrysler's Dodge Coronet/Plymouth Belvedere 426 Hemi, the GTO was the most celebrated of that genre, if not the most muscular of all muscles.

Singing about the GTO was one thing; riding in it another. That's where the real fun was to be had. Very few got to experience that. Fewer still, especially teens like me, could ever hope to own one. But that was fine. I'd be happy to just ride around in a GTO now and then. It was in my senior year in high school when my cousin, Anthony Genovese, who had already graduated, showed the good taste and fine judgment to use his savings to buy an early GTO. That was some car. It rolled off the GM assembly line fully decked out in its golden glory (Tiger Gold, if not mistaken), complete with the usual high-performance engine and transmission, and a state-of-the-art sound system. How lucky could one guy be? Not just him—me! Why? How?

Well, cousin Anthony took me out in his GTO several times, and it was great fun just being with him as we cruised eastern Long Island. He and his family (Aunt Betty, Uncle Joe, and Anthony's sisters Rosemarie and Lorraine) were living in Rocky Point, on the North Shore of Long Island, 50 minutes from our bungalow. Sometimes Anthony drove out to Southampton; sometimes I met him in Rocky Point. Either way, we had a ball tooling around in that GTO.

I loved that car. But owning a muscle car like his could only happen in my wildest dreams. I could barely imagine ever driving one. Sometimes a boy's dreams come true, sort of. I *did* get to drive one, thanks to a local girl I was dating. And a good bit of luck. It was the summer of '65, I was a newly minted high school grad, and I had been dating Stephanie, also from the Bay View Oaks community, for two summers. I didn't know it when we started going out but I later found out that her older brother had a GTO. And it was a convertible! Not that his owning that car did me any tangible good: it wasn't as if he was going to give it to me. Still, it was a piece of good luck just to have one close enough to touch.

It was mint green (officially "Palmetto Green" I think). On one quiet but cool and not very "beachy" afternoon, Stephanie and I were hanging around her parents' house a few blocks away from ours. Her brother offered to take us for a ride, and of course we took him up on it. That ride was sweet—and it got even sweeter: He asked me if I wanted to take the car out for a spin. Me? Drive his Palmetto Green ragtop GTO? No need to ask twice!

After he had me take a short test-drive around the neighborhood to be sure I could handle the smooth-as-silk stick shift, he got out, threw me the keys, and Stephanie and I had the car to ourselves. With the top down and big brother back at the ranch, we were free to cruise Bay View Oaks and the entire North Sea area in "our" little GTO. At the wheel of that baby, I was king of the world. Or at least king of the road, Noyac Road, that is.

As the song says, "Little GTO, you're really lookin' fine." Yes, it was, and so were we.

Saturday Night, Lights Out

Beach football in Southampton came to a screeching halt for me late on a cool, overcast Saturday afternoon in August 1966, the summer after my freshman year of college. Since I had been working most of that whole summer, I went out to the bungalow on weekends. I met up with a bunch of friends who had gone to the ocean beach at Flying Point. We chose sides for some pick-up football and found enough volunteers to make it about eight players on each team.

I was playing defense, informally in a safety position, and on one pass play I paired up against my best summertime friend, Bob. Pound for pound and in terms of speed and agility, he and I matched up fairly closely, although he had me beat in height by about three inches and about four in reach. All those factors enabled him to get up higher on passing plays.

Bob had played varsity sports in high school, but I knew I could successfully defend against him if I worked extra hard. And that's what I did on that one pass play. I stayed with him step for step and when the quarterback sent the ball airborne in our direction, Bob and I both went up for it. But Bob, being taller, reached higher. He tipped the ball and lost it, and we both came crashing down hard. Most of his weight landed right on top of me, with his knee jammed squarely into my chest. It hit me squarely in the solar plexus, a bundle of nerves I learned about the hard way after that play.

Here's what happens after a sharp blow to the solar plexus. It can cause the diaphragm, the set of internal muscles at the base of the rib cage, to go into spasms, which in turn causes loss of breath, loss of consciousness, or worse. That's the sequence I experienced that day. I got the wind knocked out of me for a good ten minutes and I lost consciousness for at least several seconds. Before my lights went from dim to completely dark, most of my short life started playing out for before me like the grainy scenes of a silent movie, going from fast-forward to slow-motion before fading to black. When I regained consciousness, still breathing irregularly, I saw someone in uniform at my side barking orders to some other people. Rescue workers and passers-by had begun the process of moving me from a stretcher (how I got there I don't know) on an open air beach-patrol Jeep into the back of a fully equipped ambulance.

And so, with that one play covering Bob, my beach-football days came to an abrupt end. With that one game summer went from beach football and fun in the sun to a full-blown accident scene complete with flashing red lights and sirens, and me in an ambulance with a police escort speeding towards the Southampton Hospital ER, a place much-visited by several members of the three beach bungalow families.

I stayed overnight, on oxygen the whole time, and got the full treatment: IVs, X-rays, EKGs, neurological work-ups. And somewhere in there I got some rest and recuperation on my big Saturday night in Southampton.

If anyone had offered to get a custom T-shirt made for me, I'd have asked them to make it read: "I got my Saturday night lights punched out in Southampton." I'd wear that T-shirt with pride whenever my friends played beach football anywhere near Southampton. But I'd be there on the sandy sidelines, cheering them on from a safe distance. Go team! Go Bay View Oaks!

Rye and Ginger

One of the hits by the mid-1960s folk singing group, The Kingston Trio, includes their song ostensibly about cocktails, "Scotch and Soda," also the first words in their bluesy tribute to that popular American highball. The next verse hails the "dry martini, jigger of gin."

Neither dry martinis nor scotch and soda ever became my poison of choice (straight Irish is fine though!). Scotch and bourbon, it's said, are acquired tastes, which I didn't acquire (few teens did) until adulthood. No, with many others, we opted for the sweeter, ickier drinks, and if I had ever written my own ode to alcohol, besides wine, I would have had to call it "Rye and Ginger," but with a different slant and a very different meaning altogether.

My rye and ginger caper starts on a pleasant evening at my then-girlfriend Stephanie's house a few blocks away in Bay View Oaks. Back

113

then, the legal drinking age in New York was 18, and so I was okay, well within legal rights. No one thought twice about offering me a drink if they were having one. It was just how things were done back then. Times have changed!

The caper continues that Saturday as Stephanie and I took a walk to the little beach. When we returned to her house, her parents and older brother were having drinks, chatting and watching TV. They invited me to join them and, being sociable and polite, I did. They offered me a drink and, sociably and politely, I accepted. The cocktail du jour: Four Roses rye whiskey and Canada Dry ginger ale, over ice from their Southampton well water. Sweet. So there it was, the all-American (and very popular) drink du jour. I was at best a rookie high-ball drinker, and that rye and ginger, my first, went down easily, very smoothly. The perfect blend of slightly smoky-sweet whiskey and very-sweet mixer.

Sophisticated. Refreshing. Delicious.

When I finished my first drink her dad offered me another. And I asked for and got another . . . until I can't remember how many I made by myself. The evening was hot and the drinks were cold and went down so pleasantly that I easily had more than a few. And, yes, they took their toll on me, the one and only time I got sick-to-my-stomach drunk.

I made my way home fine—I only had to walk a couple of blocks. But as countless people can attest from their own experience, rye and ginger exacts its price the next morning. And it did. By morning I was a total mess. I woke up in a fog. My head was spinning, but my stomach was worse, everything in it churning in painful spasms as I headed to the bathroom.

The situation would quickly go from bad to worse. Why? Well, remember, at our house, Sunday church was a must. Nobody was excused for mere physical discomfort. So I had to get myself together and with my family make it to 9:30 mass at Our Lady of Poland. No matter that my head and stomach continued churning in full revolt.

Mass dragged on at the proverbial snail's pace. I was able to stand for

114

the Gospel reading and sit through the sermon. Thanks be to God! But when the ushers started passing the collection baskets, I had only one thing to offer, and they sure wouldn't want it. I had to get out. I started climbing over people, as I clumsily dashed out of the pew, down the aisle toward the door, not so gently pushing everything out of my path. I think everyone noticed the strange look on my ash-grey face, but I didn't care. Thank God—and I mean that—I made it outside to the outer fringes of the parking lot where I found an open storm-water drainage ditch in the nick of time. I can't remember how long it was before the heaving stopped, but it was long enough for my father to come outside to check on me. This didn't bode well, especially in my weak condition. Strangely enough, he put his arms around me to comfort me. Of course he had to add a few words of fatherly wisdom about actions and consequences. Translation: always know your limit.

I walked back into the church with him and stopped at the water fountain in the vestibule for a quick sip before going in. I made it inside the church in time to receive communion. Lucky for everyone around me, communion was still just the little round wafer and not the chalice of wine, because the smell alone would have sent me and my battered stomach back over the edge.

We drove home without incident, but for the rest of that day, I couldn't stop belching. With each awful burp, the air around me reeked of, you guessed it, rye and ginger. I could almost taste it all over again. A reminder every 15 minutes or so of my youthful indiscretion.

If any good came of this episode, it's this: it cured me of ever being tempted to over-imbibe again, with rye and ginger forever on my "do not swallow" list. In fact, to this day, I can't tolerate the smell, let alone the taste, of rye and ginger. Even "straight" ginger ale sometimes gives me the willies. As for my digestive tract, anything that even reminds me of either of that dreadful concoction will forever hit me right in the gut. Once was enough.

Oh, and that Kingston Trio song? It's actually about feeling happy about a girl—with no drinks required. And I'll drink to that!

Adrienne's First Visit

After fifty years, I can vividly remember meeting Adrienne Rinaldi at a college dance (called "mixers" in ancient parlance) held on the last Friday night in June of 1967, just after my sophomore year in college. The day after meeting her, as I had planned, I drove to Southampton with my father, having previously arranged for a couple of days off from my job as a sales clerk at a family run liquor store on Yonkers Avenue.

The allure of spending a weekend in Southampton notwithstanding, all I could possibly think about was that I had met an out-of-my-league, out-of-this-world beautiful girl the prior night. Okay, she gave me her number. And it was real. But what's a moonstruck guy to do as a follow-up act when she's 2½ hours away and there's no phone at the bungalow? And cell phones wouldn't be invented for at least two decades?

I had to do something so she wouldn't think I asked for her number for nothing. So I made a special trip into town (Southampton Village) to buy a postcard to send her. I wrote it out inside the village post office. I started writing the usual blather about *"Southampton Summers"* with the obligatory "wish you were here," but then I had second thoughts, decided it would seem pompous, so I put it aside, and ended up taking it back to Yonkers. The next week I made some time to finish the card and mailed it. Was she impressed? Flattered? Amused? She never said and I never asked. But it must have landed well because I called her soon after the card arrived

and things seemed fine. And two weeks later, on my next weekend off, I invited Adrienne to come with me Sunday to spend the day in Southampton. She accepted. And the rest, as they say is history, or her story.

I had told Adrienne about my family and the other families at our three bungalows in a row near a little nondescript beach. I called the houses "cottages." In the late 1960s, using that term could mean different things. It could mean a Kennedy-style family compound of eight-bedroom, six-bath ocean front villas with lighted tennis courts, swimming pools, expansive lawns for the requisite touch football games. Or it could mean we owned classic Cotswald-style English houses tucked inside high hedgerows in the quiet lanes of the Southampton Village. Or it could mean what "cottage" commonly means: a quaint little house in the country. Which, of course, is what it means in our case, and hopefully, in her understanding too. I don't know which of those Adrienne was conjuring up when I told her. Again, I didn't ask. But I did try to forewarn her about the remote location; that it wasn't exactly *in* Southampton, although *legally* it was (still is). I did try to temper her reaction by suggesting that she shouldn't build high expectations about the place. But I don't think she expected what she found that Sunday afternoon.

So when the road signs told us we had reached Southampton, (remember the images of Pilgrims on the historic road markers), Adrienne may have started to wonder why we seemed to be heading away from the developed area near the village and into wooded surroundings. But she said nothing. So far, so good, I thought. As we drove on for several miles and the road became curvier and more rural, I sensed that she might be having some doubts. So I told her we'd arrive soon and that our "cottage" was a small, unpretentious place in a community of similar homes. Again I thought: so far, so good.

And then we arrived. When we pulled into the driveway—"Here at last!"—all I remember was Adrienne politely saying something with words like, "Oh, it's very nice." "Very nice," she again allowed.

"Very diplomatic," came to my mind, while also thinking (hoping?) that she might have been a little relieved to see that our little "cottage" was indeed little, and modest, just right for a middle-class Italian-American family of modest means, like mine. As it happens, that was the kind of family Adrienne came from, too. As for her expectations, well, as far as I was concerned, I had never lied. All I told her was that my family owned "a summer cottage in Southampton." That was true. And that seemed fine for the moment.

Mom and Dad greeted us, happily welcoming Adrienne—and the gifts of wine and chocolates she brought them. But when in the course of the conversation they learned that she lived near Pelham Parkway and Williamsbridge Road in the Bronx, Mom turned a little cool toward the wine and chocolates and she asked Adrienne, "Isn't that close to La Scala's?"

Now at the time La Scala's was a landmark bakery specializing in Italian bread, so Mom's clearly implied remark was that she would have loved a loaf of that crusty bread in lieu of the wine and chocolate. Oh, jeez, I thought, is this any way for Mom to start my Sunday with a girl I just met and was already over the moon about?

Thankfully, my mother never asked in those exact words where the La Scala's Italian bread was. Disaster averted. This time.

After the big Italian midday meal (including only mediocre, A & P type "Italian" bread), Adrienne and I spent the rest of the day at the beach, first the ocean, then the little rocky beach. She seemed to take an immediate liking to the little beach. And she met some of the relatives, as well as friends and neighbors while we were there. On the drive back to the bungalow, she confided that she felt much more at home and relaxed at the little beach compared to the ocean. She also said that swimming in the calm, warm water was just right for her. Further, she didn't seem to mind all the rocks. (She still doesn't.) All in all, in the space of one day Adrienne came away with a pretty good "snapshot" of what Southampton was, is, always will be for our family.

Two Italian Cousins and the Rice-a-Roni Caper

Most of my cousins on both sides are American Italians, all born in the USA. But I still have several cousins who, like my Italian uncle, are "Italian-Italians" born as well as residing in Italy. Two of them, Mariuccia Colitti, and her little boy, Mimo, visited us in Southampton in the summer of 1968 when I was 20.

Mariuccia had married Tonino Colitti, my mother's first cousin, and they had two sons, Mimo and Michele (now veterinarians in Campobasso, Italy). Mariuccia and Mimo visited us in June of that summer. Mimo was about eight years old, and a very active, strong-willed kid. His parents had other names for him because of that, but I'm not repeating them here. Let's just say he was a handful. Here's my recollection of one story that gives the "flavor" of Mimo's visit.

Even with all the wonderful Italian foods that were being cooked at the bungalow, Mimo somehow took a liking to Rice-a-Roni (which, curiously enough, an Italian in San Francisco invented). How did Mimo discover "the San Francisco treat?" From my mother, of course.

As did lots of moms in the '60s, my mother had served it as a side dish during Mimo's visit. Twice. After his first taste, Mimo loved it. He put in a standing order for his new favorite food and later demanded it at every meal, including breakfast.

"*Io voglio Rice-a-Roni!*" He'd chant (in English, "I want Rice-a-Roni!"). So for every meal, the family had to weigh the pros and cons of a separate serving of Rice-a-Roni vs. Mimo's whining. Whining and Rice-a-Roni won out, but my parents suggested, and Mariuccia agreed, to draw the line at breakfast. So they refused to substitute it for Wheaties or other healthy choice, all-American breakfast foods (like doughnuts).

On his first Rice-a-Roni deprived morning, little Mimo stomped outside, sat down under our crab apple tree, sulking and sobbing. His mother let him cry his heart out, figuring he'd eventually yield to hunger and eat what was on the table. Five minutes after Mimo's Rice-a-Roni tantrum, who should amble over for a mid-morning coffee and daily chatter? Who but Aunt Helen Saracino, who found  Mimo "orphaned" outside. This upset her, thinking something terrible had happened. Concerned and curious, she asked him why he was crying his eyes out.

"*Mi fanno morire da fame*," Mimo stammered through his tears, tugging on Aunt Helen's heartstrings. Literal translation: "They're starving me to death."

Without a scond's hesitation Aunt Helen became his champion. She marched into the screened porch, Mimo in tow, only to discover everyone having a carefree breakfast. She was surprised and confused, asking in both English and Italian, what was going on. All she could see was a poor little waif, forced outside and starving at the hands of an indifferent family.

Everyone started yelling at the same time. They tried to explain the unexplainable, what we now fondly call the "Rice-a-Roni caper." Then Aunt Helen got it and broke into a relieved smile, and most everyone started laughing. Except Little Mimo. The poor starving child still had not scored that much-desired breakfast bowl of Rice-a-Roni that morning.

But the story has a happily-ever-after ending: later that week they bought several boxes for Mimo to eat before leaving for Italy. They also got him some to take home. Mariuccia (and probably Mom and maybe even Aunt Helen) slipped a few contraband Rice-a-Roni boxes into Mimo's suitcase, which safely found their way past Italian customs inspectors. Rumor has it that the now 60-something Mimo never lost his love for the San Francisco (via Southampton) treat.

The Shinnecock Boat Ride

Shinnecock! What a great name. It's one of those strong, powerful Indian names that's fun to repeat out loud. I love saying it again and again. It just rolls off the tongue.

Shinnecock. It's a word with several meanings. It's the name of Southampton's indigenous Native American Tribe (or Nation). It's also the name of one of the hamlets within the Town of Southampton. The name also pertains to several bodies of water: Shinnecock Inlet, Shinnecock Canal, Shinnecock Bay. Stretching the water metaphor beyond breaking point, it might mean water hazards on one of the nation's oldest golf clubs, Shinnecock Hills. Of note, that famous Southampton country club has hosted several US Opens, and is said to have been one of the first clubs, if not *the* first club, to admit women as members.

But this story relates to the three major contiguous bodies of Shinnecock waters—inlet, canal, bay—and a typical mid-August Sunday afternoon in 1968 when Adrienne, my brother, Eugene, and his friend Jimmy (our next-door neighbor, whose family owned a boat) and I cruised all three.

We eventually made our way into the ocean. Yes, the Atlantic Ocean. And we did it in under eight hours in Jimmy's family's 15-foot runabout with a small 35hp outboard.

Clearly we had broken some—probably most—of the US Coast Guard's safe-boating rules, not to mention the rules of common sense, and our seagoing adventure could have turned disastrous. But no, luckily, the four of us in the little runabout made it back safely, although much later than anyone expected. Our excursion caused enough of a stir to upset members of both my family and Jimmy's family, but for different reasons and with different results.

The story begins: when the weatherman had forecast great weekend weather, I invited Adrienne to join my family in Southampton, her second time there. We arrived early Saturday and spent that day at ocean beaches. Sunday was reserved for the bay. The day started routinely, with the twin aromas of perked coffee and Mom's slow-simmering Sunday gravy wafting about the house. We had a light breakfast so that we could make the early mass at Our Lady of Poland. Then we'd come back to spend the rest of the morning and early afternoon at the rocky little beach before the customary three-course Sunday dinner at the usual time of 1:00 p.m.

So after church, Adrienne and I walked down to the beach for a couple of hours of peace and quiet. Soon after setting down our blanket on the sandiest strip of the rocky beach, Eugene and Jimmy slowly cruised by the shore in Jimmy's boat. They waved, inviting us aboard for a ride. Sure! I jumped into the boat and after some gentle persuasion and prodding from the three guys, Adrienne got on board too. And so our adventure began.

After several quick and breezy routine passes up and down the beaches of Roses Grove and Bay View Oaks, we (OK, it was clearly *my* fault, so *I*) forgot all about the 1:00 p.m. Sunday dinner. Instead, I suggested we head to Towd Point, about three nautical miles away. We could get gas, sodas and snacks at the marina there, and maybe do some water skiing in calmer, more sheltered water. So we went back to our beach blanket, packed up our towels, revved up the outboard, jumped back aboard, and off we went. We filled two portable gas tanks at the marina for about $5 (marine blend costing just over 50 cents a gallon), which I gladly paid. That was enough gas for two hours of boating and skiing around Towd Point for the next two hours.

The sun was still bright, so I suggested spending the rest of the afternoon in the boat. We decided to go further west, into the Great Peconic Bay and maybe as far as Shinnecock Bay, where we could get more gas at another marina. I convinced the other three that I knew the way to Shinnecock very well (at almost a straight line northwest along the beaches, little coastal navigation prowess was needed). Jimmy wasn't so sure. Despite his half-hearted objections, off we went, with me now navigating at the wheel. I stayed at the helm for the rest of the day.

Like most young people having fun, none of us kept track of time. Nobody paid attention to how long it took to get from our beach through the Great Peconic Bay and into the Shinnecock Canal, which was our ultimate destination. Consequently, nobody knew how long it would take to get back, and nobody seemed to care. Nor had we filed a float plan with anyone. Float plan? We were just going out for an impromptu joyride. That meant nobody knew where we were, where we were headed or when we'd return. On top of that, we had no maps, no charts, no radio. We didn't even have basic tools and parts (nor the know-how) to make any emergency repairs.

So with reckless abandon, we continued on our merry way to the real fun part of the trip. I noticed the time on the lockmaster's control-tower clock when we lined up to pass through: it was nearly 4:30 p.m. But the waning afternoon didn't really hit us. We had plenty of time for this excursion. Besides, to my way of thinking, I had travelled this route twice with Bob and others. What I failed to take into account was that Jimmy, Eugene and Adrienne hadn't. That day, the requirement for "rafting up," or getting tied to other vessels in the lock (an inherently difficult task for experienced crew), proved extremely challenging to the novices on board. Ours was the smallest boat that day—we were dwarfed by several ocean-going vessels, some more than 40 feet long. To avoid damaging our boat or the ones we lashed to, we had to use our paddles, boat hooks and fenders almost nonstop while in the lock. Even so, we still managed to do more than our fair share of bumping into all the bigger, better, more expensive boats.

Once we passed through the lock and into Shinnecock Bay, the Atlantic lay directly before us. Why not venture out a bit more and make our way through the breakers and into the ocean itself? After all, we had come this far! We three guys thought we had done very well. Adrienne wasn't so sure. So without any show of hands we clearly outvoted her and pressed on.

It must have been 5:30 p.m., maybe 6:00 p.m. by then. With the sun behind us, we didn't realize about two hours of daylight remained. But we did realize something: we may have taken on more than our little boat could withstand. Encountering some of the first swells made us consider the limits of our little runabout weighed down by four persons. As we pressed into the full force of the ocean, the boat started to pitch and heave, and take on water from waves crashing over the bow. That quickly worsened and we were now taking on water over the gunwales. We had two homemade bailers: bleach jugs with cut-out bottoms, the kind often stowed on small boats. It was all Jimmy and Eugene could do to keep bailing at the same rate we were taking on water. Adrienne was splashing out as much water as she could, although it looked like she was just heaving her hands to heaven in prayer. But we couldn't keep up. Were we nervous? Near total panic was setting in! Things were looking so bad that we thought this might end in a life-threatening disaster. We needed to turn around and head home *now.*

And that's what we did—or at least tried to do. Making a 180-degree turn in that boat was easier said than done given the conditions. As we nearly completed a full turn, an extra=large breaker hit us from behind. Crashing over the transom, the rogue wave swamped the outboard motor, stalling it for a couple of seconds. In that interminable 2-3 seconds of time, nobody dared speak. Our four hearts skipped a collective beat. We held our breaths in that moment which felt more like a lifetime. Finally, the motor stammered, choked and spewed out an ugly stream of gas, oil and brine, before coming back to life and revving up to its normal RPMs.

Now back in Bay View Oaks, at about the same time we were retreating from the wave that almost swamped the motor, young Jimmy's family was becoming seriously worried. Without any knowledge of their son's location or who was with him, they were now considering calling in an official SAR (search and rescue) request to the Coast Guard station. Before doing that they drove back and forth between our little beach and the Bay

View Oaks beach several times. After many turns around the salt pond to check their mooring site, they scoured other nearby beaches. Without finding any trace of us, they grew increasingly upset. As it was getting dark, they finally did make that SAR call.

Meanwhile, with the setting sun providing good backlight, we pushed that tiny 35hp motor to its limit as we crashed over the now much choppier waves of the Great Peconic, heading for the more sheltered waters of the Little Peconic and home. With the last bit of daylight fading behind us and with only a quarter-tank of gas left, we let out a united sigh of relief when the bulkhead of our rocky little beach finally came into view. We maneuvered safely through the Bay View Oaks channel into the salt pond and over to the mooring just as dusk set in. It was perfect timing—just enough light to see Jimmy's parents hailing us from the boat launch and to hear his mom's shrill screams and shouts, her arms flailing in every direction.

As the "adult" in the group, it was up to me to explain things to Jimmy's justifiably angry parents. They were upset; they verbally jumped all over me. Without any reasonable explanation, I conceded that I deserved their dressing down. And they didn't know the half of it! We clearly held back telling anyone just how far out we actually went and the risks we took. We just told people we were having fun water skiing on the bay and lost track of time. A likely story.

My parents, notably my mother, reacted differently from Jimmy's mom. My Mom was stewing, too, but for different reasons. (Dad, for some reason, wasn't. I don't remember how he reacted or even *if* he reacted. Now there's a switch!) With Mom it wasn't about my being reckless and irresponsible or daring. She didn't seem to care about that. No, she was angry with us being more than five hours late for Sunday dinner!

Mom was the first to say something when we got home.

"Didn't I tell you to come back in two hours and that we were going to eat at 1:30 today? Whaddaya think this is, a diner or something?"

124

She started reheating dinner for us. "We waited as long as we could," Mom said, "but as you see, the macaroni and the meatballs got all cold and mushy."

Adrienne, Eugene and I were too hungry to care. We devoured everything she put on the table, and then some. My brother and Adrienne began to discuss, then to argue, over the last meatball in the bowl of gravy meats. (Yes, it all turned out okay; they eventually split it in two!)

But to Mom, it was still all about the food she had cooked that now didn't taste too good *because we were late*. That was all that mattered to her. Not the waves that came crashing over the boat, dousing the motor and scaring us half to death. Not that we might have been lost at sea. No: she was talking *food* here—*Sunday Italian dinner* food. In her view, we had spoiled Sunday dinner, and not just dinner as the sacrosanct ritual of mid-day Sunday, but the food itself. And all because we were late getting back from the Shinnecock Canal. In her view, "getting back" was a given. Being on time was the true variable here.

In our view, "getting back" was more than a variable; it was more like a miracle.

Uncle Eddie and the Planet of the Apes

My Uncle Eddie displayed a polar opposite personality from his two brothers. With his wife, my Aunt Mary and, after her death, his second wife, Aunt Helen, Uncle Eddie became a welcome visitor to Southampton. We remember him as an easy-going guy, everyone's favorite uncle, as much for his jokes as his engaging stories. Using greetings such as "Whaddaya say, Ace?" He mimicked characters from a 1940s Bogie film. We found that great fun. And years before Cassius Clay/Mohammed Ali uttered his signature "I am the greatest," Uncle Eddie had trademarked that phrase as part of his shtick. Not that he meant anything by it. In fact, he was always laid back and low-key. And whether in the city or Southampton, he showed a zest for the finer, and "funner," things. Everything he did he eagerly described as "the best, always the best."

125

Eddie, our family's affable "Ace," often spent summer vacations at the bungalow with his daughters, Diane and Marie. They even spent some time "alone" there with me while my Dad and sometimes Mom returned to the city. On other occasions, Uncle Eddie and his family stayed on with Grandma and Grandpa Marra; or the grandparents with their granddaughters.

Eddie always wanted to do something, anything, rather than sit around, unlike many of our relatives. One night in the early 1970s, my parents, Aunt Helen, Uncle Eddie and Adrienne and I were hanging around the bungalow, bored to tears. Uncle Eddie hatched an idea: he invited Adrienne and me to join him and Aunt Helen to see a movie at the Sag Harbor Cinema, the classic little picture house seven miles down the road. (It was obvious my parents wouldn't want to go.) With no newspaper (or internet!) to check movie times, we'd just drive there.

We knew him to be an easy-going guy, but we never thought he'd go into that theater once he read the marquee. He wasn't the kind of guy to renege on an offer, so in we went, to see *Battle for the Planet of the Apes,* of all things! The film was the not-so-good, campy 1973 sequel to the original Charlton Heston hit. When it was over he didn't say a word about whether he liked the movie. (He couldn't have liked *that* movie!) He simply invited us to coffee and dessert at the Paradise cafe a few doors down, and happily we all talked about other things.

Always as a kid and even now as a mature adult, I enjoyed knowing my Uncle Eddie a great deal. He left our world in 1987, and we miss him. To this day I always try to follow his simple guidance about having a good time and always seeking, finding and enjoying "the best," even if that means watching a bad movie now and then.

The Seven-Mile Ice Cream

In the 1960s, when tobacco companies could still freely promote the widespread sale of cigarettes, the slogan "I'd walk a mile for a Camel" remained a common catch phrase in the American lexicon. That catch phrase reverberated with people who didn't smoke at all, let alone smoke

Camels. Advertisers knew even then (TV's "Mad Men") that people seemed comfortable with the concept that some things are so special that they are worth the extra cost or time and effort.

As with cigarette brands, so too with beverages, fast food, and in the summer, ice cream. With brand loyalty, the proverbial brass ring for advertisers, people go out of their way for their favorites. My family was no different: our preferred brand of ice cream wasn't Breyer's or Baskin-Robbins or the handmade kind at local sweetshops. For us, there was only one: Carvel.

Okay, so technically it's not ice cream, it's "soft-serve," or what my parents and grandparents' generations called "custard." We didn't care about the technicalities or who called it what; we craved Carvel. Back then, it wasn't sold in grocery stores. The only place to get it was at that glistening temple in white, your local Carvel store.

In our early years at the bungalow, it was hard enough to get any kind of ice cream other than in the frozen food section of the A & P in Southampton village. The nearest store of any kind was Garamone's, the general store a mile down the road. They sold pretty ordinary stuff—treats like pops, dixie cups, rockets, pint boxes—out of a small self-serve freezer. You could get good ice cream at places like the Sip n' Soda luncheonette, a little establishment that still has an old-time lunch counter dating back to the late 1950s. But there was nothing close to us.

For true devotees, when a Carvel craving hits, nothing else will do. But as I said, you could only find it at Carvel stores—and the nearest one was on Montauk Highway in Bridgehampton, not far from the windmill and the drive-in movie. Our bungalow is about seven miles away via back roads winding north from bay to ocean through woods, farms and fields. It was the same seven miles it took to get to Southampton village, which had no temple in white.

One hot, muggy late summer night in the early 1970s, a scant year or two into married life, while Adrienne and I were at the bungalow with my parents, we both got the urge for a Carvel. It came on (as it frequently does!) about an hour or so after dinner, just as it was getting dark. There was no way around it: we had to have a Carvel. So we decided we'd make the seven-mile drive to Bridgehampton and we asked Mom and Dad to join us. We didn't know if they'd want to or not, but we certainly didn't expect the negative reaction we got. Both of them shot us an incredulous look, and Dad said something like, "There's no Carvel around here. The closest one is way out on the Montauk Highway!"

Translation: What, are you crazy? And you want us to come with you? At this hour?

"Way out"? Well, yes, it was about seven miles. But we pointed out that it would be a pleasant, traffic-light-free, 15-minute drive. And I was driving, using our VW Beetle, our pre-gas crisis 40-cent per gallon gasoline. And the Carvel would be on us, our cost, our treat. Still no sale.

Dad's retort, etched almost verbatim in my memory: "I can't believe you would drive *way out there* just for ice cream. Isn't there any place closer? Besides, your mom bought good ice cream in town the other day. What's wrong with that?"

Plenty. We countered by explaining that the trip wasn't "just for ice cream." It was also about the experience: we weren't going for *any* ice cream; we were going for *Carvel*. And besides, it wasn't "way out there." It was just seven miles away. Seven little miles. Still no sale.

Mom and Dad went inside to watch TV, and Adrienne and I headed for Bridgehampton. We enjoyed the short drive on curving roads through some of the densest, darkest woods around Southampton. We made it in under 15 minutes. Adrienne ordered her usual, a chocolate cone, the soft-serve rising high to a squiggly alpine peak. I opted for the "hard stuff," a Flying Saucer, that round, soft-serve sandwich, frozen hard as a rock. We ate them then and there as we left the counter, nearly polishing them off before we got back in the car for that "long" drive home.

With those two ice-cream treats from the seven-miles-away Carvel, we just might have reached the pinnacle of a lifetime of great ice cream experiences. Sorry, Ben! Sorry, Jerry!

My Southampton Years

Sal Anselmo

I was only 12 when my grandparents, Helen and Joe Saracino, built their Southampton bungalow and I spent every summer there while I was growing into adulthood. As the oldest of "the cousins" generation, I enjoyed almost all of the family's early summers at the beach. And it was not just for summer. Since I was living in my grandparents' house in the Bronx, I went to Southampton with them in the off-season too. Members of the extended Saracino family who spent summers at the bungalow usually did not go out in the off-season, but I did. So spending year-round time there I developed a special relationship with Southampton. As a result, I had a different perspective: I got to know the area and the people who lived there year round. So it's no surprise that I ended up living in the Hamptons for eight wonderful years from 1985 until 1993.

Strategically jutting out into Atlantic waters just south of New England, Eastern Long Island and its small coastal towns were mere fishing and whaling villages through the 19th century. They still retain some of that original charm and beauty. That, and the water, attracted me to the Hamptons. The entire Eastern Long Island has been blessed with water all around: Atlantic Ocean on one side, and the sound, bays, coves, and inlets on the other.

The water wasn't the only attraction though. The air was special too. Not just that it's salt air; it somehow seemed almost always crisp and clear. Was it actually cleaner? It sure seemed so. It even smelled nicer! Maybe the surrounding bodies of water also made it somehow sweeter. Maybe it was

129

the soil, and the usually abundant annual rainfall. Maybe that air is one of the elements that attracts many year-round people. And it seems they're willing to pay (and dearly!) for something as simple and yet in such short supply as sweeter, cleaner, more breathable air. All of that may be worth the high prices.

I spent my childhood with my mother and my grandparents in a row house on Carpenter Avenue in the northeast corner of the Bronx. I was 10 when I first heard something about my grandparents' plan to build a "bungalow" in Southampton. Our lot was the one on the corner, the largest by just a little of the five lots my grandmother's siblings had  purchased. Even so, the lot measured something like only 75 feet wide by 175 feet deep. The interior plan called for more than 900 square feet, which isn't that much. They never talked of living in Southampton on a year-round basis, not us or my grandmother's siblings who built their own bungalows. No, these little houses were clearly being built solely as summer beach houses.

The Drive

I first saw Southampton, or at least our part of Southampton, in 1953. My mother, Nancy Saracino, drove my grandparents and me "out to the country," as the family called it. I was stuck in the back seat of our car for what seemed like forever, but in reality, totaled something like three hours from the Bronx to our place on Noyac Road. That was a very long ride for a kid (especially in the summer, with no air conditioning). And I didn't know what would be there when we got there. I knew about beaches, but I didn't really know what the place was like or what there might be to entertain a school-age boy.

So there I was, spending half a day (six hours round-trip) stuffed in the back seat of my mother's car with my grandmother, slowly wending our way to the site of the bungalow. The Long Island Expressway still remained a dream or a paper plan. The only major east-west highways were the

Northern State and Southern State parkways, both of which ended far short of our far-out East End destination. So we'd have to wing it trying various back roads.

Montauk Highway, Route 27, the east-west route on the south shore of Long Island, passed through so many towns with so many lights that we eliminated it as an option. The roads that turned out to be more favorable were on the North Shore, Route 25 and Route 25-A. These took us into Riverhead, Suffolk County's largest town. There we'd pick up another southbound road, Route 24, moving across open country. It was on that stretch of woodsy roads where we'd reach a special Long Island architectural landmark, the Big Duck.

The Big Duck was a kitschy two-story structure in the shape of a big white duck with an orange beak. It was built in the 1930s as a store selling a local farmer's ducks and duck eggs at a time when much of eastern Long Island was famous for potato farms and duck farms. Scant few farms remain, but the Big Duck's still there. The Big Duck made it onto the National Register of Historic Places in 2008. But years before then it had made it into our family's "register" of cool kids' places. Every time we were about to drive past the Duck we had to open the car windows, stick out our arms and wave. That's how we knew we had made it "out to the country." From there, with little traffic or delays, we entered the Shinnecock area, the beginning part of Southampton, then "home" to Bay View Oaks and the family bungalow, all in ten minutes.

It was easy to get lost once we got off the main roads however. On one of those Sunday trips my mother had to stop for directions. Thankfully, she saw a police car on the side of the road and she pulled over. But before she could say anything to the policeman, my grandfather stretched more than halfway out the passenger window and yelled in heavily accented English: "Ay, you, meestuh, 'ow we gonna go Sow-ampuh?" My mother quickly offered the officer a litany of explanations and sincere apologies, and less-than-gently she reproached grandfather. To my surprise, the friendly cop gave her clear directions, and we were on our way to our property.

The Picnics

In the late winter and early spring of 1955, just after construction began, we'd take Sunday day trips to the bungalow site. And we always brought a three-course picnic lunch, which we ate right there on the lot. What a special treat! We sat on cast-off pieces of lumber and dirty construction debris set among thick, thorny briars and some of the world's healthiest poison ivy vines. There was no grassy spot to set a blanket down and enjoy the sun and fresh air. To this day I wonder how we, particularly my grandparents, never got sick, hurt or poison ivy.

Being Italian, my family didn't use paper plates or plastic utensils, not even for a picnic at a construction site. No. We always used dishes and utensils at least as good as the everyday sets we used at home. And being Italian, we never had just sandwiches on a Sunday and call that a meal. No way! For us and most Italian families, the Sunday midday meal was sacred. It required generous servings of some form of macaroni. Without that, the world might end! So our picnics always featured some form of macaroni (never called "pasta") with meatballs or other "gravy meats" that my grandmother cooked the day before and served from a pot. We also brought bread, salad, vegetables and fruit to complete the meal. To this day, many members of our extended family still follow the midday macaroni protocol on Sundays. And as we can see, the world hasn't ended. Yet.

Summer 1955

The bungalow was completed in the summer of 1955, and I have pleasant memories of that summer and the many that followed. These were the years when we spent most if not all of the summer in Southampton. It was a special time of growth for me, moving from childhood into adolescence. I had a nice circle of friends there, especially among the many visiting cousins, and we would do what kids did in the mid-1950s en route to becoming teenagers: games, toys, comic books, music, snacks. We went to the beach just about every day and had a good time. We also loved family shopping trips, infrequent though they were, into "town." Almost as good was a trip to Garamone's general store a mile down the road. Oh, pardon me, that's the Country Deli now. But to our family it's still just Garamone's.

And the movies. Not just the movie theater in town, but the drive-in. It was especially fun on those rare occasions when one of the aunts or uncles packed a bunch of kids into one of their cars and took the whole group to the Bridgehampton drive-in. What a special treat those nights were. I hardly remember the movies. But the fun of jumping on the old-fashioned carnival rides that were there, watching the cartoons, eating all that movie-theater food. All that's permanently etched in my memory.

The Fort

Those were simpler times in America, especially in our part of Southampton. So we all enjoyed a great deal of freedom in those days, freedom to move around unsupervised by adult family members. I could walk down to the beach, or to those special places we called our own: the secret clearings we had carved in the nearby woods that my cousins and I called "the fort." I remember very well how much fun we had together there. Working with rudimentary tools, we created a pretty spacious clearing deep in a wooded area down Pine Tree Road, the dirt road on the side of our house. The fort was ours and ours alone. It was a dark and quiet refuge for all the cousins. It had become our very special place for noisy, active fun. All of us (the girls too, of course) played the full range of games played back then: kick-the-can, ring-a-leevio (a version of hide-and-seek), cops and robbers, and some games we made up on the spot.

In those first few summers, the fort took on a life of its own. It had evolved into something like a fully functioning kiddie community, complete with social structure, division of labor, membership rights—and rites! We designed the fort to feature two secret, hidden entrances, and we even constructed some unapproved building projects, such as a fully functional tree house with ladders, and a lean-to shelter. We used a clever combination of natural and man-made materials scrounged from our families' trash bins or left over from building sites. And we did it ourselves with no adult assistance. That's no surprise. We were Italians, so art, craft, and building things were all in our blood!

133

We somehow managed to keep the fort's location a secret from the grown-ups, the neighbors and just about everyone for several years. We had strategically placed tree limbs, branches and brush across the main entrance to camouflage it. We hid it so well that none of the adults knew where the fort actually was, although they heard us talk about it. We also added top-secret "escape trails" in case some 1950s-era enemy spy or guerrilla fighter were to penetrate the defenses of the fort's perimeter. We posted daily guards (i.e., the naïve, younger cousins) at all the entrances. And we all had our assigned chores to guarantee the maintenance and improvement of the structures, the grounds and any other amenities. As the fort "community" grew more complex, it became for each of us a symbol of our own growth and development toward adolescence and adulthood. But before we moved on, we passed the responsibility for its upkeep to the crop of younger Marra and Saracino cousins coming behind us. And the fort was sustained until the actual property owners decided to build on it in the mid-1960s.

What a shame that years later groups of people we jokingly thought of as latecomers "desecrated" the hallowed grounds of our fort by building their large houses on it. Sometimes it feels to me like they "violated" our sacred traditions by building their summer Mac Mansions on the exact site where our fort and the trails we cut once reigned supreme over those virgin forests. All vestiges of the fort are gone, of course: bulldozed, built on, landscaped. But they can never erase the fond memories attached to our forest playground, nor the bonds all the kids had formed. Through the many good times we had there, I became close friends with many of my cousins, most notably Albert, whose grandfather (my great-uncle Arthur) and father (my mother's cousin, Frank) had completed their own bungalow a year after ours and just two lots down.

The Visitors

In that first summer of 1955 and into 1956, my mother, my grandparents and I were among the first few who were able to enjoy all the pleasantries of summers at the beach. That was fine with us. But word quickly spread. By the second year, when the Marra family completed their bungalow, my grandparents' bungalow became a mecca for visiting relatives. Everyone wanted to come to the bungalow, and my grandmother pretty much encouraged them. So they all came: aunts and uncles and their spouses and kids; my aunts' and uncles' cousins on both sides; and *their* families too. Some, mainly aunts and uncles, stayed a week, sometimes two. Some just came for an odd weekend here and there.

Being the matriarch of a typical Italian family, my grandmother never turned anyone away, even if it wasn't their turn to visit or they made a last-minute request. She didn't say no to limit the number of overnight guests, so the bungalow at times resembled a college dorm or army barracks. Somehow as many as 13 or 14 people jammed in for the night, totaling as many as 20 or so people in the house the next day. That meant, of course, they would get at least one full meal, and now we had to fit everybody at the table on the screened porch. Remember, the bungalow was just a tiny, two-bedroom, one-bathroom house designed to sleep six people.

Sleeping arrangements became a supreme challenge; at times even a contest. Every bed was full, with kids doubled up in the twin beds. Visitors were dispatched to folding beds or World War II Army cots in the kitchen or the screened porch. At least once there was a baby sleeping in a baby bed perched on top of the TV set (honestly!). As for me, I always ended up having to sleep on one of the folding Army cots in the kitchen or on the screened porch. I often had the dubious pleasure of listening to the refrigerator (which the old Italians called the "ize-a-boxa") lull me to sleep. And we were the nightly special for mosquitoes and eastern Long Island's notorious gnats.

Mama, Papa and Mom

My Italian-born grandparents were very colorful characters, but very different one from the other. My grandfather, whom everyone called Papa, almost never went to the beach. My grandmother, whom we called Mama, was the polar opposite. She religiously walked those two blocks down to the rocky shore nearly every afternoon, more often than not with one of her contemporaries, usually her sister and next-door neighbor, Sylvia Maffei, or her sister-in-law, Mary Marra. At the beach grandma quickly

135

and thoroughly engaged with friends, neighbors and visitors. Sometimes she seemed to hold court with relatives and neighbors who also spoke her Neapolitan dialect.

My grandmother had a unique personality. She was a real character. She acted deceptively charming at times, strong and domineering many other times, and got into everyone's personal lives, business and relationships almost all the time. She could take on the characteristics of a loving and generous old woman, which she was. That and more to me! But she was also a very influential, highly opinionated, persuasive individual. She may have written the book on how older women can interfere in younger peoples' lives. Her reputation was such that the mere mention of her name probably still elicits uproarious laughter up and  down our little beach community. I'm grateful for knowing her, for living with her, and for all the loving care she showed me until I was a young man of 21. I think she may have even spoiled the hell out of me.

With Mama supervising the Southampton kitchen, we never lacked good food, and lots of it. How great was that! Relatives from both sides of the family—at times even some from the Maffei and Marra bungalows—came to eat with us. Mama had an open-door policy, and none of the people we knew in the Bay View Oaks community went hungry.

Papa didn't contribute much to the actual preparation of meals, except for barbequing chicken, streak or sausage on his homemade grill. But he had an innate talent for growing vegetables, so he brought abundant supplies of fresh vegetables from his backyard garden into the kitchen all summer long. He grew tomatoes, zucchini, cucumbers, basil and more and it seemed like there was nothing he couldn't grow. The secret of his constant success? His own specially blended natural fertilizers.

On one occasion in particular, I can clearly see him inside his chicken wire-rimmed vegetable garden at the far end of the property toward the dirt road leading to the beach. We had just walked home from the beach and saw him sitting quietly in the middle of his little garden, seemingly not doing anything. It was a curious sight. We were about to ask him what he was doing and if everything was all right, but when we got closer we understood, not that it made things any better.

There he was. He was sitting in the middle of several large mounds of freshly spread cow manure. He looked very serious, quietly absorbed in meticulously separating the larger pieces from smaller ones. He looked like a modern-day Midas counting and sorting his many gold coins. Well, needless to say, when he finished, he had a proud look on his face. The surface of his newly dressed garden looked wonderful with its perfect ebony tones of rich lustrous soil so evenly spread out. My grandfather, on the other hand, looked not so lustrous: his labors turned him nearly as dark as his precious garden soil. And who knew how he smelled. Nobody dared get close enough to him to find out.

My grandfather played the role of the typical old-fashioned Italian head of the family, and always behaved like the strong, silent type. He never said much; he never had to. And he was the most steadfast member of the family. To his children and especially to his grandchildren, he was the family's rock, its firmly set anchor. He was intelligent, knowledgeable, and highly intuitive. Much of the guidance he gave me about the ways of the world is still relevant, and still holds exceptional value for me today.

Papa was also creative: there was nothing he couldn't do, nothing he couldn't fix better than new. He also made things; and he made things happen. For example, the bungalow. He built it, improved it and passed it on. In earlier years he sent his older son, Savino, to college and then dental school; and he bought the Carpenter Avenue house, all without incurring any debt. He did it on a tailor's salary that never peaked much above $100 a week. How he accomplished all that still amazes me.

Any recollection of my good times in Southampton of course features fond memories of my late mother,

Nancy. She divorced when I was very young and never remarried. For a good portion of her life, to support herself and me, she worked very hard in the garment industry in one of New York City's many sweat shops. We had to live in my grandparents' house, where she did a good deal of the housekeeping and cooking. Once the bungalow was built, she spent a lot of time there with my grandmother, and for many years she helped my grandparents keep it going strong. Were it not for her, the place may not have held up as long as it did.

And that was what she was all about. My mother's role in life seemed to be one of sacrifice, to do more, to make life better for others rather than for herself. She was positive, giving, fun-loving, and greatly loved—everyone had a special affection for Nancy. I revel in the memory that she was a positive, generous person to the end, loved and respected by family and friends alike. And she is missed.

Growing up and spending summers in Southampton under the influence of these three wonderful people with totally different personalities was in some ways strange but totally worthwhile. I didn't think that at the time, but I know I wouldn't change a thing about any of it. The limitless love they showed me enabled me to love others throughout my life.

And while staying at the bungalow during those summers was a fun part of growing up, I don't really miss it. Those were good times, but I not only grew up, I grew *away*—from the bungalow and from the Hamptons. As a matter of fact, I haven't been back to the Hamptons for many years. I can't even remember how long it's been. I know that the little bungalow has stood for years in the face of wind, bad weather, dampness and mold. I know that it was renovated using the same basic foundation. I'll see the house in its "reborn" state soon enough. But for now, I prefer to remember my summers and that little bungalow just as they were—and with the name "Saracino" hand-painted on a little sign proudly hanging over the entrance.

Espresso Summers

Ellen Saracino

Many of my fondest childhood memories are of Grandma Saracino and the little Southampton bungalow near the beach. Here are just a few of my favorites.

Grandma's Double Shots

The tiny house had only two bedrooms, but somehow that little house found a way to accommodate ten or more people. It seemed that every piece of furniture in just about every room—there were only four, plus a screened porch—could open up, fold out, slide out and, poof, there's another bed! For good measure, there were also old moth-eaten, mildew-smelling US Army cots left over from World War II. Along with my sister and brother and a bunch of cousins, we were the ones tucked into these sleeping sleights of hand.

Grandma and Grandpa always drank strong espresso coffee, as did all the great-aunts, great-uncles and other relatives up and down the ancestral line. They'd have none of that weak brown stuff, which they disdainfully called "brown coffee" or "American coffee." My parents and their generation usually drank brown coffee in the daytime and espresso ("black coffee") after dinner, but the older family members drank espresso any time of day from breakfast on. But it's the breakfast part I remember best. Or to be more precise, it was really pre-breakfast.

139

Every morning, Grandma rose first. She'd go to the kitchen and make espresso in a very large *machinetta*, a simple, cylindrical, aluminum drip-type espresso pot. Oh, it was nothing fancy, but it made lots of strong, jet-black espresso.

When the coffee was done, Grandma poured. She never used demi-tasse cups. No, she saved those for "company." That's something I still find funny because there never was any *real* company. *We* were the only "company," our immediate family or other relatives. Goodness knows, there was no room for anyone besides family anyway! She would serve those morning shots of black coffee in a motley collection of chipped coffee mugs and juice glasses in assorted sizes. Actually, referring to all of those glasses as juice glasses is a bit of a stretch. Some of them were old Welch's jelly jars with engravings of the Flintstones or other cartoon characters, clearly meant only to serve as small glasses for kids. Others were the glasses from store-bought, pre-made shrimp cocktails that we ate on what were still meatless Fridays back then. Thinking back, we were recyclers way before recycling was cool!

So each morning I would slowly wake up to the rich aromas of Medaglia d'Oro (the only brand they'd tolerate) brewing and the sound of cups and glasses gently clinking as Grandma took them out of the cupboard and set them on a tray. But I wouldn't stir hardly, much less get up and out of bed. No, I pretended to be asleep as I heard Grandma making her way from the kitchen to the living room, where I bunked on one of those moldy cots. She carried that tray with all those steaming

Children, (L to R): Linda, Ellen, and Ray Saracino with Grandma Helen, circa 1955

cups and glasses to the table by my bed first. She'd lean down close to my face and say in a soft, Italian-accented, sing-song voice, "Good-a morning, Elena bella!" With that I'd pretend to wake up, wish her a good morning too, and give her a kiss on her tanned cheek as I picked up my favorite Flintstones glass. Then she'd go to every other bed occupied by her grandkids and repeat the ritual until her tray was empty. Sweet!

140

But it gets sweeter still. Grandma added something extra to each cup and jelly glass for all the grandchildren: a drop of whisky. It was rye or blended whiskey or sometimes anisette. That's how the adults drank black coffee after dinner, with anisette or similar. But in the morning? And for the kids? I don't think my parents knew—but *we* sure did. It was a little "wink-wink" between Grandma and each of us kids. And of course we never told anyone. Till now I guess!

So, first picture a tiny house. It's filled with normally high-energy kids jumping out of bed ready for a glorious day at the beach. Now picture these same kids having just knocked back a double-shot of espresso laced with 85 proof alcohol and sugar—and no breakfast yet. We were literally ping-ponging off the walls. Pandemonium reigned. The parents went nuts trying to control us while Grandma beamed at this caffeinated chaos by the sea, a chaos I'm certain she reveled in having created. She couldn't have been more delighted with her beloved grandkids menagerie on those espresso mornings.

Endless Scrabble

We were big Scrabble fans, my cousin Eugene Marra and I. One summer when we were 11 or so, we played what felt like endless hours of Scrabble. It seemed like the games went on the whole summer. Okay, maybe it was only two weeks or so. But we played every day. And on rainy, cloudy non-beach days, our Scrabble-mania turned into all-day marathons. Each evening, as soon as both our families finished dinner, Eugene and I would get together in my grandparents' screened porch, the one with the hard, cold cement floor. We'd break out the Scrabble board, pick up our first round of letter tiles, and play under the bright fluorescent lights glaring down on the dining table. Night after night, Eugene and I would play nonstop until we were told it was time for bed.

I enjoyed those quiet evenings of endless Scrabble with Eugene so much. And we agreed that we both got pretty good at it! What's more, our relationship went beyond cousins: we became very close friends.

The Drive-in

How we all loved to go to the Hampton's Drive-in Theatre in Bridgehampton to watch movies under the stars! We didn't go often but when we did, oh boy! The whole family piled into our big 1962 Olds 88. Dad would maneuver that boat of a car into one of the inclined parking spots in a "good" row. Good meant near this guy, but not too close to that car, and as far as possible from that carload of noisy teenagers. Then he'd roll down his window, unhook the brown metal squawk box from its post, and hook it on the inside of the window. It was our own private sound system,

Sag Harbor Express, June 30, 1955 edition

albeit usually scratchy and all staticky, and certainly not in stereo, with one small knob for simple up-down volume control.

When we were very young, Mom would put my brother, my sister and me in our pajamas to go to the drive-in. This was pretty smart, and we weren't the only PJ-clad kids at the drive-in. Why do that? Because it would be late when we got back to the bungalow, and all we'd have to do was hop into bed. Or, we could be carried to bed, as one or another of us always fell asleep in the middle of the second picture.

After the cartoons, and before the feature film started, we always made a trek to the "snack bar" to get popcorn. If for some reason someone didn't get popcorn or soda or other delectable movie fare, the giant screen out in the field showed a cartoon of a singing hotdog and box of popcorn that extolled their available yummy treats: "Let's all go to the snack bar, let's all go to the snack bar, let's all go to the snack *barrrr*, and get ourselves some treats." To this day I can't help but hum that stupid tune every time I pass the microwave-popcorn section at the grocery store.

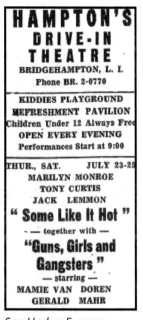

HAMPTON'S DRIVE-IN THEATRE
BRIDGEHAMPTON, L. I.
Phone BR. 2-0770

KIDDIES PLAYGROUND
REFRESHMENT PAVILION
Children Under 12 Always Free
OPEN EVERY EVENING
Performances Start at 9:00

THUR., SAT.   JULY 23-25
MARILYN MONROE
TONY CURTIS
JACK   LEMMON

" Some Like It Hot "
- — together with —
"Guns, Girls and Gangsters "
— starring —
MAMIE VAN DOREN
GERALD MAHR

Sag Harbor Express,
July 23, 1959 edition

One of those drive-in trips was especially memorable. I was real little, maybe five or so. We went to see *Some Like It Hot* starring Marilyn Monroe, Tony Curtis and Jack Lemmon. It's not only my favorite movie, but it has been named American Film Society's number one comedy film of all time. It's a hilarious movie, even for a five-year-old, one who didn't get any of the subtext, but who knew funny when she saw it.

Besides the thrill of going to the drive-in wearing PJs way before it was bedtime and stuffing my face with drippy buttered popcorn (hey, I was five: everything's thrilling at five), we got an even bigger thrill one special night. It derived from the station wagon parked next to us which was filled with people the adults said were celebrities. It was none other than the super-glamorous Gabor sisters, Zsa Zsa, Eva and Magda, who often vacationed in the Hamptons. It was all we could do to watch the movie and not the station wagon stars. Gabors, Marilyn, Gabors, Marilyn . . . What a place. What a night.

Sadly, as with many/most drive-ins just about everywhere, the Bridgehampton drive-in is no more. It's now a shopping center right off the Montauk Highway, with a big King Kullen supermarket and other stores. Now way over fifty years later, when I stand in front of that King Kullen, I can't help but think back to that starry night of the Gabor sisters and *Some Like It Hot*. I close my eyes, easily remembering. Then I smile.

Clamming, Italian-Style

One of the stories I love to tell about Southampton, one that consistently amuses my friends, especially the ones who live in the East End of Long

143

Island, is about clamming. Well, it's clamming "Italian-style." They often ask me to tell that story again (and again), so here it is for everyone who may not have had the pleasure.

When I was little, three generations would spend their summers at our three family bungalows two blocks from our little rocky beach on Little Peconic bay. There was my Grandma, Helen Saracino, my great-aunts Adeline, Sylvia and Mary, my mother, and various other aunts. They all went into the water about chest deep at low tide to find clams. But this was not your usual bunch of clammers. The Clam Ladies, as I called them, wore black or navy-colored bathing suits that looked very much like padded dresses complete with skirts. The Clam Ladies were all well-endowed, so there was good cleavage. This, as it happens, was a huge benefit. Many clammers go in the water lacking this.

With this being the early 1960s, women also wore bathing caps, the tight, head-gripping, hair-ripping rubber kind, complete with chin straps. Some caps were fancy, with rubber flower appliqués stuck all over them. But most caps were plain white or a dull pale pink. The clam ladies always cinched the chin straps tightly, in case some giant rogue wave came up unexpectedly, knocked their caps off and, heaven forbid, wet their hair. Mind you, the average wave height in the Little Peconic is measured in inches, not feet. Not one hair got wet under those well-anchored bathing caps.

The Clam Ladies, thusly clad, clustered together in the water ready to start clamming. Normal people used clam rakes. But not the clam ladies: they stirred up and felt around the sea bottom for clams. They really did. They used their toes and then their fingers, and had the abraded, scraped feet and broken nails to prove it. Why? Because you can't know where the clams actually are with a rake—you need to *feel* them. That was their secret; that was their way. Which, they would tell you, is much more efficient: either you have a clam or you don't, not a heavy rake full of useless mud and seaweed and stones you have to pull up and sort through and then go back and try again. I am not making this up.

Their technique was like underwater Braille for bivalves. And it was a sight to see. The Clam Ladies first felt with their toes or fingers for the sharp edge of the clam's "lip," the hinge at the other end, or the rough surface of the shell, all the while gossiping or telling stories in Italian, laughing and having a grand time. However, feeling around in the mud and sand was not fool-proof. Many times one of them shouted, "I got one!" Only to come up with a rock, which they promptly tossed back. But when it really *was* a clam, great joy abounded in the water and on the beach. The other Clam Ladies would stop feeling around the sand and mud just long enough to "Ooh and ah" over the clam's size—the bigger, the better for clam sauce and chowder. If it was a small one, they'd wax poetic about how sweet and tender it would be. They'd hold it high to show their beach-chair cheering section, who rewarded with a chorus of cheers and applause. This would go on until the tide came in or the sun went down.

Normal people who go clamming deposit each clam in a bucket inserted into an inner tube so that it floats around next to them within easy reach. The Clam Ladies had a better storage method: Clam Lady décolletage! The cleavage I mentioned made for a nice, big pocket to store their dug-up treasure. After a half-hour of using the "Braille for bivalves" method, they found a lot of clams, and so these well-endowed women became even more heavily (although unevenly) endowed as their treasures migrated down the sides of their suits, filling every cubic inch of space until there was no more room at the top to stuff in another clam, not even a Littleneck. At that point they'd walk out of the water, go to their chairs and unload. And that was an event in itself. Cackling loudly, they waddled over the rocky sea floor, holding up the tops of their bathing suits. When they reached their chairs they spread a towel on the sand, bent from the waist over the towel and let the clams fall from their bathing suits. Sometimes one of us kids held up another towel to shield beach-goers from this alarming sight. And that was that.

After drying off, the Clam Ladies always admired their catch, then assessed the damage to their hands, and compared their broken, jagged nails caked with black mud, all of which they wore as a badge of honor. The worse her hands, the prouder the Clam Lady. That all just added to the bragging rights.

I still go to the same beach and I sit in the same spot. At low tide, I can almost see the Clam Ladies in the water, all at about chest deep. And I can hear them laughing.

Such Tripe

Grandpa ate anything on land and sea except sea robins. Even he had limits. He loved chunks of tripe swimming in Grandma's spicy tomato sauce. Not me. The sight of it made me cringe. It was especially icky when I went shopping with her at the old A&P in town. When they had tripe, it would be found in the meat case, all white and weird-looking with its spongy, geometric, bee-hive compartments.

When I was eight years old, I stayed at the bungalow "alone" with just my grandparents for a week. Just me. One day, Grandma made tripe in sauce and served it to Grandpa. I tried hard not to look at it because it was super-skeevy (i.e., disgusting) looking. But I also learned something about Grandpa that day: he was not above bribing little kids.

Some background: red wine was always at the table for lunch and dinner. A warm gallon jug of the Gallo brothers' best stayed parked on the floor next to Grandpa's chair during meals. And it was always wherever Grandpa was. On the dock when he was fishing. Next to his lawn chair when he was grilling on the cinderblock "barbecue" he built or in reach if he was sitting outside reading the paper.

The grandkids were allowed a Flintstones-glass worth of watered-down wine at dinner. It was all fine, because the younger you were, well, the more water. So a real little kid's juice glass of wine showed a mere blush of pale lavender-pink. The color got darker as you got older, and by your late teens, it was full-strength. That's just the way it was, and it seemed perfectly fair. For us little kids, it was a great grown-up treat to drink sour, pale lavender-pink wine-water.

So there we were, Grandpa and I, and Grandma brought him that dish of tripe. Grandpa looked at me from across the table, and without a word poured wine into a second glass, almost to the top. And no Flintstone's glass, either: this was a small tumbler, edges surrounded by gold stripes.

"If-a you eata some o' this-a tripe," he explained in his heavy Italian accent, "I give-a you this glass of wine with no water." Then he pushed the glass towards me. No water! Pure full-strength wine! What a dilemma: I really wanted the wine. But at the same time, looking at the tripe, I really skeeved.

My grandfather just waited.

I sighed, took a long, hard look at the tripe. Then I stared at the wine. Then the tripe again, for what felt like a full minute. My lips were pursed tight. I was thinking really hard for an 8-year-old. Wine! (Tripe.) Wine! (Tripe.) OK. With a slow sigh and my voice full of defeat, I declined the wine.

Grandpa, well, he just grunted . . . picked up the gold-striped glass . . . and drank what would have been my prize. He went back to eating his tripe, and I went back to eating my own lunch.

Moral of the story: tripe trumped Gallo. Darn.

Three generations of the Saracino family dining "al fresco" under the grape arbors, circa 1959

Bungalow Clam Broth

Linda Saracino

Those of us who are old enough to have been in Southampton in the early years love to talk about clamming, and with great fondness. Clamming was a sport, and more than a little competitive. It was also serious business for my grandmother, Helen Saracino, and the other Italian ladies. They even came up with an Italianized word for it: *acclemsiare*—to go clamming.

They'd gossip together in chest-deep water while expertly using their toes to feel for clams (vs. the good-size stones that covered the sea floor), digging them up with one hand and tucking them down into the tops of their bathing suits, those shiny black ones with skirts and V-necks. They'd keep digging and gabbing until they had enough clams or until their suits ran out of room. Sometimes they'd put the clams in pails kept afloat by inflated swimming tubes emblazoned with images of Donald Duck or Tinkerbelle which they borrowed from the grandkids. Eventually— comical yet kind of sweet to watch—all lumpy and uncomfortable with those muddy, mossy clams in their suits, they'd slowly make their way back to the beach, gingerly crossing the carpet of beach stones, sometimes holding hands or onto each other, to get to their chairs safely.

Somehow they discreetly transferred the clams from bathing suits to pails of salt water, then covered the pails with wet towels or sometimes just covered them with damp sand and stowed them under their chairs, as much to hide them as keep them shaded and alive, as a little inter-family pilfering was not unknown. At about 4:30 p.m. the going-home ritual

149

began: shaking out blankets, folding up chairs, gathering up kids, toys, floats—and grabbing the clam pails. Then began the 10-minute trudge back to the house schlepping this stuff, always with a watchful eye on the pails and those carrying them.

If the clamming was good that day, there were enough clams for sauce that night. And if there were more than enough littlenecks and cherrystones, and if someone was in the mood (usually my dad, while he was making martinis and gin-and-tonics), the call would go out from the kitchen: "Who wants clam broth?"

Who didn't! So while we kids were scrambling out of bathing suits and into the shower and dry clothes, Dad or Mom got the clam broth going.

You could smell the magic start the instant the garlic hit the oil . . .

The Simple Recipe

There are no actual measurements here. Never were! This comes directly from my mother, dictating the recipe to me over the phone. I wanted to use Mom and Dad's actual recipe, but she doesn't use actual measurements and she really doesn't even know what those measurements would be. Oh, the quote marks in the "recipe" that follows? Well, that's Mom speaking to us in those quotes. Dad didn't use any measurements either.

As happens with family favorites, this one's been made successfully for years just by "feel," taste and experience. So start here, and then experiment if you want it to be more this or less that the next time . . .

Ingredients:

"Some" good olive oil (which doesn't have to be extra virgin either).

Six or more medium to large garlic cloves, cut into medium-thick slices.

"Some" crushed red pepper flakes (Go easy; you won't want to overpower the clam flavor.)

Salt, to taste (Again, go easy: clams live in salt water. You can always add some later.)

"Several" sprigs of fresh parsley (Preferably Italian/flat-leaf), chopped Littleneck or

Small cherrystone clams in the shell, scrubbed clean, about 3 or 4 per person (Use more if you got 'em.)

Bottled clam juice, optional. (Dad sometimes added clam juice, so then "maybe half juice and half water.")

Or, add more juice. It's up to you!

Steps:

One: heat the oil in a large pot over medium-high heat. Add garlic; "sauté lightly" (don't brown). Add red pepper flakes, salt and parsley; stir. (They'll likely make a sizzling sound as you add them.) Add "a little water." (You're on your own here. Is one cup really "a little?" Maybe. But you can correct that later: see section five.)

Two: add the clams. Reduce heat to medium. Cover and simmer just until the clams open, about two minutes. "Don't overcook. *Watch!*"

Three: then "maybe add a little water," again, if needed. The clams give off juice as they cook, but you may need to add water and/or clam juice to make enough broth.

Four: discard any clams that didn't open. They are either dead or bad. And you too may quickly become either.

Five: for each serving, put 3 or 4 clams in a large shallow cup (not a mug) or small soup bowl, and ladle about "an inch or 2" of broth over the clams. *Delizioso!*

Serving options:

* Sprinkle with chopped fresh Italian (flat-leaf) parsley.

* Sprinkle with chopped fresh tomatoes. That's a new twist: we didn't back then, but it's good.

* Not usually done and certainly not recommended: grated cheese (cheese + seafood = not really Italian); black pepper; lemon.

Serve with:

* Crusty Italian bread for dipping.

* Well-chilled Pinot Grigio, Verdicchio or Soave for sipping.

* Ice-cold pale lager, pilsner or saison.

Buon Appetito!

Woods and Water: A Boy's Hamptons Paradise

Eugene Marra

It was my favorite time of year—the last day of school. Slamming my locker door shut, eating my last lunch of twin oversized Italian heroes (subs), and searching for lost pencils and erasers all meant the onset of summer to me. And summer meant just one thing: going out to the country, to our little piece of paradise at the Southampton bungalow.

"Going out to the country," seems like a strange way to describe trips to the beach, but that's how my family referred to our trips to Southampton. Fifty years ago, "Goin' Up the Country" was the band Canned Heat's signature song. But that was different. "Going out to the country" meant one thing for this 10-year old boy: our little beach house.

The place held great wonder and magic. I felt like I was among the first to enter an enchanted forest. From the dark oak stands on the dirt lanes near our house to what we called "mountains" (sand dunes) the "country" had become a land of wonders. And that land and its diverse flora and fauna were mine for ten straight weeks of exploring, navigating and probing. The land became my own living laboratory; I went on a new field trip each day.

Our summer ritual began the same way each year. On the second Saturday of June, after waiting all year for his two-to-three-week vacation, my father stuffed us into his 1961 Chevy Impala. We then drove off on our annual pilgrimage to our Southampton house. But first, Mom had to pack the car with copious groceries, leaving our refrigerator and cupboards bare. Coolers, some of them makeshift, were jam-packed with homemade pickled vegetable jars and Italian delicacies destined for our screened porch.

And ours was no ordinary screened porch. Although it looked pretty basic, it was the focal point of the family. Black and white linoleum tiles straight out of the 1950s covered the cement floor. They still do! Jalousie windows framed the tree-shaded wraparound views. My grandfather, a master carpenter and cabinet-maker, had added to all that natural wood paneling, and, with the wainscoting, period charm.

We often used words like "tiny" or "modest" to describe the house. At just over 900 square feet of interior space (not counting the porch), by any standard it was a small summer bungalow. But that little bungalow became a home that hosted more than its share of family gatherings, some of notable proportions. On many Sundays, 20 or more convened for sumptuous Italian feasts. Our porch became a grand hall in miniature as it easily surpassed its capacity.

Apron-clad female family members scurried in and out to bring out food and drink to male family members who loudly argued everything from politics to sports and weather. Freely poured wine complemented the banter. We celebrated, enjoyed family, and reveled in the tranquility of "the country" as a necessary escape from the heat of the city.

Grandma Rosa, circa 1955

Our bungalow, humble in size and style, boasted a pedigreed location in its Southampton address. Although it fronted a busy road, it was situated on a pretty, heavily treed lot in a row of similar family-owned houses. And, more importantly, it was just two blocks from the beach. That put the Little Peconic Bay a stone's throw from our back door. Our twice-daily excursions to that rocky little beach turned into effortless jaunts. By age five, when I had learned to swim, the beach had become my second home. Having a wily and seasoned fisherman for a grandfather didn't hurt either.

The Beach and the Bay

From early on I helped my grandfather, Nonnon, carry bait, tackle and lunch to the beach. There he would cast two or three lines far into the bay. Nonnon, who hailed from Palizzi, then a small town (now a British resort!) on Calabria's coast, had salt water coursing through his veins, for if patience were the *sine qua non* of fishermen's virtues, he was well-endowed. He could fish nearly all day without getting bored, and many times he did just that, casting from the rip-rap or the rocky shoreline. He could endure tedious spells of pounding waves, relentless wind  and unforgiving sun without catching a fish. His sure hands harvested all manner of species from the bay, from bi-colored flounder with double-eyed flat heads to eels well over two feet long. Occasionally he caught gruesome monsters known as sea robins, arguably the world's ugliest fish. Porgies, bluefish, sand sharks and a good supply of ubiquitous blowfish were all fair game for Nonnon. His catches were bounty destined for the skilled hands of Grandma Rosa, the world's tiniest but most accomplished cook.

My brother and I loved to hear the sheer joy in Nonnon's voice each time a fish would strike. A series of events, signaled first by bobbing and lurching, then an arching in the rod, evoked an almost incomprehensible expression in his unique, accented English. It sounded like "Heeah id iz" and only we knew that meant "Here it is," and that the fight with a fish had begun. As he deftly reeled in his catch, we'd watch with guarded enthusiasm, then run toward the wiggling, jumping fish to steady it and coax it off the hook and into his bucket. If we didn't succeed, we'd get a stern reprimand in Italian. But fishermen we had become, and the sea was our playground for both fishing and swimming.

Every sunny day I made two trips to the beach, even if the water had turned rough. Those angry waves were best for rafting and body surfing. But on the days when the bay turned into a large expanse of flat, calm water,

I became a fisherman like no other. Not trying to rival my grandfather, I taught myself how to harvest the sea's bounty in two unique ways: by snorkeling for conch (scungilli), which Aunt Helen Saracino stewed in an exquisite *fra diavolo* sauce; and by catching blowfish with my bare hands. When it came to those cute puffers, the hand—at least *my* hand—was always quicker than the eye.

By trial and error, I learned to catch those squat torpedo-like "squab of the sea." I pushed aside rocks, dug into sand and unleashed trails of inky muck that held great allure for the fish. To them, mud meant food. The stakes rose when I dropped a clam shell or a slipper snail (two favorite foods of blowfish) and watched it helicopter down into the mud. That was all it took. As an amphibious predator, I quietly anticipated teams of puffers. They flew to the exposed shellfish like a covey of quail to corn. Just after a convoy of blowfish converged on the shell, with near lightning speed I'd snatch an unsuspecting puffer in one fell swoop. With speed and agility I would land 15 or 20 of them on a good day. When my luck and skill reached greater heights I'd catch a "two-fer." Grandma Rosa would later turn my puffers into the most sublime fried delicacies. Better yet, blowfish *alla marinara. Che fantastico!*

Puffed-up blowfish (also called sea squab)

Sometimes the Little Peconic stopped being a benevolent source of food and fun and turned threatening. That usually occurred in August, when currents, tides and wave patterns helped massive schools of jellyfish invade local waters. We identified one of the worst of those invaders as the lion's mane, a species found throughout the North Atlantic. The lion's mane is frightening: it looks like a huge mushroom cap with long, trailing strings attached. And they grow to two feet wide. To children, they look as big and powerful as the feared Portuguese man o' war. When lion's mane migrated, they crowded the little beach, making our water playground very dangerous and potentially lethal.

And can they sting! One sting can cause serious pain and a paralyzing, numbing effect. Multiple stings intensify the effect. And anyone who's allergic can also swell up, or worse. So woe to the swimmer who falls prey to their stingers! When they threatened our fishing and swimming, it was only on a dare that any of us kids would go in the water. And I was inclined to taking risks, so . . .

One hot August afternoon I ran afoul of a school of those floating menaces. Without checking to see whether they had overtaken the water, I jumped in and swam out to deeper, cooler water. Venturing out neck deep obscured my vision, so I didn't notice that the football size lion's mane, with tentacles measuring six feet, had arrived. I came into contact with them and they began stinging me all over, multiple times. I was so gripped by the pain that I began to panic. Frantically paddling, I swam into more of them. Some wrapped their tentacles around my arms, chest and face. The pain became excruciating, sending my body into shivering contortions. It hurt like nothing I had ever felt before.

Somehow I made it to shore, where Jimmy, my swimming buddy, best summer friend and fellow "explorer," was waiting for me. I could see the fear on his face. As I shook with pain and oncoming nausea, Jimmy took deliberate, but incredible action. He knew just what to do. He began to pee. Yes, he urinated all over my body, except my face (thank God)! He claimed regret for doing something so offensive, and swore that this was a remedy. He read somewhere about ancient tribes using pee as a cure and he assured me that it would quickly soothe the stinging. After I got over my best friend peeing on me, I actually began to feel better. No matter how gross it was, soon my pain subsided. It worked just like Jimmy said.

Into the Forest

The only thing more fun than the beach were the fields and forests. In the early 1960s, thousands of acres of woodlands near our bungalow were undisturbed. At that time, animal life in North Sea was still abundant. When I was about 10, my friends and I were lucky because whichever direction we took, we could experience new and fascinating adventures. After breakfast, especially on mornings too cool for the beach, we ventured into the woods and fields. All I could think of was how much more land there was for us to explore.

I recall those first breaths of morning air when I stepped outside, how the sweet scent of fresh-cut timothy grass permeated the dewy atmosphere as we planned our trek. Those forays into the forest took us through fields thick with brambles, blackberries and poison ivy. I was lucky. I wasn't allergic to poison ivy, much to the dismay of my hyper-sensitive brother. Poison ivy landed him in the hospital twice, but it never bothered me.

I began most days with Impy, a giant black Labrador retriever belonging to nearby friends. That dog had become my fearless tracking escort and hunting pal. Big for his breed, Impy had a head like a grizzly and paws like one, too. We could have ridden him like a horse! He plowed through fields and forests like a crazed beast when he was pursuing an animal. And every living thing around became his prey.

We usually started our hunts in the woods and fields behind our house. The forests next to our houses had become tangled with vines taller than a man. These thickets were the perfect habitat for pervasive cottontails, where they multiplied exponentially, "like rabbits." Those balls of fur were just about everywhere—and they were ideal prey for Impy.

Little did I understand Impy's acute sense of smell. He was born with the tracking instincts of a hound dog. Embarking on his search-and-destroy missions he'd scour those briars and brambles head first, tail wagging like crazy. Impy's zeal combined with his tracking skills resulted in finding numerous dens of newborn rabbits. We had to be on constant alert, ready to yank him back with a strong, quick jerk whenever he dove into a burrow. Sometimes we had to pop him on his huge skull to make him drop an animal. Strong threats sometimes kept him at bay long enough for us to save many litters. I adopted many newborns orphaned by Impy's relentless charges and always attempted (although not always successfully) to nurse them back to health with eye-droppers of warm milk.

In addition to rabbits, our part of eastern Long Island was replete with pheasants. In those years, the whole area seemed to have as many pheasants as well-known pheasant-hunting areas in the Great Plains. Impy once located a nest with a pheasant squatting on a clutch of beautiful blue-green eggs. When the mother hen saw him she let out a screech that pierced the morning calm and scared us to death. We managed to hold Impy back before that crazy dog scrambled all those eggs right in the nest.

Impy also uncovered deeply entrenched turtle dens, something I never knew existed. To me, the only thing cuter than a baby rabbit might be a baby turtle. Holding a soft, leathery, greenish brown baby turtle, all of three inches long, eyes still sealed shut, is something to behold. I kept boxes of these prehistoric-looking baby reptiles during the summer, but never for too long. My parents always made me set them free.

On turtle excursions without Impy, we considered it a bad hunt if we didn't find a bunch. A cry of excitement erupted when one of us found a turtle. We made each hunt a contest to see who could find the most. Back then, the common box turtle lived all over the Hamptons. They came in various shapes, sizes and vivid colors, from tortoise-shell brown to yellow ocher. They were fun to catch, to playfully nudge their heads back in their shells and even to race them. But we didn't keep them long. We sometimes marked them with our initials before releasing them. Re-capturing a marked turtle warranted an even bigger celebration. It was amazing how many times we found the same turtle. That would take the "grand prize" of the day. Since these magnificent turtles live an average of 40 years and can go beyond 100, I often wonder how many of "our" turtles still roam those woods.

King of the Wild Frontier

I was still little when frontiersmen like Daniel Boone and Davy Crockett turned into pop culture heroes of TV and movies. In the late 1950s and early 1960s, stories and characters of the "Old West" and the frontier were all the rage, front and center in the public consciousness. Frontier and cowboy images appeared on everything from lamps and lunch boxes to toys and clothes. When I was about six, my second summer in Southampton, I dressed up in full Davy Crockett regalia nearly every day: coonskin cap, fringed faux-deerskin

Left to Right:
Eugene and Albert, circa 1956

shirt and leggings, and an "authentic" Bowie knife in its matching rubber sheath. Thus attired, I blazed new trails in the woods around the family bungalows.

On one excursion I climbed a fairly tall tree to stake out some "uncharted" territory and managed to wedge my leg between two branches. I got completely stuck. The more I struggled to free myself, the tighter it got. I was trapped. When I realized I couldn't get out, panic set in, and I started to cry. And then I started to yell for help. But nobody came. After what seemed like hours and with dusk setting in, I yelled louder. But these woods were deep, and my cries eventually subsided into faint murmurs and inaudible whimpers between sobs.

Where was everybody? Weren't they getting worried about me? It was dark when I finally heard someone calling me by name—*both* of my names. *Eugene! Davy Crockett!* It was a woman's voice and it emanated from my father's first cousin, Nancy Saracino. She delighted in always calling me Davy Crockett, and she was the only person who did that. I knew that voice.

When I responded to her she shouted to the bungalows for help, and a throng of rescuers finally arrived. But by then they had turned into a very irritated group, my mother chief among them. I was glad to be rescued, of course, but essentially that didn't change a thing. I was undaunted. Like my frontier hero, I knew there was still so much new territory to explore. "Tomorrow" always meant a new day of adventure, and I could hardly wait.

Crossing the Great Divide

At age 10, a few years after my Davy Crockett days, my friend Jimmy and I crossed the "great divide," Noyac Road, the two-lane highway in front of the bungalows. We headed for deeper woods across there. It's hard to imagine now, but in those days we could walk south toward Bridgehampton all day and see nothing but woods: no people, houses, farms or cars. Only heavily wooded, Tolkien-like forests of half-dead, weather-beaten pines and scrub oaks forming a sandy, barren, desolate landscape. I got lost on more than one occasion in those woods.

Once I stumbled upon what looked like the ruins of a colonial-era house. We saw pottery shards, arrow heads and old bricks scattered all around. I imagined early 18th Century Shinnecock Indians stealthily crawling toward the house in a pre-dawn raid that turned into a total massacre. Scary thoughts for a 10-year old boy. But not for this Davy Crockett.

If we continued in that direction we'd eventually come to another mysterious place, one that resembled the crossroads of Indian footpaths. An opening in the brush surprised us. It was a glen hidden by a dense canopy of trees and bushes. Handsome tall, pointy cattails outlined a pond about the size of a football field, but to us it could have been one of the Great Lakes. The water was covered by a carpet of green and white water lilies. It was a find that promised limitless opportunity.

By arriving early in the morning and keeping silent, we knew that the area's abundant wildlife would congregate freely. Deer, fox, raccoons, otters, weasels and maybe a black bear would cautiously make its way to the pond for a morning thirst quencher. Camouflaged by thick undergrowth and besieged by relentless gnats and mosquitoes may have caused our "Walden Pond" to remain virgin and evade development. The only sound piercing the calm came from a chorus of bellowing bullfrogs, some the size of dinner plates. They were everywhere, sunning on the water lilies and singing. The frogs made Jimmy and me feel one with all Earth's creatures. Maybe we had formed some kind of bond with our Noyac Walden. But the main thing for these two 10-year-olds was that the pond was a fun place.

Jimmy and I eventually shared the pond with other friends, but only after they had pledged secrecy. One of those boys was Finn: a chubby, freckled, boy capped with a shock of carrot-red hair and dubbed "Red" by my grandfather. We swore him in, but we had some reservations about adding other new members. We were young, but we were smart and pragmatic. Plus, we had an ulterior motive: Red owned a gun.

Okay, it was just an air rifle or BB gun, but it was a gun nonetheless. Unarmed jaunts into the forest were no longer enough. A gun now took these explorers to the next level. How could we consider ourselves great white hunters without modern hunting tools? That meant rifle power, and Red had it. So now armed with Red's gun we began to take a fair amount of game, starting with those ubiquitous, lazy frogs. We plinked at them relentlessly, taking one trophy frog after another. But it was too easy, and we got tired of it. Having caused the near-extinction of a frog population meant very little to us, except that there were now fewer frogs to shoot at. So we "moved up" to rabbits and squirrels.

A Special Skill

I remember feeling as if I had been born with a particular God-given talent, something like a fortune-teller or horse whisperer, and something Grandpa Marra told me he shared with me. Born in a mountain hamlet in the province of Salerno, Grandpa grew up with his seven siblings on rural land that provided the wood for the family's successful lumber and charcoal business. It was on that land that Grandpa realized he had a "gift."

The "gift" we shared was much like the one David used against Goliath: we could turn a stone into a formidable weapon, a deadly missile. Even with small hands, I could hurl that stone with the accuracy of a marksman. And so I built that skill into a hunting routine that involved stalking, tracking and killing. I could take my prey with my hands and the rocks I found all around. I was so adept and so swift that I could pivot, whirl and release a stone in a flash, before my target sensed what was coming.

And I got better and better. I started with noisy catbirds, then a thrush or a towhee. I could hit them whether they were perched on a branch or hidden in a jumbled mess of brambles. Clearly I was good at it, but not as good as Grandpa! He had actually taken out a bird in flight, knocking it out of the sky like a rifle would. That sounded unbelievable to me, but then his sister, my great-aunt Helen, told me she *saw* him knock down several birds in flight and that people back in their village began to call him *sparacille* ("bird shooter").

After birds I went for chipmunks, which are not only fast but cagey. Hitting them with a stone would be a true test of marksmanship. Tiny, frenetic and easily spooked, they challenged my skills. In fact, a chipmunk later proved to Grandpa that we did indeed share the same gift. We were on my uncle's property, and a chipmunk appeared on a log. With a blur I whirled around and without seeming to take aim, I nailed that little critter in a second, knocking it right off its perch. Grandpa was astonished, then impressed and finally ecstatic. That's when we agreed that our shared talent must be in our blood, and he proudly welcomed me into his select "fraternity."

An even greater challenge was my next prey, cottontails. Rabbits, being wily, quick and nervous made them a formidable challenge. But I learned that rabbits have an insulation zone, an impenetrable ring. If that ring isn't disturbed, they stayed immobile and frozen like a statue. But once anything disturbed that thirty-foot comfort zone, they instantly take off. So I taught myself a technique for rabbits. I'd stalk them silently, taking small steps, but never penetrating their comfort zone. Since they have a wide field of vision, I first had to make sure they thought the thirty-foot zone was intact. But I found I could get within 20 feet. From that distance I averaged one kill per three tries, with three my self-imposed daily bag limit.

I'd hang them on my belt and bring them home to Grandma Rosa, who turned them into the world's best cacciatore. She always seemed amazed at my ability to bring home wild game since I had no gun and I was only ten. Looking back, I find it strange that she didn't find anything odd about that. Then again, Grandma Rosa asked very few questions and, to her, meat was meat, food was food, pure and simple. She just smiled that knowing smile.

When Nature Fought Back

Every explorer knows that taking to the woods is never without peril. Sometimes the perils come in the form of comic relief. One day, my second cousin William Cioffi (Aunt Helen's grandson) and I set out down the dirt road turtle hunting. We were about 9 or 10. Willie (as we called him) lived in the Bronx, and came to Southampton with his family less frequently than I did. I remember him as a big kid, but more of a city kid. We ended up in overgrown woods where we hadn't ventured before. It looked almost impassable, but since we had yet to explore it and exploit its potential turtle bounty, we couldn't resist. The property looked like it was below the road grade in a slight depression, with some of the thickest, meanest briars. A giant oak log that had fallen years ago now looked like a strange horizontal monument. That should have served as a warning, but what did we know. Besides, we weren't looking for warnings, we were looking for turtles.

We didn't have Impy with us, which meant we had to unearth turtle dens

164

on our own. I'm not sure who made the first wrong move, but somewhere near that log we were enveloped in a whirling cloud. They were the worst kind of bees, nasty swarming yellow jackets capable of multiple stings. Infiltrating their territory was, to them, a frontal assault. To us, we were looking for turtles. But we had disturbed their nest, hidden for years in a soft cavity of that giant oak. And they went into full defense mode. I still remember their intense hum resonating all around us. These were not happy bees, and they showed us how unhappy they were. They started stinging us in a wild frenzy.

We ran as fast as we could, screaming like banshees through the briars. We shot up the road like rockets from Cape Canaveral, heading for the safety of Aunt Helen's bungalow. We covered the distance from hive to home at near-lightning speed and got there in what seemed like an instant. We flung open the door, scared our relatives half to death and frantically tugged at our T-shirts. And as the shirts came off, the bees came out by the dozens. And then they started buzzing around the relatives. Arms were flailing, and many yellow jackets met their demise from frenzied swats. I received more than ten bites, Willie a few more. Fortunately, no one had an allergic reaction. Vinegar and calamine lotion assuaged the pain, but it took several aspirins—and several hours—for us to feel better. And it took years before we could laugh about "the great bee stinging" episode. We still laugh retelling that story, which is now legend, and everyone who remembers that day will swear that Aunt Helen's house was full of crazed bees for hours.

Snappers Run; Summer Wanes

Italians have a saying about August 7th, the feast of Saint Donato (Donald), signaling the beginning of the end of summer. *Per San Donato, l'inverno e' nato:* From St. Donald's [day], winter is born. And that saying fits the pattern of our Southampton summers. Right after the first week of August, just when swimming was at its best, summer showed signs of waning. But that also signaled a great run of fish.

Before Southampton was home to native tribes, pilgrims, wealthy families, artists, or Italian Americans like us, great runs of snappers (baby bluefish) invaded the brackish waters there every year. These voracious feeders begin life in the salt ponds and protected inlets of bays like the Little Peconic. As they mature, they migrate to larger bodies of water and grow into more predatory feeders, some up to 40 pounds. Some get so aggressive they sometimes attack humans and have been mistaken for sharks. Fortunately, that didn't happen to us.

When snappers run, you simply can't find a better fishing experience. But to be successful, you need good bait. That meant going to the beach to gather "shiners" (eastern Atlantic whitebait), one of their favorite foods, in seines. We formed four-man teams to drag our rudimentary nets, with floats on top and weights on the bottom, in waist-deep water to scoop up those little fish. It was a good system, and we caught huge numbers of fish. On a good "sweep" we could net several pounds of jumping, wriggling fish. And it was great fun.

Not all of them went into the bait bucket, though: sometimes they'd turn into a meal for us. Dredged in flour, deep-fried whitebait sprinkled with lemon juice is a culinary delight. (It's an acquired taste, though: they're eaten whole, "nose to tailfin.") And if Uncle Joe Saracino happened to amble down to the beach while we were working our nets, we were luckier still. He'd treat the kids to a very entertaining performance with his antics. Like a sideshow carney or a street performer, he'd snatch a live shiner from the net, hold it up as high as his arm reached, drop that wriggling fish dead on into his mouth and swallow it whole with a comical, exaggerated gulp followed by an equally exaggerated sigh as he flashed a big, devilish smile to his stunned audience of laughing kids.

Any shiners we could keep away from the frying pan (or Uncle Joe) we used for snapper bait, as intended. Attached to a silver lure and, at two to three feet a red and white bobber, we fished the channels and the bulkheads with seven-foot bamboo poles with no reels. We didn't need anything more sophisticated than that. Our shiners worked like a charm. Cast after cast yielded quick strikes, short but enjoyable fights, and then a nice baby blue usually weighing up to a pound, sometimes two pounds on luckier casts. (We always threw back the very small ones.) At dusk, when clouds of gnats swarmed, we'd call it a day and bring our catch home to Grandma Rosa. She turned them into marinated, broiled fillets.

Toward the end of August, the nights get appreciably cooler. So does the bay, making swimming less pleasant. The lower sun takes on a different hue on those noticeably shorter days. And so beach time becomes briefer, and marshmallow roasts end earlier. Even the crickets' chirping becomes a barely audible hum. And at bedtime, blankets suddenly appeared (thanks, Mom!) to ward off the nighttime chill in a bungalow with no heat.

I began the end-of-summer countdown during the last week of August, making a point of staying on the beach or in the woods as long as I could. Those days were bittersweet. It all seemed so unfair: we had only just arrived and now we were getting ready to leave. And eventually the day would come when my friends and I exchange regretful farewells while at the same time hatching plans for next summer.

Summer's ending meant that my adventures in the woods and the water were ending too. As impossible as it seemed, I was powerless to stop our move back to the city. And so Impy and Jimmy, turtles and rabbits, fishing and hunting and endless hours of bucolic bliss would recede into memory. When Mom scattered those smelly mothballs around the bungalow, it meant another summer was about to be logged into our family's history book. And next summer couldn't come soon enough.

THREE LITTLE HOUSES IN A ROW

Top to bottom:
Saracino House, Built 1955 / Maffei House, Built 1963 / Marra House, Built 1956
All Photographs, circa 2009

Our Little House in the Middle[1]

Frances Maffei

As hard as I try, it's nearly impossible to remember my first visit to Southampton. That's probably because I was only about two when my parents [Gilbert and Marion Maffei] first took me there. Then again, I can't remember *not* spending a summer at our Southampton bungalow. I've been going there every summer for over 50 years.

A similar pattern holds for my children. Selena, Victoria and Anthony. They're even luckier. You see, those kids have never missed a summer vacation at our bungalow. So we can say we've all grown up in Southampton. We can also say that we've been very fortunate, and we owe our good fortune to my parents, grandparents and other relatives of those generations.

My family's bungalow is "the little house in the middle." It stands between the first family house that was built, the Saracino's, and the second, the Marra's. Our house was built by the same builder who built the other two family bungalows, so it looked just like the other two. And as with only a few other houses in the area, our three bungalows are still in the hands of the families who built them.

I barely remember my first trip to the newly built bungalow. It had to be in the early to mid-1960s, a year or two after that first visit, the one my parents had to tell me about. I have only the faintest memory of the trip: a long ride by car with my mother and father in our blue station wagon.

[1] This story by Frances Maffei was recorded by the principal author. It was then faithfully transcribed just as it appears.

But the memory is so hazy that I can't even remember if my younger brother, Louis, was with us. But I do remember several other things about those early years.

My mom and dad often drove to Southampton in separate cars so that Dad could leave us there when he went home to Yonkers for work in the middle of the week. Once Louis and I went with Mom in her white Ford Falcon, and I think my cousin Charlie came with us. My parents put a small white flag or some kind of a streamer on the antenna of each car so we could maintain visual contact on the road and not get separated in traffic. It's a good thing that they did, because Mom's car broke down and Dad had to come rescue us.

The Great Tomato Caper

One afternoon when I was about four years old, on our way back from the beach but before getting cleaned up and ready for supper, my grandmother (Aunt Sylvia to other family members) met me at the door. She had already started cooking and said she wanted to add fresh tomatoes to the gravy simmering on the stove. She asked me to go next door to Aunt Helen's and get a couple of ripe tomatoes from Uncle Joe's garden. She said not to worry, that it would be fine since we were all family. That made sense, and who would miss two tomatoes? Besides, I was so little, I could just breeze in and out and nobody would even notice me. Or the tomatoes!

Like most Italians of his generation, Uncle Joe set out tomatoes, zucchini, peppers and other summer vegetable plants. Just about everyone knew about his garden! After all, it was one of the better ones. That's because regardless of weather conditions, Uncle Joe seemed to defy the odds and reap a bountiful summer harvest year after year. I don't know how he got such tasty produce from that small plot or what he was always adding to the soil. Whatever the stuff was, it produced great crops. So that made it even less likely that any tomatoes would be missed.

The garden was at the end of his property down a slight hill, and quite close to ours. He secured it with a chicken-wire fence all around to keep out rabbits and other pests. It had a homemade gate. And he hung several nutty contraptions, like tin pie plates, on broom sticks or on the wooden fence posts. These were designed to make noise to scare away birds and any possible other pests. To scare the kids away, there always was Prince, his huge German shepherd guard dog. As a last resort, there was always Uncle Joe himself.

Acting on my grandmother's orders, I meandered down behind the bungalows, eased that flimsy old garden gate open and entered that precious preserve to pick some nice ripe tomatoes. I tried to scoop up several of the biggest ones, but I couldn't even manage three. Those beefsteaks were so huge and my hands were so little that I could only carry two. I started back up towards our house, not knowing if Uncle Joe was home or if he or anyone else had seen me. Well, either he saw me or he tracked the muddy footprints that led from his fence to our back door.

And he wasn't more than a minute or two behind me, running towards our house at breakneck speed—all this despite his obviously crippling arthritis—and yelling non-stop in Italian. He continued yelling through the screen door. I didn't know what the heck he was saying. But I sure understood him well enough to know that it wasn't good and that it had something (probably *everything*) to do with me and the two tomatoes I had "borrowed" from his garden per my grandmother's orders. She, on the other hand, knew exactly what he was saying. And that's when the fireworks began.

Never one to back away from a fight, my grandmother started yelling right back at Uncle Joe, matching him word for word (and at the same fever pitch) in Italian. I made myself scarce, backing away from the door and from all the family trouble I had started, albeit unintentionally. I knew my grandmother didn't hold me responsible for doing anything bad. I was glad my parents didn't either. But I learned an important life lesson: stay away from Uncle Joe's garden!

Then again, I didn't have to worry much about his tomatoes anymore.

That's because, on my way back from the beach a day or two later, I saw a big, new lock on the garden gate. Next time, if there was ever going to be a next time, whoever was sent to "borrow" a couple of tomatoes would have to be big enough and agile enough to scale the fence, and then run like the dickens before Uncle Joe noticed. Or better yet, fly over it between the pie plates like the birds used to do. Either way, I wasn't going to be the one ever again.

Hose Encounters

I remember, when I was nearly six years old, that the other two family houses were full of kids who were all older, some teenagers and others pre-teens. All the older Marra and Saracino cousins would make plans to go out together almost every night after supper. Of course I always wanted to go with them. And of course I was way too little. They knew that; I didn't.

So one night I really started pushing my point. And like every other night, they said I couldn't go. Why not? I'd been with several of them all that day at the beach. Now they tell me I was too little? That just didn't seem fair to me. I complained and started whining to all the cousins, to their parents and, finally to my parents. But the answer was still a big "no." So I decided to get even. And I made a plan.

While all the older cousins were still together finalizing their plans, I quietly left our bungalow and walked down the hill, just far enough to get behind the Saracino's. Making my way along the back of the Saracino bungalow, I came out near Uncle Joe's shed while they gathered sort of close by, near his stone barbeque grill. With the backyard shed as cover, I made my way to the outdoor water spigot, carefully picked up the attached hose, turned on the water full blast, and aimed it right at them. I sprayed them with a torrent of water as if they were on fire until they and their clothes were soaked to the skin. They were all screaming at me as I turned to run away, and I screamed right back at them: "You didn't want me to go with you! So now nobody's going!"

Well, they did go out, of course—they weren't going to let a little hellion with a hose subvert their social plans—but not until they went back inside to change into dry clothes.

Memory Fragments

I can still vividly remember…

Falling on the bungalow's back stoop at age three or four and everybody screaming and yelling. I was cut so badly that they took me to the Southampton hospital. I had seven stitches in my chin. I was very proud of my "boo-boo" and my seven stitches, and I thought of myself as a big kid, and a brave one too. But that ended when they told me I couldn't go to the beach because sand might get in it.

Going to the drive-in movies, many times in pajamas, the kind with "footies." My father always drove a bunch of us kids, including Uncle Eddie's and Dina's kids, in that old blue station wagon. I can't remember many of the movies, but we always had a great time.

Walking down to the beach when I was very little with my grandmother, sometimes just the two of us. And I remember how she would put me in a little inflatable swimming tube, take me out into deep water and make me feel safe just being near her, no matter how big the waves or how cold the water. And sometimes she'd take me to watch people dig clams and scungilli.

Being fascinated by my great-aunts, especially when they went down to the beach. While there they always talked in an animated way to all their friends, sometimes in English, sometimes in Italian, often times using their hands. After the beach Aunt Mary, Aunt Helen, Aunt Adeline and the others sat on the porch, knitting in the fading light of the late afternoon or early evening.

A bunch of us little kids going down to the channel in mid-August to fish for snappers with bamboo poles. I used one that my father bought for us at Garamone's general store and put together himself. That pole lasted many years.

Watching Aunt Helen and Uncle Joe at the stone grill Uncle Joe had built as he cooked all kinds of meat. I clearly recall the smoke and the aromas drifting toward our house, and Uncle Joe sitting on a folding beach chair near the grill with whichever of his sons or sons-in-law were there. They'd be drinking beer and wine as they cooked.

Taking what seemed like endless day trips with my brother and parents to Montauk and East Hampton and many other towns in between.

Buying toys and stuff at the 5 & 10 cent store right there on Main Street in Southampton, and freshly made fudge at the candy store.

Seeing my mother and grandmother putting clothes through the ringer—literally—that was on top of the old-fashioned washing machine my father carted out to the bungalow. And I remember then helping them hang the clothes on the network of clothes lines strung between the trees in our backyard.

Sylvia Maffei

As a teen, arranging for rides to go dancing at the teen clubs between Water Mill and Amagansett, and longing for the day we could drive there (or anywhere!) by ourselves.

As a mom, visiting Paul's Pizza with my kids [Selena, Victoria, and Anthony] and delighting in how well he got to know our family, even to the point of usually knowing exactly what we were going to order.

Delighting in the knowledge that like me, my kids have been sharing such similar, positive experiences and understanding the joy of more than one generation of our family. We all see the strong impressions that vacationing in Southampton made on us. We all see several generations enjoying precious quality time together.

I didn't realize it then, but now I can appreciate how different my grandmother and the older family members born in Italy were, when compared with my relatives who were born here. All of these memories, from the vague to the most vivid, enable me to make powerful connections with my family's past. It's something quite special. It has enriched the family greatly. And it's a tremendous legacy that I hope to pass on to my children.

Southampton Summers: Boomers to Millennials, Early 1980s to Early 1990s

CHAPTER FOUR:
Fourth Generation Stories: Generations X, Y, and Z

Albert Marra

They comprise the family's fourth generation to enjoy summers in Southampton. They are the sons and daughters of the Saracino-Marra-Maffei family's generation of Baby Boomers born in the late 1940s through 1960s, whose stories are included in the previous chapter.

They have all spent memorable summertime years in Southampton with their second generation grandparents; some even spent time bonding with their Italian great-grandparents. And one or two of the older, luckier ones can actually recall those very special times!

They were born in the years spanning the 1970s to the dawn of the new millennium and they loosely fit the following three non-scientific, popular demographics: Generation X, for those born in the mid-1970s to early 1980s; Generation Y, (more frequently called "the Millennials" by the mass media) for those born from the mid-1980s to mid-1990s, up to the year 2000; and Generation Z, those who were born from the late-1990s to the year 2000 and beyond.

They may be at widely divergent stages in their lives, with some still in their late teens, while others now have become seasoned professionals with growing families of their own. And while the first of the fourth generation visited Southampton as early as the mid- to late-1970s, most were not even born then. Some were not born until the ending years of the 20th century.

But the members of the family's fourth generation share a common thread, something that binds them all closely together: their vivid memories of good times in Southampton with parents, grandparents and, in rare cases, even with great-grandparents. Those experiences have led the older members of the Saracino-Marra-Maffei family's X-Y-Z alphabet soup generation to write the stories about Southampton that appear on the following pages of this chapter.

It should be noted that only the "older" members of the family's fourth generation at the beach have written stories included in this chapter. Their younger cousins include: at the Marra bungalow, Clara and Gabe Marra, the children of Gene and Montell Marra; and at the Maffei bungalow, Selena, Victoria and Anthony, children of Frances Maffei, and John and Joseph, the children of Louis and Bianca Maffei. It is definitely planned that the second edition of this book would ideally include some of the stories of this younger group as well.

Bungalow buddies! Marra-Maffei millennials (L to R): cousins Gabe, Anthony, Selena, Anna (a Marra-Genovese cousin), Clara, Victoria, circa 2007

Small Stories

Jon Resh

Many years have passed since I spent long stretches of time at the Saracino bungalow. In my childhood I was there every summer, sometimes for weeks on end, with my grandparents, Savino and Sylvia Saracino. Since growing up, having a family of my own, and moving away from the New York area, I only go there from time to time, schedules permitting.

The bungalow itself isn't the dominating aspect of my memory of those visits, though, nor was it the little beach that was our daily destination at just a short walk away. Those days at the beach blur into a sunny, pleasurable fusion for me—bobbing up and down in the water one moment, eating salami sandwiches on a blanket on the sand the next, searching for seashells in between. That was the routine, and it was bliss.

My recollections, the ones that remain the most distinct, the most vivid, are smaller but sharper: those singular occurrences, bright sensations and powerful impressions that so many years later continue to divert my day-to-day thoughts and, on occasion, inhabit my dreams.

National Velvet

There wasn't much for a kid to do at night if you were staying at the bungalow. Aside from reading and playing cards, it was pretty quiet. So we talked.

During those evening conversations, some adult family members—not telling who—would often read the movie listings in the newspaper aloud, although all of the theaters listed were too far away to actually visit! Okay, easy guess, so it was Grandma and Granddad. As a movie-obsessed youngster, this drove me literally bonkers. The idea that movie listings might be recited for fun—as an entertainment in itself—seemed totally deranged. The conversations between me and my grandparents went something like the following.

Grandparent: "That movie 'Airplane' is playing in Islip. I hear it's funny."

Me: "Yes! 'Airplane!' Let's go see it!"

Grandparent: "We can't. It's in Islip. Islip's at least an hour away."

Me: "Let's make the trip!"

Grandparent: "No, it's too far. The movie starts in 20 minutes, so by the time we get there, the movie will be over."

Me: "*Then why would you even tell me it's playing?*"

Grandparent: "Oh, it's just interesting."

And there I sat, trembling in dismay.

One afternoon, however, knowing how I craved *any* cinematic experience, my grandparents proposed an option while one of them was reading the paper.

Granddad: "There's a movie playing tonight that we could go see. It's 'National Velvet.' And it's not too far."

Grandma: "Oh, that's a nice movie. I think you'd like it."

Me: "What's it about? I've never heard of it."

Grandma: "Well, it's about a horse."

A horse? Instant skepticism. "Did this movie just come out?"

"Oh no," she said. "It came out a while back."

"How long ago is 'a while back?'"

"The '40s, I think. It stars Elizabeth Taylor. She plays the girl who rides the horse. I think she's about your age in it."

It's worth mentioning here that, at that moment in 1982, the movie I most wanted to see was "Blade Runner." I'd heard it was dark and futuristic and intense and, according to reliable witnesses, featured brief nudity. In other words, everything an 11-year-old boy *wants* in a movie.

"What's this movie called again?"

"National Velvet," Grandma said.

"What does 'National Velvet' mean?"

"I don't remember," she said, raising her eyes as if the answer might be fluttering above. "Maybe that's the horse's name. Or the girl's. Or it has something to do with riding horses. But that's what it's about, a girl and her horse. It takes place in England, I think."

This all made zero sense to me.

"Are you serious? You're saying we should go see a movie about a girl and her horse in England—*from the '40s*?"

"Well, if you want," Granddad said. "It is a good movie."

On those boring Southampton evenings, I yearned to see a movie, any movie. Except, it seemed, *this* movie.

"No thank you," I said, fully crestfallen.

That night, Grandma and I played gin rummy in the living room. It's likely that she let me win. Oh, yes, that's right, I still haven't seen "National Velvet." For all I know, I never will.

Local Critters at Large

Dead horseshoe crabs appeared on the shore of our local beach now and then. They resembled a cross between a long-extinct Paleozoic predator and a Nazi helmet. I never came across a live one, so I have yet to see a horseshoe crab in action, but I'm sure it's marvelously creepy. It brings me comfort that small monsters like this exist even in genteel Southampton.

The jellyfish at our beach were generally small, flat and unspectacular, colorless or faintly white, and floating innocently up toward the bay's surface. Without the lurid tentacles or glowing translucence of their sexier and more colorful jellyfish cousins, they were easily overlooked. But those little bastards could still sting. Hard. Nondescript and yet no less painful, they were all bite and no bark. I sort of admired that.

Tadpoles and baby frogs lived throughout the vegetation in the marshy part of the fresh pond that emptied into the bay near the beach. I saw only a few full-grown frogs, but I chased after little ones by the hundreds. My cousin Louis and I decided to collect as many mini-frogs as we could find and put them in a large bucket. Within an hour, half the bucket was filled.

Louis's father, Granddad's first cousin, Gilbert, upon discovering what he considered an inhumane endeavor, ordered us to empty the bucket immediately. So we did. We poured the frogs into a pile on the sand, and for a few seconds this unnatural mound of amphibian mass held together. Then all at once the frogs scattered, dissolving the pile and darting away in every direction at speeds seemingly too quick for so small an animal. It was an explosive mini-frog exodus. I really couldn't blame them for wanting to get the hell away from us, but their velocity in doing so still astounds me.

Wasps inhabited Southampton, as they do in almost any American locale in the summer. They made their nests in sandy patches below the surface of the bungalow's yard. They didn't have the decency to nest above-ground where you could keep an eye on them. And so stepping on unseen hordes of wasps beneath the grass was a perennial problem. I have bad memories of those wretched insects, and so I hate wasps to this day.

Montauk and the Shark

Jonathan with his grandparents, Sylvia and Savy Saracino

Grandma likes recounting our visit to Montauk (the fishing mecca and beach town east of Southampton at the very eastern tip of Long Island) and how we came upon a group of fishermen who caught a very large shark. She still laughs about it.

The fishermen hung the shark's enormous body on the dock by their boat. As a 9-year-old, I loved *Jaws* and was fascinated by anything related to sharks, so this was a real thrill. I asked Grandma, "What are they going to do with it?"

So Grandma went and asked the fishermen. They said they were disposing of the body. They had already taken pictures and removed the jaw bone (their trophy for the catch, as I learned) but they had no intention of keeping the carcass.

I became incredulous. Wasn't the body the best part? Sensing a once in

183

a lifetime opportunity, I begged my grandparents.

"Can we keep it? Can we take the shark home?"

I pleaded my case to my grandparents. Strongly. Granddad tried to reason with me: It couldn't fit in the Lincoln Mercury, he said, even if we did want to cart off a giant, smelly, quickly rotting shark carcass. Which he didn't do. But it made no difference to me. I still wanted this big dead shark.

"What are we going to do with it, make soup?" Grandma said. (And she still says that. I love that saying.)

Surprisingly, I remember only a few details of this event. I recall the fishermen letting me touch the shark. The skin, wet and sleek, felt like sandpaper, but fleshy and cold. I actually remember saying to myself, *I'm finally touching a shark!*

I clearly remember how disturbing I found the shark's mouth stripped of its teeth and jaw. Bleeding and raw, with flies hovering around the shredded tissue, that huge gory cavity was, to me, an excessive symbol of how thoroughly this shark had been vanquished. Trophy or not, extracting its jawbone and the ensuing damage to the shark seemed a violation of the animal's wholeness.

If I ever visit Montauk again, let's say with my daughter, Colette, and if we see a fresh shark carcass hanging, and if my daughter begs to bring it home as I once begged (and she just might!), I doubt I'd be able to refuse. Because after all those years, I still sort of want one, too.

And yes. Maybe we *can* make soup.

The Road

The road (if you can call it that!) on the side of our bungalow has always

184

been a wreck. Dirt and sand were pitted with broken, rutted chunks of black asphalt, some as much as six inches thick. Driving on it felt like traversing the front line of a war zone.

We walked this road [Pine Tree Road] to the beach every day. Between the sand, asphalt chunks and loose gravel, the walk was an uneven prospect. But I loved how ramshackle and forgotten the road was. It was one of the many aspects that, back then and even today, keeps our little corner of Southampton a tad rustic and coarse and endearing, well, at least for a city kid like me.

How the condition of that road came to be—as I understood it—is quite a tale. The road started out as just a sandy dirt road. Then at some time in the '60s, a block party of sorts was held along the road when it was still just sand. Drinking at the party started early, and conversation eventually veered to the sorry state of this road, how cars often got stuck in it, what happened when it rained, and how it could be improved.

As the gin and tonic flowed, an intoxicated, ambitious group-think— ideas on how to fix the road—seemed to take hold. Somebody thought of a cousin in Queens (a guy named Arthur, I think I heard) who owned a business involved in laying asphalt. A drunken phone call was made to this Arthur, demanding that he make the trek to Southampton that evening to pave the sandy dirt road. Well, within a few hours Arthur arrived. *With* his asphalt truck. The partiers plied him with lots of drinks and soon enough he enlisted his family members to help with the job, overlooking the fact that these men were at this point totally pickled.

Night soon fell. With no lights to illuminate the street, the inebriated relatives, subbing for trained professionals, were ready to lay the asphalt. With Arthur at the helm, who by now having knocked back a few too many, the slow pouring of the black asphalt began. It went directly on top of the sand, with no foundation, no crushed stone base, no road bed. Just sand.

Hours later, finishing the job well past midnight, the men celebrated their labor with one last drink, then retired to their homes, and probably all promptly passed out.

The following morning, the residents went outside one by one and took in their first look at the "improved" road—the gnarled, caked, globular expanse of asphalt already in the process of cracking, already exposing the sand underneath. They were aghast at what may have been the worst paving job in New York state history. Their collective hangover immediately worsened. So did the road in the years to come.

And that's the story, at least how I remember it being told to me. As a paragon of epic comic failure, it's nothing short of spectacular.

And, as it turns out, it's entirely false.

Not only is it false, no one has ever heard of it. And yet I thought that was the story. It's cemented in my brain, right down to the gin-and-tonic detail. No matter how convinced I was, and despite how many times I've told this story at parties, none of it actually happened. I'm only now finding that out. So what about the broken asphalt?

I recently asked Grandma about the details of the road. I was shocked to learn that its sorry condition was, by and large, just a botched county "paving" job. It should surprise nobody that again local government had screwed up. Happens every day everywhere; happened here too.

There's no cousin "Arthur" in Queens. No gin and tonic. No midnight laying of asphalt by "Arthur" and the homeowners. As for the horrifying day-after results, well, there may be some truth to that, except it was more like a couple of weeks later.

Where and how this story and its details originated remains a mystery. My absolute belief in it for years is baffling, and a little troubling. I still wonder how such a wild yarn, with positively no basis in reality, got planted in my head.

I just wish it were true.

I really should stop telling this story at parties. But maybe not. It's really a great story!

I Remember ...

The small black-and-white TV in the bungalow living room that received some semblance of proper reception maybe one hour a night, at best; the rest was just static. This stood as the embodiment of hell for a TV-starved young wretch as myself. There was, however, that one glorious evening when the heavens properly aligned and a five-hour marathon of original "Twilight Zone" episodes aired, uninterrupted too. I watched the whole thing in thrilled disbelief, feeling as if this clear broadcast of my favorite cult classic was divinely conveyed. That this sad half-pint of a TV held strong for the one evening that mattered was total happiness.

Grandma's linguine with red clam sauce, among the most sublime assemblage of flavors I've ever encountered. This dish seemed to gain an uncommon potency at the bungalow. We'd dig into the linguine on the Formica-topped table on the enclosed porch next to the kitchen, the jalousie windows filtering the incoming light with the soft saturation of an old Polaroid.

The small utility closet on the other side of the porch. This is where we'd stash our wet old sneakers after we returned from the beach. These sneakers were a necessity, and a ritual: the beach was painfully rocky on bare feet. So the still-damp sneakers were set (thrown?) on the closet's concrete floor or wooden shelves and left to dry there overnight, rendering the air around them musty and slightly sour, and smelling of the nearby sea. A subtle but sustained waft of that closet air made its way onto the porch year after year. (Maybe that's what made the red clam sauce taste so good.)

The time I sneaked a slim bestseller to Southampton called *Truly Tasteless Jokes.* (for example, Question: What do you call an epileptic in a lettuce patch? Answer: Seizure salad.) It felt like the dirtiest, most illicit contraband ever smuggled into our wholesome G-rated family bungalow. Naturally, I loved it. Accompanying the book was Men at Work's "Overkill," which just might be the most melancholic Top 40 hit ever written about clinical depression. I listened to it repeatedly on my Sony Walkman alone in my bungalow bedroom. The combination of book and tune made for an interesting stay.

The cute little hand-painted wooden sign that hung in the kitchen: "Enjoy yourself! It's later than you think" emblazoned with a '40s-style cutie-pie with a big smile. It had been there from the very earliest days, apparently; someone gave it to my great-grandmother as a little house-warming gift. I once asked Grandma what the sign meant. She sang me the song, which had been played by the likes of Guy Lombardo and Tommy Dorsey. It was a chipper little tune, at least the way Grandma sang it. One day, years later and far from Southampton, the full weight of its meaning hit me. Adulthood ensued.

Generations

There was our Great-Grandma. I knew her only in her later years, and I recognize with sorrow that as a child I wasn't terribly warm to her. I usually rebuffed her (often exuberant) affection, as boys often do. Only when I reached my teens did it dawn on me that this woman—who seemed so frighteningly ancient, who shuffled feebly from room to room yet appeared suddenly around corners, her worn frame like that of a small, frail ghost—was so persistently kind and loving to me. I came to appreciate her sweetness, and truly reciprocated it, during the year before she died.

There was Grandma: loving the beach; loving to cook. Loving to have us with her to look after (and *scootch*). Ever busy, funny, and smart. She still is. And she still spends her summers there. I love the idea of bringing my family to Southampton to spend time with her at the bungalow.

And there was Granddad. He is inseparable from nearly any memory I have of the bungalow. How he'd splash a little wine into my empty water glass at the end of a particularly robust dinner. How he'd carefully spoon his shrimp scampi onto my plate in an exacting, masculine manner, clearly proud of his masterwork. How, driving together on errands, he'd passionately discuss any subject with me in the Lincoln Mercury—and one time sitting in the sand driveway for 20 minutes, with the air conditioner blasting, to ensure that I comprehended the finer points of why Richard Nixon was a misunderstood, under appreciated president.

How he'd joyously bound up the large rocks of the channel along the beach, carrying a pair of old, primitive fishing poles, transforming this middle-aged dentist into the spry lad he once was . . . And how, as I'd walk past him in the bungalow, he'd sometimes pull me over to get a quick hug. Why? For no apparent reason other than just to hug his grandson.

Sylvia Saracino (2nd generation) and great-granddaughter Colette Resh (5th)

There was the mild sea air always permeating the bungalow, and the unstirred depth of the nights. There was the comfort of falling asleep knowing that this small house was filled to the brim with family—as was the neighboring bungalow, and the bungalow next to that. There was also that un-fragmented serenity, that warmth, which I've found to be so rare in the summers since.

And then there was us. And that was our Southampton.

189

Southampton Summers: The Later Years, circa 2000 to Present

Driving to Grandma's Southampton Bungalow

Mark Saracino

I've been going to Grandma's Southampton Bungalow for as long as I can remember. The little house on Noyac Road, which has undergone significant renovations a few years ago, has always held a special place in my heart and in my mind.

Car Ride Crescendo

It usually begins early on a Saturday morning. I awake just before sunrise. I venture out to my garage, muster the hose and sponge, and start washing a week's worth of dust, pollen and greasy sediment from our SUV. After that, I water the flowers in the yard as I catch the first sunlight of the weekend. My wife, Dawn, comes outside—sunglasses on, hair quickly tied in a half-ponytail—with our baby, Nicolas. She buckles him securely into his car seat. She walks to the back of the SUV and heaves suitcase, chairs, diaper bags and beach umbrellas into the trunk. With the car packed and the fresh iTunes playlist I created earlier that morning cued up, we settle in and off we go, letting the hustle and bustle of everyday life recede in the rear-view mirror.

That's how the ritual of a family drive to Grandma's Southampton bungalow begins. At least, that's how it begins now that I'm an adult. It started differently when I was a kid and my dad was rounding up the family—Mom, my older brother, Greg, and me. But one key aspect of the drive to Southampton has never changed and likely never will: my eager anticipation of fun in the sun with family. It's an exuberant excitement that

191

builds in stages, as if on cue, at strategic spots along the way.

To me, the ride from Westchester to Southampton has always been a climatic upsurge, like the familiar crescendos throughout the *Marriage of Figaro* overture. It starts softly as I am about to leave my hometown. I feel the first rush of happiness just minutes into the two-hour trip. It picks up as I round the sharp curve of the exit ramp that connects the Sprain Brook and Cross County parkways just outside Mount Vernon. This is where my senses come alive: I begin to feel it. I begin to smell it. I begin to hear it. It's been this way since I was a kid in the backseat of my parents' car with Greg, and it's that way now as I drive my own family to Southampton. I don't know what it is about this turn, but this is the point where my vacation officially starts. This is where the road screams "Southampton" at me.

The excitement, the crescendo, continues to build as I get closer and closer to the pinnacle: arrival in Southampton. It builds at the Whitestone Bridge, with the view of the Long Island Sound on one side and the haze-covered Manhattan skyline on the other.

It increases again getting off the Long Island Expressway at the Manorville exit onto Route 111. This is a good spot to stop for a cold drink, a snack, a restroom stop, if needed. Anyone want to stop? Hopefully, not; I just want to *get* there.

We pass Linda Scott's huge *Stargazer* sculpture (aka "the deer eating a bent tree branch") while merging onto Montauk Highway, and then remarks on the hard-to-miss remnants of the massive brushfire of 1995. Thousands of eerie, twisted, blackened skeletal remains of pitch pines now show new life sprouting around them. The throaty roar of a vintage Ferrari whizzes by us—yeah, we're getting close!

Stargazer Sculpture

192

Soon we're passing all my personal landmarks, the ones I can recall since I was a child: Atlantic Hotel, Schmidt's market, etc. Then the turn-off to Noyac Road, followed by the North Sea firehouse, the small bridge at Fish Cove Road., the one with twinkling sea water to the right and left. The crescendo rises yet again at the marina at the Coast Grille near Roses Grove. It's only a matter of minutes before I spot my final two landmarks: the quaint row of mailboxes that signal the Herne Place neighborhood, and then—at last—the utility pole on the corner of the Pine Tree Road with the ancient wooden sign that reads "Saracino."

Yes! We've arrived! Cue the cymbals!

As we carry our things up the slight backyard slope, Grandma sees us from the kitchen window. She's excited. She comes out on the deck with a big smile, waiting to exchange hugs and kisses. She pays extra attention to Dawn, who's carrying Nicolas.

"Oh, let me see the baby! Do you need anything, Dawn? What can I get you? Here, come in, sit down and relax," she says, as Dawn and Grandma walk into the house. I stay on the deck a minute. Brief memories of my childhood flash before me. I stood on the deck, thinking back on nearly three decades of events, the memories that came running across the tracks of my train of thought like a commuter running to catch the last train home.

And that's when I realized it. It occurred to me what Southampton, at least as I've always known it, was all about. It was about being a kid.

It was being there as a grandchild and being taken care of by Grandma. It was being there as my parents' child. Being away from the monotony of the school year was part of it. It was also having a chance to laugh, play and feel carefree—and build the memories I'm remembering at this moment and many more. In that moment on the deck, an inexplicable feeling washed over me: a feeling of change. This was a new "first" for me.

It was my first time in Southampton as a *dad*. I thought of all the things my dad and I did together in Southampton, and I had visions of my son someday doing those same things with me. What I didn't know then is that I'd have a daughter, Alessandra, to do them with, too.

Since I was too young to remember my first trip to Southampton, I drew a mental illustration of it. It was the summer of 1982. I wasn't born yet. I assume my parents enjoyed that summer with my brother, who was just shy of three years old. I'm sure Mom and Dad reveled in the fact that by the next summer, my brother would have a little playmate on the beach, and that they would the excitement of a new baby as they strolled down the narrow dirt road to the beach. About 27 years later I'd feel that same excitement as I walked hand-in-hand with my pregnant wife down that very same dirt road. The excitement of knowing that our son, due the next January, and the first of his generation to carry the Saracino name, would learn to swim in the Little Peconic Bay. He would learn the rules of the sea and so much more in Southampton, just as I had.

Thanks for the Memories

It wasn't until the summer of 1986 that my brain began to record episodic memories. I was three then. This is about the earliest age I can recall the house, the people, and all the "events." Southampton was never just a vacation to me. It was a place where these "events" consistently took place. Being in Southampton we escaped from the norm, and of course, something out of *my* ordinary *always* happened when we were there. These events included many "firsts" for me. Some were personal milestones, others simply nonsense but always *seemed* to be much more than what they actually were because we were on vacation. Everyday inconsequential happenings my young mind inflated into "big deals," but not just because I was a child. No, it was because we were in this magical place.

I vaguely remember learning how to build a sand castle, watching my brother demonstrate transforming an upside-down plastic bucket full of damp sand into a structure. From then on, the beach was an opportunity to test my architectural acumen by replicating the magnificent mansions that lined the Atlantic beach-front. We frequently rode down Meadow

Lane, which is lined with stately homes built on dreams. A fixture for me was the Dragon's Head Estate. Each year, for as long as I could remember, we would cruise Meadow Lane just to see what changes billionaire Barry Trupin made to his home, which we called "The Castle." Trupin constantly transformed the structure year after year, moving chimneys, building ever higher turrets, and constantly being sued and ordered by the town to make his house smaller. At its peak, Dragon's Head was 65 feet high and had more than 60 bedrooms within its 50,000 square feet of living space. A trip to Southampton was never complete without a ride past The Castle, and then an afternoon of recreating it in the sand.

Other stellar firsts: the triumphant moment of my first "pee-pee on the potty." This miracle occurred at Grandma's bungalow. The day Dad locked his keys in the car and we were "stranded" at the beach—my first memory of feeling helpless. And the time I nearly drifted out to sea—my first memory of *fear*. The rope securing my inflatable raft to shore came loose and sent me adrift in the deeper water of the bay. I can still see Dad's determination as he frantically swam out to rescue me. Of course, I probably drifted no more than 10 feet offshore, but as a toddler, the distance between my raft and the beach seemed like four football fields.

Another stellar episode: the time Mom and Dad ate a slew of raw clams and *then* realized the clams were infested with tiny, white parasitic worms. They rushed themselves to the emergency room while my brother and I stayed at the house with Grandma. Greg and I were worried sick, but Grandma calmed us. "I'm sure it's nothing," she said several times, and then she cooked us macaroni and cheese as we waited to hear. (Upshot: the worms were harmless; Mom and Dad were just fine. And yes, they still love raw clams.)

More of these little stellar moments: when Aunt Nancy's cat got stuck behind the refrigerator, and the fiasco that ensued . . . My father's frustration when Greg broke the cassette deck in Mom's *brand-new* 1988 Volvo because he kept playing the same track over and over. The kind, elderly man in the yellow house next door who gave us his old green bicycle; that bike held even more meaning for me when he died. The enormity of seeing a car on fire for the first time. We had just pulled up to the Carvel on Hampton

Road for an after-dinner sundae when we saw a beautiful silver Jaguar partially engulfed in flames. The image of the once beautiful Jaguar, with its hood (bonnet) ajar (the real British kind that opened "backwards") being devoured by flames stayed with me for weeks.

And how about the week our family friends came with us. That was in the Batman era. All of the kids ran around pretending to be the various characters. Their boys gave me a toy-scale Winnebago, large enough for me to sit on at the time, and I rode it around the indoor porch for hours on end that week. And the week my brother's best friend, Justin, came with us. We met Alec Baldwin twice in one day (and yes, he remembered us the second time and graciously gave us his autograph), and Justin got stung by a jellyfish, the first time I witnessed what a jellyfish sting can do to a person's skin.

Other moments, other memories: Mom and Dad lounging on the beach, eyes closed, catching rays while Grandma and Aunt Ellen are out in the water, digging for clams with their feet and shouting every time they dig up a big one. And my brother, Gregory, he's there too, off in the distance, exhibiting his usual exploratory nature with a metal detector along the rocky sand, eager to locate buried treasure.

Other times, Aunt Celia and Uncle Frank Marra are at the beach, too, as usual. Uncle Frank is there making me laugh, time and again with his infectious humor. Uncle Frank was one of the relatives I always wanted to be around when I was a kid. He was just always so silly and he paid special attention to us as kids. Maybe it was because I knew that he was my late grandfather's cousin and that they were close, so it felt like I was with a part of Granddad. In any event, being around Uncle Frank was always great. And as a car fanatic from age two (yes, it's true!), I always looked forward to seeing his latest Cadillac Sedan De Ville. I never knew what color it was going to be. I always admired those huge, elegant sedans of his, sparkling clean and all steeped in chrome.

I remember: doing my required summer reading for school on the porch. The many evenings before dinner, home from the beach and awaiting an awesome meal on the porch: Aunt Nancy enjoying her favorite cocktails, Grandma and Mom slaving away in the kitchen, Dad manning the grill, Aunt Ellen setting the table, and Greg and I chasing fireflies in the yard. Then the many after-dinner rides to Carvel, and coming back to watch late-evening television with Grandma, while learning a card trick or two. Greg and I were allowed to stay up late in Southampton, and every night ended with me falling sleep on the old orange and white polka-dot sofa, the one that always smelled like Southampton.

To Grandma's (On My Own)

I was about 19 the first time I drove to Southampton on my own. I took my then-girlfriend on a day-trip. It was to be a surprise-visit to Grandma. I actually did that a few times, showing up unannounced, just to enjoy Grandma's surprise and to see that warm, happy smile on her face. Once I drove out there late and arrived after dark. She nearly had a heart attack when I knocked on the door!

Dawn and I often took short weekend trips to Southampton when we were dating. We went on Memorial Day one year to help Grandma "open"

Enjoying "Southampton Summers," 94-year old Sylvia Saracino

the bungalow and get it ready for the coming summer season. First, we made our traditional pit stop at North Sea Farms to pick up a bouquet of flowers for the house. After we arrived, I'd grab a bottle of Windex and paper towels, and wash every individual glass louvre of the jalousie windows that surrounded the porch. Later we'd drive Grandma into town for a gelato at Sant' Ambroeus, a place which she loves.

My mind could race on for hours with all the memories. The trip my parents, Greg and I took to Shelter Island, where we drove around sightseeing and even caught a movie. The dozens of fishing trips with Dad and Greg to the Shinnecock Canal and the time Dad reeled in a huge, magnificent rubber tire. Our regular trips to the dumps, where we hurled garbage bags and empty wine bottles into the gigantic pits. Visiting the zoo. Lifting up the rock in the backyard of the bungalow to see where the septic line ran. Breakfasts at McDonald's, eating hot cakes and sausage while Dad read *Dan's Paper*. Running back and forth across the yards of the three family bungalows with my Marra cousins, Andrew and Alex. Seeing Chevy Chase and Sigourney Weaver jogging along Dune Road.

And more memories: a van on Noyac Road, smashing into Aunt Ellen's car parked right out front. Exploring the utility closet on the porch that always housed the coolest, most interesting tools and knick-knacks that had belonged to my great grandfather. Riding the blue and white boogie board that Mom bought us for the ocean. The pains in my feet after walking on the rocky beach. Mom and Dad showing me how to listen to the ocean inside a curling scungilli shell. The concrete slab off the back steps with my great-grandmother's name carefully inscribed in beach stones.

Also: roasting marshmallows over the charcoal grill. Dad getting a ticket in town because Greg and I weren't wearing seat-belts. Buying cassette singles at Sam Goody's in town. Being afraid to climb down into the three-foot crawl space when Dad wanted me to fetch something. The tap water that always tasted like metal. No stove because one of the cousins nearly blew up the whole kitchen while staying alone in the bungalow. Watching the reconstruction of the fuselage of TWA Flight 800 at the Coast Guard hangar in Hampton Bays. Grandma and Aunt Nancy alone in the bungalow during a hurricane and rushing to fill the bathtub with water so the toilet would work.

And how well I recall the last trip I made to the old bungalow with Dad and Grandma, just prior to its renovation. We sorted through the furniture and helped Grandma decide what to keep and what to carry to the dumpster out front. It was then that I caught myself and nodded toward the backyard and the rest of the property, as if to say, "That's right, thanks for being a part of our family, and yes, we'll keep on keepin' on." I walked back inside, joined the conversation with Grandma, Aunt Ellen and Dawn, and began the process of building some newer, adult memories.

New Look, New Life

It's been over 30 years that I've been making the same exciting trip from my permanent home in Westchester County to our family's bungalow in Suffolk County. The main difference now is that I'm no longer just a son, grandson, brother, nephew or cousin. No, I'm a husband and now a father too. Many things in Southampton look a bit different now than they did when I was a child. The quaint little beach cottages along the bay shoreline aren't nearly so "quaint" anymore. Heck, many of them are certainly no longer cottages. We find the town—actually Southampton Village—much more crowded and certainly more diverse. Barry Trupin sold The Dragon's Head Castle to Calvin Klein, who tore it down and built an Art Deco (and, to me, fairly ugly) house. The Castle, well, it's gone forever.

And the kids running worry-free around the backyard are no longer Greg, Alex, Andrew and me. Now it's cousin Gilbert's grandchildren, our distant cousins, at the house next door, all of whom just adore my grandmother and my parents.

And the biggest change of all, well, that's easy: the old 1950s-era bungalow has been totally rebuilt, by Grandma. And she did it all at age 87. The antiquated, pale green asbestos shingles were replaced with beige vinyl shakes. The once-ailing interior is no longer tired; it's new and up to date. The old jalousie porch that saw more than a half-century of family meals was also demolished. It's now a gorgeous living room that will see new memories made for many years to come. All in all, Grandma's bungalow has been transformed into a beautiful little year-round beach house. And it's a house that's all ready for the future, for a whole new generation of Saracino's, including Grandma's six great-grandchildren (so far!), who have already visited and will soon be making their own memories there. It's my hope that the small, everyday happenings they experience in Southampton will seem like world-stopping events that stick with them all their lives, just the way they did, and always will, for me.

Southampton Generations: Sylvia Saracino (2nd generation), her grandson Mark (4th), with wife, Dawn, children Nicolas and Alessandra (5th) at the little beach.

Feeding Frenzy: Summer, 1987

Gregory Saracino

In the innocence of my youth, any swagger associated with the Hamptons is irrelevant. There has never been anything lavish or swanky about my Southampton experiences. My connection to the place runs deeper than any trivial allusion to celebrity, high society or anything chic.

The summer of 1987 was about a year after my grandfather, Savino, died. I was only seven years old then. I can surmise now that his passing may well have been the reason my family drove to Southampton on numerous occasions that summer. Perhaps it was to bask in Granddad's memory; perhaps it was to forget his untimely illness. But above all it was to reconnect with family, and the sea, the clear night skies, and the clean air.

I've been to Southampton every year of my life with few exceptions, but the year 1987 is burned in my memory. Maybe that's when I started to become aware of "time," and that years can be *counted*. For whatever reason, the summer of 1987 serves as a nexus for me: when called upon to put my Southampton memories into words, my mind immediately unlocks a series of images from that special year, that special summer.

One image reveals me with my father on the western jetty at Shinnecock Inlet, named for the Shinnecock Indians (a tribe now relegated to a reservation that occupies just a little more than one square mile). The inlet, which connects the Atlantic Ocean to the Shinnecock Bay (and then to the Peconic Bay), was first formed by the devastation of the "Great Hurricane"

201

of 1938. In 1956 the Army Corps of Engineers dredged the inlet and solidified its formerly sandy edges with two dark stone jetties, wharfing into the ocean on either side of the waterway. My Aunt Ellen once pointed out that the Corps is most adept at building things in *straight lines*. And this was no exception.

Brothers Greg (L) and Mark (R) Saracino, "On the Dock of the Bay," circa 1987

Despite the dark and resolute stone quays, the inlet is very much alive. In geophysical terms, the seasonal flooding and ebbing of the shoals influence an endless cycle of eroding and redepositing sparking white sand. Aquatically, violent currents boil, swirl and sweep seaward with the tide. And there is indeed much life: seabirds, seaweed, the errant dolphin or seal, and the fish. Oh yes, the fish.

On that beautiful day in 1987, my father and I weren't there to bird-watch. We were there to stake claim to an enormous jetty rock and drop our lines into the swirling inlet, with the intent of pulling up a few bluefish. Or a striper. Or a fluke. We were simply fishing.

About an hour in with no catch—something perfectly normal, since fishing often requires significant downtime before even a little bite—we noticed a brood of gulls, gannets and terns acting very strange. They were in formation hovering over the water like a massing fleet of Stuka bombers. And, alarmingly, they were increasing in number, as if preparing for something big.

Suddenly my father and I felt even more than we heard a disturbance or rumble in the tide. The inlet's normal eddy-like current was replaced in the distance by a boiling shimmer of foaming white water rapidly approaching us. Like a sleeping sea monster had been awakened, the surface tension of the water exploded with an armada of fishy game! The Stuka birds took their cue to dive-bomb like in a blitzkrieg. We took our own cue: to replace our bait with sharp three-barbed lures (treble hooks), in order to yank our quarry out of their world and into ours.

It was a feeding frenzy. The bluefish were chasing the bait fish, their favorite prey, mossbunker (or menhaden), from the ocean into the bay, right through the inlet at prodigious speeds. The blues were biting at everything, and we reeled them in as fast as we could. That means that for every one fish I landed, my father reeled in five!

I struggled to lug one particularly large bluefish out of the water. It dangled helplessly on my hook. All of a sudden an *even larger blue* jumped high above the fray and in one lightning strike, cleanly bit my catch in half from the gills on down, like a katana slicing through an apple. Without question it was the most finely executed display of cannibalism I have ever witnessed. When I pulled the sad, pathetic head of my half-fish onto the rock, its mouth still kept twitching open and closed, like it was crying "Ow...ow...ow..." Then with a final twitch, its eyes glazed over, and I knew it was dead.

When I composed myself I looked up, and the frenzy was over. It ended as fast as it began. It was as if nothing had happened. The birds were gone, save a few stragglers ogling our catch. The monster had gone back to its watery slumber. At least our bucket was filled with about 25 bluefish. (I threw the head back—I think.)

The life lesson here? There's always gonna be a bigger fish. Or, maybe this: if you let your guard down, you'll get chomped? Maybe the only real lesson is just that bluefish have pretty sharp teeth, so watch your fingers.

Now, 30 years later, my father fondly recalls that day as well. He does that at least once a year with these words: "We couldn't reel them in fast enough!"

The frenzy was one of those finite moments I also hold dear. For me, it was a father-son bonding experience. You know, coming of age, manly stuff and all that. And I guess it couldn't have happened at a better time in my life.

My father and I will most likely never experience another feeding frenzy, but we do find time to fish at the Shinnecock Inlet whenever we can. However, for a variety of factors (such as environmental problems and over-fishing), the fish are now sparse. It's been a long time since the Summer of 1987, but at this time in my life I've learned that years mean more than just something to count. When my children are old enough, I'll bring them there, make new memories, and share the old ones too.

Greg and Sarah Saracino's children at the beach: twins Mason and Chloe, with older sister Annabelle

Three Decades of Hamptons Heaven

Andrew Marra

Even though I've been going to Southampton for over 36 years, I should start my story at the time of one of my last trips to the Hamptons, over Labor Day weekend in 2010. I can remember almost all of what we did then, and I can vividly picture our return trip from that visit perfectly.

There we were, my Dad and I. It's now already dark, even at about 8:30 p.m. and we were on our way back to Virginia Beach and home. We're stranded near the small farming town of Millsboro, Delaware, off US Route 113, trying to return home, now about 100 miles away.

Our supposedly bullet-proof car (a late-model, low-mileage, fully loaded BMW 330-ci convertible) lies stopped and helplessly dead. That car, perfect for cruising several Hamptons villages the previous day, stopped dead in the middle of a rural highway. We pushed it to the side of the road, not knowing what to do. Meanwhile every indicator on the dashboard kept flashing like a pinball machine on full tilt. We had literally rolled dead near a darkened Food Lion shopping center, with no mechanics' garages or service stations in sight, much less expected to be open anywhere around. And forget finding a Beemer repair guy on a long holiday weekend. I'm thinking to myself "How on earth was I going to get back to work the next day?"

A local guy in a battered old pickup truck with Delaware tags pulls over and asks if he could help. He's the kind of guy some might have called a redneck, hillbilly, yokel or worse, but on that night he proved to be a friend. Here was a true Good Samaritan. With an air of total confidence, he took out his well-worn but trusty tool set, looked through our owner's manual and tried everything to figure out how to get that motor going again. But nothing worked. He just about declared our car DOA, dead on arrival, even though we hadn't really arrived anywhere yet, other than off on the side of the road in "nowheresville" Delaware.

With our new friend we pushed the car a little further, to a small "mom and pop" motel just past that little shopping center. Dad and I got a room, phoned Mom, and left voice-mails at work and our Virginia Beach BMW dealer. After all, the car had fewer than 40,000 miles on it, was still under an all-inclusive full-service warranty. Plus, the BMW dealership's service people were the only ones who had ever lurked under its hood.

Actually, the car problem's really the second part of the story. The first part—yes, the really exciting part—happened well before we left Southampton. It was our last full night at the beach house.

The Sunday night before Labor Day was long, hot, and sleepless. Grandma had to spend that night in the hospital. In fact, we had to leave her there for two more days of observation. How Grandma got to the hospital is in itself a crazy story, but even that's not the whole story. Before she got to the hospital, we were all just trying to get a good night's sleep. After a long struggle to fall asleep in that un-air-conditioned room, I must have been sleeping several hours when I heard a loud knock, a bang or maybe even a kick on our front door. I heard a woman's voice yelling and screaming.

It was around 2:30 a.m. and things were happening next door, at the Maffei's house. Grandpa's cousin and neighbor, Gilbert Maffei, had fallen on his bathroom floor in an apparent diabetic shock, and his wife, Marion, ran over to our house for help. She had already called 911, but she needed our help to get Gilbert off the floor and move him. She was banging on our door and screaming "Celia!" for my grandmother. We were all sound asleep.

Who was the first to jump up to answer the door? Not my Dad, who was out like the proverbial light. Not Grandpa, and not me. Grandma got up first. Grandma, with her poor eyesight is really as blind as a bat on a good night. She gets up, walking through the bedroom that happens to have extra furniture and other stuff piled all around. Of course she bumps into something, loses her balance, tries to grab onto something to steady herself but instead grabs the fabric runner on the TV table and pulls the big, heavy, defunct, old TV on top of herself. It crashes into her chest and face, a full frontal attack that fractured several ribs and cut her forehead and into her eye sockets.

When I got to her moments later she was on the floor yelling in pain. We were all still in almost total darkness; there's not even a night light on. I could barely see her, only the shape of that old clunker of a TV sitting on her face, chest and head. She can't move the TV or herself. Grandpa and I ran to help her, grabbing and lifting the TV. We realized in two seconds that the ambulance Marion had called for Gilbert would now be needed at my grandparents' house, too.

In the midst of all that commotion, Dad gets up and tells me to handle Grandma while he responds to Marion, still at our front door, still screaming something about getting help for poor cousin Gilbert.

The ambulance arrived almost simultaneously, and the paramedics promptly administered to my grandmother. They ran tests and except for some scratches and bruised ribs, she was okay. But she had to spend two days in the hospital and a few quiet weeks at home to recover. A separate ambulance came and took Gilbert to the hospital, where he got through the night safely. Then all of us drove to the hospital, too. I spent the rest of the night and early morning there with Dad, Grandpa and Marion, watching and waiting, trying to sleep in a chair. I don't remember catching another wink of sleep that night.

And that's the weekend that was. But as bad as things got on that double-ambulance night, and after our Beemer getting stuck on a rural road, I still think of that as a great weekend. And I have nothing but love for Southampton and our family's little house. Maybe it's because those memories, almost all very pleasant, go way, way back. How far back?

Well, I can't remember exactly, but I've seen several pictures of me in Southampton at about four to five months old. There I am, a happy little guy comfortably chilling on the beach with Mom, Dad, Grandma and Grandpa. (My brother, Alex, came two years later.) I spent time at the Southampton beach house every summer until high school. Plus, starting at about five years of age, Dad took me there for a unique experience: spending a week alone with my grandparents. I can't remember many details, but again, we have several photos.

Andrew, age 5, 1986

In my grade-school years I'd spend weekends or whole weeks there with my brother, either with my parents or sometimes a week or so "alone" with Alex and my grandparents. One such time was the summer of my parents' 20th anniversary. I was ten and Alex was eight, and Mom and Dad left us in Southampton for a whole week alone with my grandparents.

I remember well how Grandpa, the undisputed head of our family, had put in place what seemed to us like a list of strict rules. Did you read my Dad's take on Grandpa's rules? Same rules. And we had to follow each one to the letter, too—or else! So many do's and don'ts! Grandpa had rules for swimming, ball playing and almost any other activity. For example, after eating—even just a snack—he ordered us to sit still and do next to nothing for at least 30 minutes. To us kids it felt like two hours. That's the way it usually went with Grandpa. And that's the way things were with him for many years after that week we spent with them.

Despite Grandpa's irritating rules, we still had lots of good times: playing many different board games on the screened porch with my brother, and playing with our cousins, Gregory and Mark Saracino, who were nearly the same exact ages as my brother and me. Those two guys turned out to be very cool friends. They would come over from the Saracino house and often they stayed at our place until quite late. And that was okay with everyone. Alex and I also played a lot of Wiffle ball, sometimes alone, sometimes with Mark and Gregory or other cousins, and even several times with Grandpa. He always amazed us with his athletic prowess, even when he was well into his mid-70s.

Other times we had to persuade, cajole and nearly force Grandpa to take us into town. In those days Alex and I and even Dad were avid baseball-card and sports-memorabilia collectors. As it happened, one of Dad's childhood friends, Charlie, lived very near our bungalow. He had opened a coin and trading-card shop in town just off Job's Lane, one of the little streets with several trendy shops and designer boutiques. Grandpa would give us a dollar each, and with that paltry sum we found a way to coax Charlie into selling each of us a couple of packs of cards.

That same summer I had little arguments with Grandpa about one of his stupid rules. He always insisted that because our bay beach was so rocky, we had to wear sandals or sneakers to protect our feet from the sharp stones and shells. Everyone did that. But for me, it just wasn't cool. I refused to look like a dork there or anywhere.

Being a more stubborn kid than my brother, I really fought with Grandpa about it, so I didn't wear them all the time. When I was 10 and my parents had left us there for over a week, I got cut by a sharp shell or rock or something. For the rest of that week I didn't think much of it. On second thought, I probably didn't want to draw anyone's attention (especially Grandpa's) to the cut. But toward the end of the week it got worse. That little cut became badly infected. Just before we went home the pain in my foot got really bad, so bad that I couldn't walk on it. On the last day of that visit I finally told Grandpa and asked him to take me to the hospital to treat the infection. He did. Seemed he was right after all. Lesson learned, the hard way.

As an adult, of course I see that Grandpa and the other adults were right: it was a sensible "rule." Now I always wear those awful-looking foot protectors, or water socks, or any pair of old sneakers to go down to that little beach. I may look and feel stupid in them, but the last thing I want is to cut my foot again.

It's small and very, very rocky, but that little beach is unique. I've never seen anything like it on the East Coast, not on the Delmarva peninsula, not in Ocean City, Maryland, or Virginia Beach, and certainly not Florida. There's not a lot of sand, and what sand is there is mixed in with pebbles, small rocks, and millions of shells and a lot of shell fragments. At first glance, it seems like such a scrappy little nothing of a beach. But it's actually quite beautiful in its own little way. And when we were kids, that's the beach we went to. The only beach!

At the time that was fine, because it was just two blocks away and so easy to get there. We could walk there, and often did—by ourselves! As young kids, Mom and Dad would never let us do that in Virginia or in Ocean City. But in Southampton, Grandma and Grandpa didn't have to do much persuading to get themselves or us to the little beach. On the other hand, if we pleaded enough and caught them on a good day and they were in a good mood, they'd agree to take us to one of Southampton's fabulous, scenic oceanfront beaches, which were only about seven miles (a short ten minutes ride) down the road. Those beaches were something special.

For drives to the beach, especially on the few occasions we did go to the ocean, Grandpa packed up the Cadillac (he always drove a big sedan, always a late-model Caddie) with everything normal people might pack for a long trip. Along with the usual beach gear, they always packed lots of food and drinks. It looked like enough to cover breakfast, a snack and lunch. For some reason they had to make it an all-day event. And so we'd spend the whole day there, on a beach with sand and big waves, which was much more exciting than the puny waves at the little beach. Try using a boogie board at the bay. It's pointless. But at the ocean, it was awesome.

When I was just a kid I thought Grandma and Grandpa's little house and the whole surrounding area were stupid and totally dinky. But in my adult years I gradually came to know that I was sadly mistaken about everything. I was dead wrong about how Grandma and Grandpa's little bungalow and the little beach didn't compare at all with Mom and Dad's condo two blocks from the surf in Ocean City. As kids we always preferred the condo, where there was a pool, the ocean beach was just two blocks away, and there was a big boardwalk. Summers in Ocean City meant that we had all kinds of fun stuff right at our doorstep, even on rainy days.

When I got older, I started to see that Southampton and "the Hamptons" weren't just about our row of three tiny family bungalows in the woods near the little beach. I started to realize that this vacation place has historically been exclusive and prestigious, a place where celebrities own houses and the wealthiest of the wealthy from the New York City area spend their summers. My whole outlook had changed. As I grew up I became much more open to and appreciative of Southampton and its look and lifestyle. I've taken note of the area's classic and spectacular homes, the old-money wealth and the new-money glitz. There's no boardwalk—but with my newfound respect, I can proudly boast, "who needs a boardwalk anyway?"

I've come to love visiting the whole Hamptons area—the small towns, the beaches, the woods and more. I see its natural charm. I see what my parents, grandparents and great-grandparents must have seen years ago. Even our little no-name rocky beach takes on a more positive image. To me, that beach—so quiet, so peaceful, so unspoiled—is more special and more beautiful than all the glitz, glamour, wealth and celebrity that people usually associate with Southampton.

During that last fateful visit, we spent much of the afternoon at the little beach. By the end of the day, maybe 15 people, friends, neighbors, relations, had gathered around talking. Several were our cousins, others were all old friends of my parents and grandparents, many also from Italian families. It felt almost like a private "Italian" beach. In a way, it was, and still is.

The last time we were in Southampton we rode through town with the BMW's top down. That was fun, and without looking like a couple of crummy wannabees, we looked like we "belonged" to the upscale, wealthy, trendy Southampton. But in the final analysis it paled in comparison to what was the highlight of our trip: spending that final sunny afternoon at the little beach in the company of all of those relatives and neighbors. What I took away from that day on the beach is how pleasant it was to be there, and how beautiful and tranquil that beach has stayed over the years.

Getting back to our story, we never did find out what had caused my car to die on the road. The tow truck arrived the next morning, ready to take it to a BMW dealer some 40 miles away in Georgetown, Delaware. But that didn't happen. Instead, the tow truck driver asked for the keys and what do you know? The car started instantly! All the lights, gauges and computer

controls came back online, re-setting themselves as if nothing untoward had ever happened. The Beemer took us home with no problem, and it's been running perfectly ever since. Even our local Virginia Beach BMW dealer's mechanics couldn't explain it. But there had to be an explanation.

Maybe the cause wasn't mechanical or physical at all. With its excellent German engineering, no apparent defects, and all of its scheduled maintenance up to date, maybe the car was offering us an explanation of another kind: maybe my BMW wanted to tell me it didn't want to be in Delaware and points south. That car wanted to be back in Southampton.

And in many ways, I do too!

Rocks, Horseflies and Grandparents

Alex Marra

When I was a kid and my folks told me I was going to "Southampton," it meant nothing to me. It's not that our family's Long Island beach house, really just a beach "bungalow," meant nothing to me. No, my grandparents' bungalow meant and still means an awful lot. You see, it's a part of who I am.

What I mean is that "Southampton" became shorthand for Grandma and Grandpa's "beach house." I put quotation marks around "beach house" because it wasn't on or even within sight of the beach. Well, to be fair, it was *near* the beach; you could walk to the beach in 10 minutes if you cut through woods on the dirt paths they call roads to that little beach on a body of weak-wave water they call the bay. I don't know the name of that beach, or if it has one. I doubt cartographers or even the Google people know that beach exists. If they do, it's probably too small to be worth naming.

My grandparents' beach house isn't like the beach houses my DC-area friends' families rented in the Outer Banks. It's not one of those beach houses built on pilings that look like daddy-long-leg spiders to keep them safe from hurricanes, as the pounding surf takes the sand for a long, bumpy ride. Nor is my grandparents' house one of those high-in-the-sky condos 14 stories above and 100 yards from the ocean, as in Florida, New Jersey or Maryland. Our beach house never fit those stereotypes. But it meant the world to my grandparents, and to all four generations of us. Still does.

213

Goin' to Town

Every time I've gone to the Southampton house, I can count on one hand how many times I've actually been *in* Southampton—that is, what my parents and grandparents called "town." And that term (town) can mean any of the nearby villages of Sag Harbor or one of the other nearby beach towns such as East Hampton, Bridgehampton, Shelter Island or Amagansett.

When my Dad, Mom, my brother and I went "out to Southampton," it was mainly to stay with my grandparents at their bungalow near the beach—the beach with tiny waves, lots of rocks and practically no sand. "Southampton" also meant that place where raccoons ransacked Grandpa's rusty old garbage can every night. In those dark battles, what was Grandpa's defense? Easy, just place two bricks on the lid, a solution which he considered preferable to: 1.) Carrying the trash all the way home to Yonkers in the trunk of his Cadillac; or 2.) Paying for private trash collection; or 3.) Driving those stinky bags to the Southampton town landfill, which Grandpa still calls "the dumps."

But we hardly ever went there; or anywhere for that matter. No, we had to stick close to the house—we were allowed to travel only between the bungalow and the beach. Whenever we said we wanted to go to town to dump the trash or for any other purpose, Grandpa's face would contort into a look of utter disbelief. "Why would you want to do *that*?" he'd ask, as if we had asked him to help us sell all our worldly goods and join the Basque sheep herders in Utah or Wyoming. Were we insinuating that there might be more exciting things to do than eat, sit around the house, read the newspapers, spend time in his company and take the daily (and admittedly refreshing) dip in the wave-less, crowd-free, rock-strewn beach on the bay?

I'm not complaining, though. I was privileged. Even though I went to public schools, and we didn't even have cable until after the new millennium, our family had a house at the beach in Southampton. How cool is that!

214

In fact, we had *two* East Coast beach houses, if you count our own family's place in Ocean City, Maryland. It was just a two-bedroom condo, but only a five-minute walk to the Atlantic, to a beach with tons of white sand to play in and "real" waves for all-day boogie-boarding. And unlike our Southampton visits, in bad weather we still had plenty to do along Ocean City's century-old boardwalk: rides, arcades, tacky T-shirt shops, and all kinds of tacky-wacky people. Plus, Ocean City seemed very kid-friendly, whereas Southampton didn't. In Southampton things were too quiet for kids. In fact, it always seemed to me that the Hamptons were populated mainly by a lot of middle-aged folks and retirees, although not many in their 80s like my grandparents were at the time. They have to be among only a handful of that age group who still made the summer trek (on their own, too!) well into their 90s. But whatever the actual demographics, there weren't many kids in our part of the Hamptons. If there are, they seemed to be well-hidden.

Brothers (L to R): Andrew (9) and Alex (7), at the ocean, 1990

That's not to say there weren't any kids around for us to play with. No, not at all. We had cousins, like Gregory and Mark Saracino, who were about our age. When we were in elementary school we connected with Greg and Mark for three or four summers straight. We got along great with them. They stayed with their grandparents or parents at the bungalow

215

that their great-grandparents, old Aunt Helen and Uncle Joe, had built. We were lucky our vacations overlapped, that they lived so close, and we all became good playmates.

The four of us commiserated when we got bored out of our minds on rainy days with nothing to do but play cards or board games ("War," anyone?). Southampton had no boardwalk, no rides, no wacky people like Ocean City's Boardwalk Elvis, but we did have board games at the house, although none of our favorite ones like "Chutes and Ladders," "Hungry Hippos" or "Sorry!" No, we had to play "adult" board games like backgammon and checkers. And since we didn't know how to play backgammon and you can only say "King me!" so many times before going nuts, we were SOL—Southampton Out of Luck, that is. There was "Monopoly," too, but Andrew and I could never agree on who should be the banker. It wasn't long before we started calling the board games exactly what they were: "bored" games. That's how we felt before, during and after.

So no town, no boardwalk and no good board games. But there's always television, right? Surely every American home has multiple TVs and many channels. As I've said, we grew up without cable TV, so we were OK with having only the three or four network channels to choose from during Saturday cartoon marathons. But at my grandparents,' there was just one channel. That was beyond belief.

We didn't have cable at home but we sure had more than at my grandparents' bungalow which had just one fuzzy, black-and-white image of whatever ABC decided to beam out in 13 inches of click-and-pick glory from some third-rate station across the water in Connecticut. What, was that from … Connecticut? Yes, it was, and that one stinky station brought them "Wheel of Fortune" every night, which meant my grandparents could torture us with their endless guessing to solve the silly word puzzles, and their gratuitous comments about how special Vanna looked. That one station was all my grandparents needed: it also broadcast other Medicare-approved faves, such as "Murder She Wrote" and "MacGyver." We spent many Southampton evenings like that, bored to tears, aging faster than my grandparents, watching a Connecticut TV station on a tiny TV and its crown of metal coat hanger rabbit ears-cum-tinfoil antennae. It made quite a picture.

Was I spoiled? My grandparents were in their mid-70s to mid-80s during the years when my brother and I stayed with them. They were nice enough to have us there during what would have been unproductive, day-camp filled (arts-and-crafts, anyone?) hot, humid Virginia summers. Instead we got to hang in the hippest of northeastern beach towns in a family beach pad. And my grandparents were aware that we were little kids who had lots of energy and needed attention. That's why Grandpa played Wiffle ball with us almost daily. To boys in the 1980s, Wiffle ball was the most exciting game going, and Grandpa always made our games challenging and fun. But never right after a meal. Remember, he had the crazy rule that we couldn't play or do anything after eating. We had to sit and wait a good 30 minutes before we could play. How did we know when 30 minutes are up? By counting down my brother's Game Boy.

That's one of the simple things I remember about Southampton summers, the truly simple things: sitting and staring at my brother playing Game Boy and listening to the 8-bit tweets and burps emanating from that hand-held, primitive video game console he received from my parents one Christmas. No one would freely spend 14 half-hours a week sitting in a rusty old oversized lawn chair on a dirt "patio" at the edge of the mossy woods trying to catch a glimpse of Game Boy action. But you would if you had to. And you would have to if Grandpa told you to. Oh, yes you would.

Grandpa didn't tell me explicitly to sit next to my brother (who was also coiled up on a lawn chair) and count the seconds by Game Boy sounds. But what else would a 6- or 7-year-old boy do if ordered to "sit still" for 30 minutes? Like many people of his generation, Grandpa wholeheartedly believed that old wives' tale. As I said, that meant no running, no swimming, no Wiffle ball, no nothing. Grandpa was perfectly happy with his Italian after-meals ritual of sitting with the newspaper for 30 minutes to ward off quick and certain death from indigestion. God forbid some poor fool tries to swim right after a meal. The result would be "death by lasagna" that didn't get the mandatory 30 minutes to make its way down the digestive tract. (It's funny, but the 30-minute rule didn't apply to breakfast. Maybe because there's no tomato sauce at breakfast? Or maybe bagels or eggs make their way down faster?) What was I to do? So there I was, a prisoner, a Hamptons detainee, for two half-hour spells a day.

But I not only survived this ritual—it paid off in certain ways. All my work keeping my bum glued to that chair twice a day earned me a Game Boy of my own after my mom heard the story of my deprivation.

Little Guys at the Little Peconic

Southampton wasn't just sitting, of course. We enjoyed lots of beach time at the nearby bay. My grandparents often took us there in their cool Cadillac. When we were just a little older my brother and I walked to the beach alone several times. But we were still often chauffeured to and from the beach, and that came with drawbacks going home. Did anyone think Grandpa would let us in his fancy Caddie in wet bathing suits? Or, God forbid, with sand and mossy stuff, remnants of seaweed or slimy green algae on our feet? Just enough to ruin the carpets of his like-new, late 1980s-1990s Sedan De Ville. But the preceding generation, our great-grandparents, didn't survive and thrive at that beach without knowing some tips and passing them on. No, they had taught my Grandpa, and they taught him well.

So, before leaving the beach, Grandpa grabbed a sand-castle-size pail and filled it with vintage Little Peconic Bay while we dutifully sat on the edge of the car seats, feet dangling out a bit. Then he'd "baptize" our lower extremities by pouring the water down our spindly, sand-encrusted legs, washing it off and back onto the ground. Once Grandpa (AKA "St. Frank the Baptist") was assured that our feet were sand-free, they were dried with a towel that Grandma had snapped to the ready. Now washed and dried, our feet could safely enter the car. Soon back at the house we showered the rest of our bodies San Quentin-style, naked or nearly so, all outdoors, in freezing-cold well water, hosing away every last trace of salt.

Just thinking of the simplicity of our daily routine at that Southampton beach stirs something deep in my memory. And like that pail of beach water, I wash away the bad, leaving only the good. In fact, since I haven't been back in years, I can only go by what relatives have been telling me. The word is that our stupid little rock-strewn beach might be the best damn beach in all Southampton, if not all the Hamptons. It's still quiet, peaceful and unpretentious, with a nice view, cooling northwest breezes, and warm wave-less water. But don't tell anyone.

That beach had its share of unique hazards besides the slippery rocks. One time a shell or sharp rock sliced my brother's foot bad enough to force Grandpa to take him to the hospital. My brother just walked into the water and, yikes! Blood flowed and pain hit at the same time. It must have been the rocks. Maybe it was the shells or shell-encrusted rocks that cover the beach and the sea floor. They were out to get us. Now, I was little and I didn't know much about beaches, but I sure didn't think that anything at a little kid's beach should slice your feet open. Other than Southampton, all I knew about beaches was what I learned from the sands of Ocean City, and I could easily conclude, via limited scientific observation, that there was nothing in Maryland capable of cutting a little boy's foot.

So my grandparents made this much clear: we were to only venture into the deadly bay with our "booties" on. What else to call our rubber water shoes? Honestly, I didn't appreciate sporting fluorescent pink "booties" (a slight exaggeration) during my young beach-bum days. But I wasn't going to argue. I had seen first-hand what happens to those who think they're a match for the Little Peconic Bay's rocks and shells. So I wore my cute booties until the last time I swam in those waters. And I'd wear them now, too, if I go back, which I surely will.

So what made our little Southampton beach so different, so special? Was it the lack of waves? No, that had nothing to do with it. Perhaps the voracious horseflies that made giant welts on your body and face or the gnats in your eyes, ears, nose? No again.

Southampton and that beach mean a lot to me after all. I realize that it was a big part of my childhood because of all the "firsts" I experienced there, like my first scungilli (although I never did actually eat one of those things) and tasting my first home-grown garden tomato. There were many firsts for me in Southampton. At my grandmother's Southampton garden is where I had my first unadulterated tomato, plucked fresh off the vine. Dad wanted me to try it, so I took a small, wary bite, and it was awful! Why would anyone eat those things? No wonder Columbus' crew thought they were poison. My first thought (as I tried not to throw up): *no way* Grandma's

gravy came from that! Tomatoes are sweet-salty, herby, piquant, smell great, and taste great with sausage or meatballs—right?

So what was *this*? Sour and seedy, with weird jelly-juice in the middle, and obviously I didn't know then that basil, oregano, salt, garlic, onion, wine and a pinch of sugar went into that pot of tomatoes on the stove. I just knew tomatoes—*Italian gravy*—tasted good. (My brother got a tomato, too, and he

Scungilli - When you can't find any at the beach

liked it. No, he loved it. He kept on eating more until Grandma yelled at him to stop. I couldn't believe it.)

Well, why was Dad force-feeding me a tomato? I didn't understand at the time, but he was showing us the beauty of vegetable gardens (which Italians love) and how things grow. Many people think the tastiest tomatoes come from Italy, but judging by Grandma's gravy, Southampton's North Sea micro-climate makes a good tomato grow even better. They're surely the reddest, tastiest tomatoes anywhere.

And then there's the story about my first scungilli. They say that the Indians used those large, twisted shells you put to your ear to "hear" the ocean, as "wampum." Well, I found out that scungilli, what most people call conch, seem to abound at our beach. They're known by all in Southampton by that zany Italian name, "scungilli." Many Italians (including my family members) were actually eating the slime inside. Dad taught us about scungilli at our beach. He explained the name, and that Italians really eat those ghastly, gooey creatures in tomato gravy. My grandparents and parents were nice enough not to scare the crap out of us by trying to feed us those bottom-dwellers or demonstrating how and why we can hear the ocean in their shells. Until that point I didn't know that anything ever lived in those shells or that people ripped the squishy critters from their homes and grilled, seared or boiled their rubbery bodies before mixing them with red sauce.

But at the beach it was all about connecting with and discovering our roots. That's why Dad made a point of showing us the beauty of growing one's own food and teaching us the Italian names of sea creatures. He was reconnecting with his own roots by visiting Southampton with us, and he couldn't help but share his own experiences. He did that by explaining the unique cultural experiences that this special place held for the first three generations of our family to spend summers in Southampton.

Now an adult, and as a father myself, I finally get it. Sure, there are nice beach houses in Ocean City, and there's a boardwalk. But they don't have dirt roads that take you through mossy woods to the beach in minutes. In Ocean City they don't have rocks, horseflies or scungilli on the beach. They don't have gardens to grow tomatoes.

And they sure don't have my grandparents.

TOWN OF SOUTHAMPTON
TRICENTENNIAL STAMPS

CHAPTER FIVE:
The Fifth and Future Generations at the Beach

Albert Marra

What will the future hold for our family's bungalows? Years from now what will the young children of the fifth generation, some of whom have already visited, think about the beach houses their great-great grandparents built 60 years ago? And what about future generations?

Well, nobody can say with any degree of certainty. Baseball's old sage, Yogi Berra sums it up as well as anyone could with one of his oft-cited malaprops, that the future ain't what it used to be. In the case of our Southampton beach houses, that may be truer than true.

Yet we can glean from recent natural, economic and sociological trends to make some reasonable predictions. Natural forces such as the area's cold, damp climate and its hungry termites and other pests will continue to exact a toll on the little houses. These factors may well exert additional pressure on the Marra and Maffei families to follow the Saracino family's lead and invest considerable resources in renovations. Lord knows, repairs are already overdue.

The woods we once considered ours, the site of our clandestine fort, have long vanished, with more clearings, more houses, and more growth still to come. The pleasant dirt roads we've walked thousands of times to the beach may likely be destined for certain "improvements" (signaling the demise of their "country" feel) in coming years. That would just add to the existing and accelerating changes in the area. So much for that woodsy, countrified look.

223

If natural forces don't destroy the bungalows, social and economic pressures may exert even stronger influences. Pressures from increasingly well financed newcomers and ever-rising Southampton real estate taxes could drastically affect our family's situation relative to the three simple houses. Gentrification of neighboring properties in Bay View Oaks and the North Sea district in general has already begun to change the area's demographics in subtle ways. It may take more money than our grandparents could ever have imagined for future generations to keep up with costs, as what once resembled a haven for working class families grows and morphs into an upper middle class community or worse yet, just another enclave for the well to do.

Another variable could also cloud the waters in coming years and possibly change quaint and quiet Southampton forever. This has to do with the Shinnecock Indian Nation's quest for recognition of claims to additional lands. If and when these claims are settled in the Indians' favor, with the added possibility of an Indian-owned casino, commercial activity in Southampton will likely boom.

Nicolas Saracino, age 7 - The fifth generation to fish at "our little beach"

And would our no-name little beach remain the tranquil oasis for the fifth and further generations as it once was for us and previous generations? Clearly, there is no "clear" answer. And who could predict if the descendants of the Marra-Maffei-Saracino troika will continue to appreciate the modest bungalows that their immigrant ancestors worked so hard to build for their families in the 1950s and 1960s.

While the Maffei family may be a few years away from adding its next generation of visitors, already several young members of the Saracino clan's fifth generation have enjoyed spending summer vacations at their family bungalow. These young visitors have included Colette Resh, the daughter of Jonathan (Saracino) Resh; Annabelle, Chloe, and Mason, the children of Gregory and Sarah Saracino; and Nicolas and Alessandra, children of Mark and Dawn Saracino.

Fifth generation Marra's: sisters Margaret (3) and Cecilia (1) with cousin Dominick (2 Months)

Distance factors have kept Maryland residents Andrew Marra, his wife, Kristen and son, Dominick, from visiting. In a similar way, Andrew's brother, Alex Marra, wife Isabel, and daughters Maggie and Cecilia, all of whom live in Bath, England, find it challenging enough just to make plans to visit their US family as a group once a year. Will the two Marra brothers find sufficient travel time to attempt, like "the Saracino boys," to recreate their childhood times in Southampton with their own children in the coming years. And will all of these young children and their parents find answers to the myriad questions posed above?

It's likely that the answers to these questions may not come easily. We also prefer that the answers not come too quickly. It would be ideal if the three bungalows survive; it would be doubly special if the little beach on nobody's must-see bucket list retains its simple family appeal for the children of the fifth generation to enjoy as much as their parents and their predecessors have. Then, even if nothing is certain, we could be reasonably sure—maybe as sure as the summer sun setting over the Little Peconic—that our fifth and future generations will have plenty of material with which to write their own Southampton family stories.

Annabelle Saracino (5th generation)—Sunset at "our little beach" on the Little Peconic

226

Appendix One:
About the Authors

Albert Marra

Contributing Authors

Sal Anselmo

Sal is a certified Reiki specialist, a trained religious counselor, and he has operated a home care service in Richmond, Virginia since 2001. Currently semi-retired, Sal continues to volunteer many hours weekly for several local church-affiliated agencies and other causes.

Frances Maffei

Frances has worked many years in health care management. Born and raised in Yonkers, she resides in Dobbs Ferry, New York with her family. With her mother, Marion, and children, Victoria, Selena and Anthony, Frances has spent over 50 summers at her family's Southampton bungalow.

Gilbert Maffei

Gilbert was another of the special authors who contributed narratives for this book. A Yonkers resident for almost all of his life, Gil, who passed away in 2013, spent his professional career in the steel industry. His keen wit and his pragmatic approach to life's problems are traits greatly missed by all who have frequented the Southampton family bungalows since his passing.

Alex Marra

A lex, the second son of the main author and another fourth generation Marra, resides in Bath, England with his wife, Isabel (a physician and major in the British Army), and young daughters, Margaret and Cecilia. After obtaining his doctorate and lecturing in sociology at the University of Bristol, Alex has been teaching religion, philosophy and history at Catholic schools in southwest England.

Andrew Marra

A ndrew, the son of the principal author and a fourth generation Marra family member, lives in Olney, (Montgomery County) Maryland, with his wife, Kristen, and infant son, Dominick. He has been a senior representative for major pharmaceutical companies in DC-Maryland-Virginia for over 15 years and currently works at the Gaithersburg, Maryland office of Astra-Zeneca in several capacities, primarily in women's oncology drugs.

Eugene Marra

E ugene, a classically trained chef who graduated from the CIA (Culinary Institute of America), has been a longtime restaurateur and cooking instructor. He currently owns and operates the Cooperstown Distillery and the Cooperstown Beverage Exchange (a wine and spirits café), both of which are very close to the Baseball Hall of Fame in Cooperstown, New York.

Frank Marra

F rank, whose narrated story is included in the book, has lived in Yonkers, New York for nearly 60 years. His professional career included the Bank of America in northern California, as well as management positions at several New York City branches of Chemical Bank (now JP Morgan Chase). A World War II US Army veteran, he recently celebrated his 100th birthday with 100 relatives and friends.

Peter Nardi

Peter, a Marra family friend for over 50 years, spent several summers in the Sag Harbor area. Peter, a California resident for over 45 years, has lived in Los Angeles for the past 30. Author of several books and journal articles in several fields, he retired as Professor Emeritus in Sociology after 35 years teaching at Pitzer College, which is part of the Claremont Colleges.

Jonathan Resh

Jonathan, the first grandchild of Sylvia and Savy and a fourth generation Saracino family member, has been a Midwesterner for several years. Jon currently lives in Chicago, along with his daughter, Colette (a fifth generation Southampton visitor), where he currently serves as the Creative Director of the Chicago Children's Museum.

Ellen Saracino

Ellen, a daughter of Saracino bungalow owners Sylvia and Savy, recently retired from a 30-year career with the Lilly pharmaceutical company. She maintains her permanent home in Danbury, Connecticut and also devotes a great deal of her time to her 95-year old mother, Sylvia, at her Yonkers, New York home.

Gregory Saracino

Gregory, grandson of Sylvia and Savy and a fourth-generation family member, is an attorney who specializes in commercial and business litigation in the New York metropolitan area. Gregory resides in Valhalla, New York with his wife, Sarah, daughter Annabelle, and twins Mason and Chloe. The couple and all three children have visited their family's bungalow.

Linda Saracino

Linda is the eldest child of Sylvia and Savy Saracino. An artist, as well as a writer and editor, she began her media career creating print and video projects for major corporations. Working from her home base in metro Orlando, Florida, she has recently focused on editing books, magazines, articles, online content, museum materials, and even recipes.

Mark Saracino

Mark, grandson of Sylvia and Savy and another fourth-generation member, lives with his wife, Dawn, and young children, Nicolas and Alessandra (fifth generation visitors as well), in Valhalla, New York. After spending a decade in the commodities trade, Mark founded and serves as president of a natural stone and monument building company (Saracino Industries) in New York.

Sylvia Saracino

Sylvia, who with her husband, Dr. Savy Saracino, has been an owner of the first family bungalow for over forty years, also contributed a narrated story to this book. She has lived in Yonkers, New York for many years, after raising her family in Mount Vernon. Sylvia completely re-built her family's bungalow in 2011.

Judith Marra Scott

Judith, one of the Marra family's first Southampton visitors in her youth, presently resides in Eastchester, New York. An accomplished author, journalist and newspaper reporter, she has recently retired from her career as a school reading specialist.

Principal Author

Albert Marra

The author retired from the US Public Health Service as Senior Contracts Manager after 34 years with the Health Resources and Services Administration, the National Institutes of Health, the US Department of Education, and the Social Security Administration. After moving from the DC area to Virginia Beach in 2005, he began a second career as supervisor of student teachers and assistant professor of Spanish and Italian at Old Dominion University and Tidewater Community College in Norfolk, Virginia. In 2018 he moved to Woodstock, (Howard County) Maryland, outside Baltimore, to be near his son and family. As a translator-interpreter for the United States Coast Guard (with 21 years of voluntary service), he was tasked with translating reports from the 2012 sinking of the Costa Concordia in Italy. For that act in 2014 the Commandant of the Coast Guard awarded him the Auxiliary Special Achievement Medal for Superior Performance of Duty.

A native of the Bronx and Yonkers, he completed elementary, secondary and undergraduate education in New York City. He earned a Bachelor's Degree from Manhattan College, Master's Degrees from the University of Valencia, Spain and Binghamton University, and a Doctorate from Catholic University. He married his college sweetheart, Adrienne Rinaldi, another Bronx native, in 1970. The couple has two sons, two granddaughters, and one grandson. He has published articles in several national magazines and journals as well as in Northern Virginia newspapers. A recipient of many awards from the US Surgeon General and the US Secretaries of Education, Homeland Security, and Health and Human Services, his proudest achievement is his 1995 Pyramid Award from Montgomery County, Maryland as public sector Supervisor of the Year.

APPENDIX TWO:
List of Photographs and Illustrations

APPENDIX THREE:
Documents Related to
1563 Noyac Road, Bay View Oaks

STATE OF NEW YORK, COUNTY OF *NASSAU* ss.: LIBER 3293 PAGE 447

On the 21st day of November , nineteen hundred and fifty-one
before me personally came HOWARD T. FINCH

to me known, who, being by me duly sworn, did depose and say that he resides at No. 1916
Jones Avenue North, Wantagh, New York
that he is the Vice President
of PECONIC SHORES, INC.
the corporation described in and which executed the foregoing instrument; that he knows the seal of said corporation; that the seal affixed to said instrument is such corporate seal; that it was so affixed by order of the board of directors of said corporation, and that he signed h is name thereto by like order.

Notary Public

CHARLES G. RITTER
NOTARY PUBLIC, State of New York
No. 30-2251300

State of New York } ss.:
County of Nassau

I, CHARLES E. RANSOM, County Clerk and Clerk of the Supreme Court, Nassau County, a Court of Record having by law a seal, DO HEREBY CERTIFY THAT *Charles G. Ritter*

whose name is subscribed to the deposition, certificate of acknowledgment or proof of the annexed instrument, was at the time of taking the same a NOTARY PUBLIC in and for the State of New York, duly commissioned and sworn and qualified to act as such in Nassau County and throughout said State; that pursuant to law a commission, or a certificate of his appointment and qualification, and his autograph signature, have been filed in my office; that as such NOTARY PUBLIC he was duly authorized by the laws of the State of New York to administer oaths and affirmations, to certify the acknowledgment or proof of deeds and other written instruments for lands, tenements and hereditaments to be read in evidence or recorded in said State, to protest notes and to take and certify depositions; and that I am well acquainted with the handwriting of such Notary Public, or have compared the signature on the annexed instrument with his autograph signature deposited in my office, and believe that the signature is genuine.

IN WITNESS WHEREOF, I have hereunto set my hand and affixed my
110064   official seal at Mineola, N. Y., this day of   19 57

County Clerk and Clerk of the Supreme Court, Nassau County

C12-6M-11/50

TITLE No. 18326

PECONIC SHORES, INC.

TO

ARTHUR MARRA and
MARY MARRA.

Warranty Deed
WITH FULL COVENANTS.

The land affected by the within instrument
lies in Section   in Block   on the
Land Map of the County of Suffolk.

RECORDED AT REQUEST OF

HOWARD T. FINCH
Attorney-at-Law
No. 5 Centre St.
Hempstead, N. Y.

TITLE GUARANTEE
AND
TRUST COMPANY
Offices

Main Office: 176 BROADWAY, MANHATTAN

Branch Offices

6 East 45th Street   570 East 149th Street   70 Grand Street
MANHATTAN   BRONX   WHITE PLAINS

175 Remsen Street   90-04 161st Street   Franklin Avenue
BROOKLYN   JAMAICA   MINEOLA

56 Bay Street   Griffing Avenue
STATEN ISLAND   RIVERHEAD

RECORDED

Deed: Peconic Shores, Inc. to Arthur Marra and Mary Marra, November 1951

3534 ● 4-50-40M—Warranty Deed With Full Covenants—Individual or Corporation.

LIBER**3863** PAGE**550**

THIS INDENTURE, made the   1st   day of   APRIL   nineteen hundred and fifty-five

BETWEEN   ARTHUR MARRA and MARY MARRA, his wife, both residing at
19-75 Lafontaine Avenue, Bronx, New York

party of the first part, and   FRANK MARRA and CECILE MARRA, his wife, both residing
at 3055 Bouck Avenue, Bronx, N. Y.

party of the second part,

WITNESSETH, that the party of the first part, in consideration of

TEN AND NO/100 ($10.00) -
dollars,

lawful money of the United States, and other good and valuable consideration   paid

by the party of the second part, does hereby grant and release unto the party of the second part,

their heirs   and assigns forever,

ALL that certain piece or parcel of land, situate in the Town of Southampton,
County of Suffolk and State of New York, being designated on a map entitled,
"Subdivision Map of Bay View Oaks, situated at North Sea, Town of Southampton,
Suffolk County, New York, Owner and Developer, Peconic Shores, Inc., 88 81st
Street, Brooklyn, New York, Mr. Vilhelm M. Reimann, President; Theodore F.
Squires, Civil Engineer and Surveyor of Southampton, N. Y." and filed in the
Office of the Clerk of Suffolk County, State of New York, on the 12th day of
December 1947, as Map No. 1594 as Lot Number 169.

TOGETHER with a Right of Way in common with others over the following
described premises:

BEGINNING at a monument set at the intersection of the north-westerly line
of East Shore Road and the westerly line of lands of Daniel David Daley; said
monument being situated South 43 degrees 43 minutes 20 seconds West, 180.00
feet from a monument set at the intersection of the northwesterly line of
East Shore Road and the westerly line of lands of S. J. Newberry; and running
thence from the point of beginning southwesterly along the northwesterly line
of East Shore Road South 43 degrees 43 minutes 20 seconds West, 20.00 feet
to other lands of Daniel David Daley; thence northerly along these other lands
of Daniel David Daley North 20 degrees 54 minutes 00 seconds West 171.00 feet
to the average foot of bluffs along Little Peconic Bay; thence North 43 degrees

Commission expires March 30, 1957

STATE OF NEW YORK, COUNTY OF New York   . **SS.:**

On the   1st   day of   April   , nineteen hundred and fifty five
before me personally came

Deed: Arthur & Mary Marra to Frank & Cecile Marra, April, 1955

CHARLES H. SULLIVAN
President

JOSEPH F. HUBERT
Vice President

JANE M. SULLIVAN
Secretary

HOLLIS W. MEINECKE
Treasurer

WALTER T. HANRAHAN
Vice President

NICHOLAS J. LEONARD
Assistant Vice President

RONALD F. OLLETT
Assistant Treasurer
and Comptroller

GEORGIANA TITUS
Assistant Secretary

NORTHPORT FEDERAL SAVINGS
AND LOAN ASSOCIATION

225 MAIN STREET   NORTHPORT, N.Y.

Telephone: NOrthport 3-4200

November 24, 1958

Mr. & Mrs. Frank Marra
3055 Bouck Avenue
Bronx 69, New York   RE: L-2166

Dear Mr. & Mrs. Marra:

In accordance with your letter of November 22, 1958,
we enclose herewith your cancelled mortgage payment book.

Very truly yours,

Kenneth O. Nimphius
Mortgage Department

KCN:mp
Enc.

Satisfaction of Mortgage L-2166: Northport Federal, November 1958

245

SOUTHAMPTON SUMMERS
Main Street, Southampton, NY

248

Summer afternoon, summer afternoon;

. . . the two most beautiful words in the English language.

— Henry James

CPSIA information can be obtained
at www.ICGtesting.com
Printed in the USA
BVHW011013030621
608734BV00008BA/72/J

9 780578 475257